Beyond Sushi

A year in Japan

D1474742

Beyond Sushi

A year in Japan

Kenneth Januszewski

Colken Publishers
Phoenix, Arizona

Front Cover Photos: Kenneth Januszewski

Januszewski, Kenneth.
        Beyond Sushi, A year in Japan
        1. Japan – Description and travel

ISBN 0-9663268-4-9
First Printing, February, 1998

1 2 3 4 5 6 7 8 9

PRINTED IN THE UNITED STATES OF AMERICA

To Colette

Preface

This book is about the Japan most of us do not know. When I went to Japan I knew as much about it as most Americans. My knowledge was limited to the stereotypic notions about their companies, the character of the people and some cultural items such as food. What I found was a Japan very different from my expectations.

While in Japan I kept a journal and tried to learn as much about the country as I could. I wrote letters home to my family and friends who enjoyed them and passed them on to their friends and coworkers. It was their reaction to my letters and support that made me decide to write this book. The book is based upon some of the letters I wrote home, but its scope is beyond them.

I wrote *Beyond Sushi* to provide a more realistic understanding of Japan than the media gives us. On each page I tried to include some fact about Japan that is new to the reader. I also attempted to inject as much humor into the book as my skills and the subject being discussed permitted. My goal is to entertain and educate without lecturing.

HOKKAIDO

HONSHU

Nagasaki

Hiroshima

Fukuoko

Tokyo

Kyoto

SHIKOKU

KYUSHU

Kumamoto

Kagoshima

Hondo

日本
Japan

*D*ear Dad,   August 3
          After landing in Oz, Dorothy says, "Toto, I've a feeling we're not in Kansas anymore." All I can say is "Dorothy, I know the feeling."

Beyond knowing about sushi, I landed with little knowledge of Japan but I have already seen so many interesting things, I believe my decision to take a year out of my law practice to teach English in Japan will be worthwhile in enjoyment if in no other way. The people are friendly and the language barrier sometimes can be overcome by the use of a smile, pointing and a little pantomime.

The flight took eleven hours. We left L.A. on Saturday afternoon and landed in Tokyo at 3:30 P.M. Sunday. The sun shone the whole trip. The program's 2,000 participants were brought to Tokyo on the same day from all over the world, including six cities within the U.S. The flight was overbooked and somehow with my economy-class ticket the Japanese government purchased, I ended up in the more expensive upper deck section of the 747 where there are only a dozen seats.

The language barrier reared its ugly head on the plane. The flight attendant was extremely polite, attentive and bowed so much that I thought she would need a chiropractor by the time we landed in Japan. Her English needs practice, as my answer, "No thank you, I don't want sake (sah kay)," apparently translated into "Please wake me from my nap for a big cup of sake."

To my disappointment, I realized how hard Japanese is going to be to learn. The in-flight magazines were written in English, Japanese, Chinese, and Korean. Although I picked up a Japanese-language book in April to study after work, when faced with a real-life magazine written in all three Asian languages, it took a couple of minutes just to figure out which was Japanese.

The Japanese government is putting us up at the Keio Plaza Hotel in Tokyo, which I am told is one of the better known hotels in Japan. It must be expensive. There are hostesses in uniforms at the bottom of the escalator who bow as people get off.

The hotel has unobstructed views, but smog has limited visibility to about five or ten miles. The Japanese use the metric system, which would make the distance eight to sixteen kilometers, or *kiro* (key row). The smog is no doubt in part due to the bad traffic. The bus ride from the Narita International Airport to the hotel, a distance of about forty miles, took two and one-half hours.

On Monday during "Opening Ceremonies" we had the endless speeches that the Japanese seem to love. Because this teaching program is sponsored by the government, one cabinet member gave a speech too. At the end of the speeches we had an elegant banquet.

It was my first encounter with honest-to-goodness Japanese food. Seaweed seemed to be on everything. When I smelled the traditional Japanese soup, *misoshiru* (me so she roo), I tried to attract the attention of a waiter but the woman next to me confirmed that that is how it is supposed to smell. It tastes fine and is supposed to be healthy for you, but if I had named it, it would be called stinky-tennis-shoe soup.

It is going to take some getting used to eating soup in Japan, not only the smell, but the lack of spoons. For Western- and Chinese-style soups they use spoons, but for traditional Japanese soups they take out the vegetables, roots, and berries or whatever with their *hashi* (hah she – chopsticks). They then drink the soup directly from the bowl. Soup without spoons: a concept I will be living with for a while.

I was surprised that some of the food tried to walk or wiggle off the plate when I was not watching it. Even some food that was definitely dead was definitely not cooked. We all know raw fish is popular here, but I learned that in the area where I will live this year, raw horse meat is a delicacy. I am not sure if I want to carry cultural immersion that far. Fortunately the Japanese like cooked chicken, noodles, and rice so I filled up on those. Even though they sometimes include seaweed. Disappointingly, even innocent-looking potato chips are laced with seaweed. I am becoming more courageous though. I tried broiled eel for lunch yesterday and last night even ate a little raw fish. Using *hashi* is getting easier with practice too. I am steadily improving the plate-to-mouth ratio of food that ends up in my mouth rather than on my shirt or on the floor. I miss forks.

We have had many seminars about teaching English in Japan. I learned I will be in a small town in southwest Japan called Hondo. It has seven junior high schools where I will teach on a rotating basis. Another thing I have learned is that being thirty-four makes me an old man in the eyes of the other participants, who are predominately fresh out of college. Boarding the plane I felt young and adventurous going to the other side of the world for a year and in the process jeopardizing my law career. By the time the plane landed I was viewed as an old-timer. Youth, too, is in the eye of the beholder.

After the seminars, there have been plenty of drinking parties to celebrate the new job and the new adventure. Half of us have had jet lag, the other half hangovers, or both since our arrival.

Tokyo is hot and muggy so it is just as well that many days the seminars keep us inside until early evening. On the streets, the traffic blares away as in any big town. The sidewalks are more crowded with people than in any U.S. downtown. During the day there are so many people, vending machines, parked bicycles, and displays from the stores spilling out onto the sidewalks, walking seems like I am perpetually in the aisle of a movie theater making my way slowly toward the exit.

From the vending machines, which are everywhere, you can buy pop of course, but there are other drinks I am not too sure about. One is call *karu pisu* (ca roo pee sue). I do not know what it is supposed to mean, but the way the Japanese pronounce it is sounds very much like "cow piss." The other drink I have yet to try is called *Pokari Sweat* (po ca ree – sue way toe).

There are vending machines with beer, whiskey, *adaruto* (a dah roo toe – adult) magazines, noodles, telephone cards, disposable cameras, and fruit. I have asked how the beer machines can check ID so minors cannot buy beer. The Japanese response is that their children know they are too young to drink so they do not buy beer. "Renewers" (people who have signed on for a second year on the program), who are teaching us survival Japanese skills, say high school students find the beer machines a temptation not worth resisting.

Restaurants have display cases out front with realistic-looking plastic re-creations of food served. The displays make it possible for me to eat out. I find what looks good, copy down the Japanese name for the dish, then go inside and show my note to the waitress. I do not always copy the Japanese down correctly, judging from the waitresses' blank stares. When that happens, I use my limited Japanese and ask for an English menu (many restaurants have them) or a picture menu (even more restaurants have them). If that doesn't work, I shepherd the slightly harried waitresses outside where I can point to the food I want.

Along with menus, waitresses give patrons cool wet hand towels which, as I see Japanese men do, I wipe my face with, although women seem to wipe their hands with it. In winter, these are brought to the table hot.

Food is expensive, about double U.S. prices, and the portions are smaller. Coffee and tea are about $2 a cup, and it is considered rude to fill the cup more than half full. Refills are not free. With the combination of high prices and small portions, it is no wonder that there are few overweight people here.

During the day, sidewalks near subway or commuter train stations overflow with bicycles (most have baskets on the front) and motor scooters. Renewers and our Japanese instructors say people ride them to the subway or train station, where they leave them for the day.

Finding a legal spot to park is next to impossible. With virtually no convenient legal parking, commuters universally ignore the no-parking signs. More than that, because the signs are situated near the most convenient places to park, row upon row of bikes cluster around the no-bike-parking signs. An anthropologist basing his opinion on behavior only might conclude the signs say "Crowd as many bicycles around this sign as possible."

Often bicycles flow from the sidewalk out into the street. The parked bicycles leave people only irregular narrow paths along the sidewalk which wind around the bicycles helping to make the daily commute a little more difficult and slower. By the early evening, most bicycles are gone. Some, however, are orphans. These have several "Parked illegally" stickers peeling from them. Many have flat tires, some coming off of the rims.

After the stores close, the crowds clear, revealing sidewalks not as pristine as we imagine when we think about Japan. Bicycle baskets are considered trash cans by so many people that most are full to the brim. For the casual trash thrower, making the basket is not important, so trash litters the ground around the bikes. A few homeless people arrange their cardboard box homes when night falls. Coming back to the hotel late last night I saw a group of *sarariiman* (sa ra ree man – from salary and man, meaning white-collar worker) gently swaying down the sidewalk stop to relieve overfull bladders. There are few public rest rooms, and the intoxicated *sarariiman* are in no mood to hunt one down. The Japanese who passed the *sarariiman* did not look right or left but kept on their way.

I had my own trouble finding a rest room last night, our last night in Tokyo. About two hundred of us invaded a *biagaden* (be ah ga den – from beer and garden), which is a bar on the roof of a department store. In the *erebeta* (eh lay bay ta – elevator) there was a young woman in a uniform with a hat and makeup job that reminded me of a 1950s Doris Day film. She explained what was on each floor, which seems a waste of money as there are plenty of directories in the stores to inform the Japanese, and for me, I haven't a clue with or without her help.

Beer garden decor is strictly patio furniture, but it is pleasant to sit outside in the evening to enjoy a brewski. When I needed to use the rest room, I asked a renewer how to ask "Where is the rest room?" in Japanese. The most-used word for toilet in Japanese is *toire* (toe e ray – from the word toilet). Using a foreign word apparently seems more polite.

Armed with an answer from the waiter, I confidently made my way to the elevator. The woman bowed, I told her the floor I wanted and she said something syrupy sweet which I could not understand. The doors opened, and I stepped out into the second basement of the building, which is where the subway is located. When I turned with the intent of trying to ask why she had let me off here, the elevator doors were closed. A few minutes of looking around the subway for a toilet without much success convinced me it was time yet again to do some communicating in Japanese.

I found a newsstand and after a couple practice tries to myself, I walked up to the woman and asked her where the toilet was. I knew I had said it right as she started pointing and saying in perfectly understandable Japanese, "*Kjkdf kdfkjieur hrnpildnb dnhd.*" Being a skilled intercultural communicator, I responded, "Huh?"

In that moment, I felt the irony that knowing how to say "Where is the rest room" made me not one step closer to it. Perhaps sensing my predicament the woman did a terrific job of gesture language. I mimicked her gestures back to her and she said, "*Hai* (hi – yes)." I was not sure if I actually knew the way, but I was making progress and that was encouragement enough.

I found the rest room. Once inside, I saw the cleaning lady with mop in hand. She looked up at me and I walked out, hoping she would not be too long. As I danced around, I looked for the sign I had missed on the way in saying the toilet was closed for cleaning. There was no sign of any kind. Japanese men continued going in and coming out. Back in I went, cleaning lady or no cleaning lady. When she saw me, with a sweeping gesture, she pointed to the urinals and said, "*Dozo*" (dough zoe – please).

In a counterproductive effort to make me feel more at ease, she stood near me. With both hands on the top of her mop, her chin on top of her hands, she asked simple questions like "Where are you from?" All I could think of was "Someplace very different from here." I had no idea how to say that, so I answered as best as I could. Renewers say I will become used to women in the rest rooms. Maybe, but I doubt it.

Well, I have to close now. Today we are all heading out in smaller groups to the various "*ken*" (cane) we will be living in. "*Ken*" is the Japanese word for prefecture and is not quite the equivalent to one of our counties. I am going to Kumamoto city (pop. 500,000) in Kumamoto-

ken where next week I will attend more seminars. I will write again when I get there.

$\mathcal{D}$ear Uncle Chet and Aunt Dottie,   August 10
        I was surprised to receive a letter from you so fast. Being far away, letters from home are already a pleasant treat. I am still settling in and until school starts in September I have plenty of free time and am taking advantage of that to study Japanese and write letters.

I thought I had told you all about the program I came over on, but from your letter, I gather I did not. It is called the Japan Exchange Teaching (JET) Program and is sponsored by the Japanese government. I am an Assistant Language Teacher (ALT). Each year about 2,000 people from eight countries (the U.S., Canada, Great Britain, Ireland, Australia, New Zealand, France and Germany) are invited to teach English, French, and German, although the emphasis is on English. Most of the participants are from the U.S. The stated purpose of the program is to have native speakers teach their language in classrooms across the country from the elementary school level all the way to college. German and French are taught only at the college level. Most of the participants are like myself, with neither Japanese-language ability nor prior teaching experience.

My salary is 300,000 yen a month (or about $25,000 a year), which has risen a bit since I arrived here due to the yen growing a little stronger. Making the pot a little sweeter is that Americans pay no taxes on the first $70,000 of overseas income; we on the program pay no Japanese taxes; and the city pays my rent.

To answer your questions about Tokyo traffic, picture an overweight, gray-haired old woman with hip problems walking down the street using a cane. Now slow that picture in your brain down a little bit and you have got Tokyo traffic speed. Unfortunately, I have a perfect real-world example. Tokyo has two airports, neither of which is close to downtown. Narita is for international traffic, and Haneda, the more convenient of the two, is for domestic flights.

Leaving Tokyo for Haneda Airport on a chartered bus with the seventy or so ALTs assigned to Kumamoto-*ken,* the driver took an "expressway." The airport is about twenty miles from the hotel, but due to Tokyo's traffic we spent two and a half hours making the trip. The worst part was that the stop-and-crawl traffic caused the engine to run so hot that the air conditioning shut off. We opened the windows and really felt the 90 percent humidity on the 95 degree day. The bus then crawled through a series of long tunnels with diesel fumes from the trucks choking us. I wondered if I would have been cooler back in Phoenix.

We rode another bus from Kumamoto Airport to the hotel, where our seminars were held. The man in charge of the local program serenaded us using the bus's P.A. system. He sang poorly but enthusiastically in both Japanese and English. The hotel in Kumamoto was a *ryokan* (ree yo kahn), which is a traditional Japanese hotel. The service was faultless. The elderly woman who greeted me in the lobby grabbed my bag. I gallantly (I thought) refused to let her carry it. When she insisted on fighting me for the bag, I let her carry it (or rather waddle, tilted over with it) to my room.

She spread my bed, called a futon, which is a covered three-inch-thick piece of cotton. She made tea, kneeled, and bowed. I felt a little awkward standing there looking down at her. Not knowing what to do, I smiled and offered her a tip, which she refused. People do not tip here, not hotel maids, waitresses, no one.

The floor was made of *tatami* (ta ta me) mats. A *tatami* mat (six feet long and three feet wide) is made of tightly woven straw. Rooms in a house are measured in terms of *tatami* even if the room is not a *tatami* room. The material is sturdy enough to put heavy furniture on, but soft enough to provide the Japanese some give when they spread their futon out on the floor at night to sleep. Shoes are not permitted in rooms with *tatami*. When I walked around the *ryokan*, I was encouraged to use slippers, which were provided by the hotel. The slippers were sized for Japanese feet and my heels dragged over the back edge.

The room had a small table about one and a half feet high. Since there were no chairs in the rooms, only cushions, there was not much choice but to sit on the floor. There was a TV, but no bilingual button (as many of the new TVs have) so even though some news programs and American movies are broadcast bilingually, I could watch them in Japanese only, which means I wrote letters and read in the evening.

In the short time I have been here I am already finding one Japanese habit irritating. It seems every time I am introduced to something that is traditionally Japanese they will say, "This is Japanese *ocha* (o cha – green tea)." Or "This is Japanese kimono (Japanese has no indefinite article so when speaking English people usually do not use the word "a" or "the")"; "This is Japanese *shoyu* (show you – soy sauce)"; "This is Japanese *sake* (sah kay – sake)"; "This is Japanese *yukata* (you ka ta – a thin cotton house coat)"; "This is Japanese *bonsai* (bone sigh) tree"; "This is Japanese *shoji* (show gee – the wood and paper sliding doors)"; "This is Japanese futon." As if without adding the "Japanese" I might get it mixed up with a Greek kimono, Canadian *ocha*, Russian sake, or the wood-and-paper sliding doors I might otherwise believe are found in American maximum-security prisons. Some of the other participants say the Japanese are just proud of their culture and are happy to show it off. I imagine that is true, so each time I act surprised.

As in most *ryokan* (the Japanese have no plural form for their nouns so I do not intend to write *ryokans* either), rest rooms were down the hall. The toilet bowl is about two feet long, eight inches wide, even with the floor, and made out of porcelain. Using the toilet here reminds me of tent camping. There is etiquette connected with using the toilet slippers that must be learned. When I use the toilet, I have to leave my "hall" slippers outside and change to the provided "toilet" slippers. Japanese giggle watching me return to my room in toilet slippers. I cannot tell the difference but they can.

Baths too are down the hall and communal style (not coed). The *ryokan*'s bath is composed of two rooms. The first is the dressing area. I took off my hall slippers and stepped up into the room where the clothes racks are as well as sinks. I saw Japanese men using the same communal cup for brushing their teeth which I think is stretching the communal stuff a bit too far.

The main washing room is the size of a large living room. It has a tile floor, and all around the room are small mirrors set at about waist level. When I sat down on the five-inch-high plastic stools provided, the mirror was at face level. The fifteen or so spigots were about two feet from floor level. I could either take the little buckets that were provided and fill them up, douse myself, wash, and rinse the same way or use the flexible hose to basically shower sitting down.

After showering and rinsing comes the communal dip. Unless you wash first, you are not welcome in the big Jacuzzi-like tub, which has enough room for ten. I did not indulge in this custom. For one, I do not want to share my bath water. For another, it is steaming hot, and I mean lobster temperature. I hear it is a great feeling once you get used to it, but it is a slow process. My Japanese coworkers explained that as babies, they would rebel at the hot temperatures but get pushed back in by their parents. By the time they were elementary-school age, they were addicted to it. Why they do this is hard for me to understand. The Japanese I ask all say something like "Gosh, I wonder how that custom got started too."

Men bring a thin *taoru* (ta o roo – from towel) about ten inches wide by about two and a half feet long into the big pool, soak it, ring it out, fold it up, and place it on their heads. Drying is done strictly in the outer changing room – except for me, that is. It is nice and toasty in the bathing room. Walking out wet into the colder air of the changing room gave me goose bumps, so, shock to the Japanese sensibilities as it may have been, I dried off in the bathing area.

The city I live in is dish-towel-size too, when compared with big Japanese cities. Hondo is on one of the Amakusa Islands with the Ariaki Sea on one side and the East China Sea on the other. The island is connected by bridge to Kyushu, the southernmost of the four main Japanese islands.

During the drive from Kumamoto city, I saw beaches with huge temporary-looking frames made of wood and string where the seasonal octopus catch is spread out to dry. The lack of pleasure craft on the water also caught my eye. With all the islands around here this place should be a recreational boater's paradise, but sailboats, speedboats, and houseboats unsuccessfully compete with fishing vessels for slip space. The last notable aspect of the seashore is the Japanese aversion to natural shorelines. Miles and miles of otherwise beautiful seashore is concreted in. No one I ask knows the rationale for the concrete extravaganza. The seashore around downtown Hondo is concreted in, to protect the city center, which sits on reclaimed land, from tides. The land downtown is flat, but just outside of downtown it is hilly as is most of Japan.

My house, which is about ten minutes from City Hall, sits on a hill. I pay the utilities. I am told energy costs are four times higher than ours so my energy bill will be higher than in the States. Another reason my bill will be higher is that Japanese houses do not have insulation. They do not even use the thin, Styrofoam stuff so popular with builders in Arizona. The house next door was framed since I moved in and I never saw them put insulation in. My coworkers explained that insulation is not used, but why it is not, no one can explain. No wonder my house is an oven. I am not looking forward to winter.

As I write this, I am in the living room, which is the only room with air conditioning. The next room, like everywhere else in Hondo, is hot and muggy. I am sitting on my legless chair with my legs resting on my *tatami*-mat floor writing on a table that stands four inches shorter than my knees.

The house has four rooms. When I ask the Japanese how big the house is they respond with either square meters or *tsubo* (tsu bow – one *tsubo* equals approximately 36 square feet, which is the size of two *tatami* mats). Either answer requires calculations that cause me a headache. So I just go with my eyeball estimate of 900 square feet.

Two of the rooms are "Japanese" style, which means they have floors made of *tatami*. The rooms are connected with sliding doors made of a light cardboard-like material which do not lock. No locks is typical for Japanese houses. The house has one Western room, which means a wood floor and a regular door with a knob. Then there is the kitchen. Last are the toilet and separate bathroom.

The tour starts when you slide open the front steel-frame glass door and step into the concrete *genkan* (gen khan). This is what we call a vestibule or an entryway, but slightly different from either concept. Physically, the *genkan* is lower than the rest of the house. So when I use Japanese to invite someone "into" the house, the verb I use literally means "Come up into the house." Socially, the *genkan* is considered outside the house. The front door to a Japanese house is usually kept unlocked while anyone is at home. Under Japanese rules of conduct, visitors, friends, and salespeople are allowed to open the front door, step into the *genkan* and call out "*Sumimasen*" (sue me ma sen – excuse me). I lock the door because I do not want the intrusions. Salesmen try to open my door and try again when the lock works as it should.

In every Japanese house, the *genkan* is where the shoes are left. I simply push mine to the side, but the Japanese usually have shoe racks located to one side of the *genkan* for family members to put their shoes away. They also have family and guest slippers which are often not kept in the *genkan* but reachable from it. If you are a guest at a Japanese house, the host will set the slippers out so you can step out of your shoes and slip into the house slippers. Only rude Japanese visitors fail to line their shoes up neatly with heels against the home side of the *genkan* and toes pointing to the door. *Gaijin* (guy jean – foreigners) leave their shoes anywhere in the *genkan*.

If you pretend you have properly aligned your shoes and put your slippers on, we can start the tour of the house. Immediately to the left of the *genkan* is the Western room. I use it for storage as it does not have heating or cooling. Walking down the hallway from the *genkan*, about ten feet on the left is the door to the toilet.

It is what they call a Western-style (sit-down, flush) toilet which are becoming widely used. Mine is complete with instructions on the inside cover. I am not kidding. I have heard that when some older Japanese encounter a Western-style toilet for the first time they try to squat down, with their feet perched on top of and on either side of the toilet bowl. Whether the stories are true or not I do not know, but somebody at the fixture company felt a need to include a picture demonstration of how to use the toilet. This small room has neither heating or cooling. No matter how fast I am, when I come out I have a sweat going.

The toilet, while at least sit-down style, is not connected to a sewer, but to a septic tank. Even in Tokyo's administration area a significant percentage of homes and buildings such as schools are not connected to sewers. At a school in an outlying area of Tokyo, in a rare case, a couple of children died due to refuse seeping into the well water. Some schools in different parts of Japan still have no-flush gravity toilets such as you find in outhouses in national parks. An apartment of a nearby ALT is only partially hooked up to the city sewer. The sinks, shower, and washing machine drain to the one-foot-wide, two-feet-deep concrete trench that runs alongside the building and drains into one that runs along the street in front of his building. Another ALT in the north of Japan said the waste (everything) in his house flows out to just such a system. Maybe this odd mix of old and new can be explained by nothing more than the economy surging ahead, leaving in its wake out-of-place pockets of pre-prosperity outhouses.

Leaving the toilet, do not forget to take off the cute little green plastic slippers that have the white bunnies pictured on the top. Only greenhorn *gaijin* forget to change out of the toilet slippers and back into the house slippers.

To the immediate left of the toilet is the "bathroom" sink, although it is actually located in an alcove in the hallway. It has the medicine cabinet and the only mirror in the house, which gives me back pain. If I stand in front of it, I see nothing above my shoulders. Unfortunately, this mirror is set at standard height found in all private and public rest rooms, so when I need to shave or comb my hair I have to bend over. I will be glad to get back to a country where I can look in the mirror and see my face without having to bend over or stand resembling an upside-down Y.

Standing at the mirror, you turn to the right and see the main room. Cross the hall, slide the wood and glass door and you enter into one of the "Japanese" style rooms. No slippers are allowed in rooms with *tatami* mats. A teacher my age named Honda Akane helped me move some things in. (They always put their last name first so I did too.) She wore shoes to the *genkan*, took them off, put slippers on to walk in the hallway, took them off at this room, put the slippers back on in the hallway, took them off at the *genkan*, and put her shoes back on. She did this all three trips. Slipper etiquette in a Japanese home can be complicated.

This is the room where the TV is located (in the corner to the right). To the left of the door is a bookshelf where I keep the pink phone the Board of Education bought. It is complete with a hold button and plays an electronic version of "It's a Small World After All" when I put someone on hold. Most electronic music on hold here has "Home on the Range" or some other Western music. Next to the phone is a *minicompo* (me knee come poe – minicomponent stereo, or boombox).

The room also has the table I am writing on. I eat, read, write, sleep, and practically live in this room during these sweltering August days because it is the only room with *eacon* (eh ah cone – from *air conditioning*). The air conditioner is actually a heat pump, which is sophisticated almost beyond belief. It is programmable to turn on and off automatically. It has a quiet mode for sleep. It has settings to vary the force and direction of the blown air. It has a hand-held and wall-mounted remote control. I can even program it over the phone remotely (well, actually *I* have no idea how to do this, but I am told it can be done.)

On the other hand, the house has built-in heat only in this room. To heat the other rooms when winter comes the Board has purchased a traditional and still well used Japanese heating source: the portable kerosene heater. In essence I have 21st-century technology hanging on the wall in the living room and 18th-century castle technology for the rest of the house. It is one of the baffling inconsistencies in this house and one of thousands such inconsistencies in this country.

Built in the wall next to the TV is a big closet with the futon and blankets and sheets that I have to spread out nightly and collect again every morning. Most of my coworkers still use futons instead of beds, but the trend is toward beds. The *tatami* is not as hard as a wood floor. However, to compensate for the thinness of the futon, I spread out my camping mattress underneath to make it more comfortable. Covering the entire outer wall are four seven-feet-tall sliding steel-framed glass windows. Four inches inside of these are the *shoji* (show gee), the sliding paper-and-wood doors that act as curtains, which I think gives the house touch of class at what must be a rock-bottom price.

There is direct access from this room to the next *tatami* room, which I call the guest room. It is almost identical to this room, minus the heat pump. The rooms are separated by two big sliding doors which are made out of half-inch-thick cardboard without locks.

As we slip the footwear on, we turn left and walk through the doorway into the kitchen. The swearing you hear is because I have forgotten to duck again when going through the doorway, so once again I have whacked my forehead on the low-clearance doorways. What bothers me the most is when I duck but come up too soon and smack the top of my head on the door frame anyway. In public it is embarrassing to be the second one through a low-clearance door and the second one to smack head to wood. At times like those I chuckle to myself because the Japanese witnessing these head whackings must wonder 'How did our parents lose a war to their country?'

The sink is at the proper height, which means I have to bend down to reach it. The stove sits on the cabinet next to the sink and is as close to a Coleman stove as I care to have in my house. It is only eight inches high with four burners, a small toaster oven built in, and no cooking oven.

To smooth my transition to Japanese society, the city has assigned Tsuruta-*san* (*san* is the equivalent of our "Mr." for men and "Mrs.," "Miss," or "Ms." for women), a man whom I am rapidly coming to admire, to help me. He is in his middle forties, sits next to me at the office, and has been assigned the responsibility for making sure the *gaijin* is well provided for. I call him my mother hen. The other ALT who will teach in Hondo's junior high schools, Rosemary, calls him her personal life manager.

Though I have been in Hondo only a short time, I have learned to trust Tsuruta-*san*'s judgment. Although he has no education past high school, he has a lot of native intelligence, knows how to get things done, and knows, it seems, everybody in the city. We have things in common I would never have suspected. He grew up on the same TV programs and rock and roll I did. He knows *Bewitched* and can even sing "House of the Rising Sun."

Last week Tsuruta-*san* told me the city had a few yen left to make the house habitable. He took me shopping for a *suihanki* (sue e han key – an automatic rice cooker). Every Japanese household has one. Making rice with a *suihanki* is super easy. First you buy the rice at many times the price it is in the States. Put the rice in, wash it in cold water, fill with fresh water to the line, close the top, and flip the switch. The rice cooker does the rest. The rice can be stored in the *suihanki* for a couple of days without losing its quality. Many single male ALTs who want to "go native" yet put minimum effort into cooking think s*uihanki* are nirvana. I, however, eat enough rice everywhere else so I do not make it at home.

The cultural differences between Tsuruta-*san* and I were apparent in the appliance department. I chose a microwave. I do not see the need for a *suihanki*. He could not imagine anyone living without one. He has a hard time believing that I eat rice only a couple of times a month. He finally purchased the microwave (which was almost the same price as a *suihanki*), with an I-hope-Ken-does-not-regret-passing-on-the-rice-cooker look. The microwave sits on top of the refrigerator, which is as tall as American models, but is about one third narrower than a normal single-door model.

To the left of the refrigerator is the laundry room with a washing machine. Due to the cost of energy, Japanese washing machines are hooked up only to cold water. The machine is half the size of a standard American model. Despite being new, it shares a common trait of Japanese washing machines: They are made to rip socks and towels to shreds, which is a complaint echoed by many ALTs (the Japanese say it must be cheap American socks and towels).

Clothes dryers are an almost unheard of luxury. There are clothes rods outside the house, and I bought lines to hang inside the house for the rainy days (which seem so far to be in the majority). Here again, the inconsistencies seem strange to me. The washer is so high tech that it is able to change the wash cycle in reaction to how dirty the clothes are. But I hang the clothes outside or in the house like my mom did thirty years ago.

After going through the small laundry room we enter the bathroom, which houses a four-foot-deep stainless steel tub. It is square and about four feet across. I bathe *next* to the tub on the tile area, where I sit on the short plastic stool, as I did at the *ryokan*. Again this room has no heat or cooling. I am not looking forward to winter showers. When the bathroom is not in use, I leave the window open to keep it as dry as possible. Japan is hot and humid and makes a perfect breeding ground for fast-growing mold. I already have found some on the bathroom walls – even on my shoes in the closet. Fortunately, exposure to direct sunlight kills it.

With a quick explanation of the view from the house, we will conclude the grand tour. The kitchen has a view of the orchard rising up the hill in back of the house to the east. (I do not know what kind of fruit is on the trees because each fruit has been covered in paper!). The living room has a view of Tsuruta-*san*'s house and the high school down the hill. Outside the front door a hill steeply climbs from the opposite curb. From the house, the property extends only four feet in every direction except in front where the carport is; there the property extends inches beyond the carport's support posts. And that is the end of the tour.

Like me, when putting your shoes on you probably will have to sit on the floor with your feet in the *genkan* to retie your laces. The Japanese almost never do. Whether they wear loafers or lace shoes (which they get out of without untying), they just slip into them. For the first several feet outside the house, they gently tap the toe of the shoe into the ground to work their heel into it. When a group of Japanese leave at the same time, it almost sounds like a percussion symphony. All their shoes sag at the heel having been stepped on millions of times, but the toes are not scuffed up from all the ground whacking.

I am pleased with my living arrangements and so far I could not be happier with my job. The people at the Board have been very nice. I think this is partly because this is Hondo's first year of participation in the program and they are glad to be on board. Rosemary, the other ALT, and I are Hondo's first *gaijin* on the city's payroll. We are also the first foreign teachers who will be visiting the city's seven junior high schools daily. She and I, however, will never be at the same school on the same day.

She and I are not literally the first foreigners in town, of course, but two of only five in the city. Of the other three *gaijin* in town, Angela, from California, works for the private language school. The remaining two, Joe, from Maryland, and Steve, from Nova Scotia, are on the same program as I am but work for the *ken* (prefectural government).

Joe works in the three high schools in Hondo. (High schools are run by the *ken*.) Junior high schools are usually run by the city except for the tiny villages, where they are run by the *ken*. Steve goes to all the junior high schools in the surrounding areas. Without the program there would be only one *gaijin* (Angela) among a Japanese population of about 100,000. Through the program, we four ALTs will teach every student in and around Hondo. Stories of what the *gaijin* teacher said and did will filter back to the households of darn near every family around here.

The day after Rosemary and I arrived in Hondo, the city held a banquet in our honor attended by all of the English teachers, all seven school principals, and all members of the Board, the city council, and the city mayor. There was a big "Welcome to Hondo" banner on the wall and Japanese and American flags on each table.

Everyone introduced themselves briefly in English and then we had speeches up the yin yang. Rosemary and I were each asked to give one, which were translated by Akane. She is the teacher I mentioned earlier who has been very helpful to me. After our section chief at the Board gave his speech, Rosemary and I were to go to the podium where he would introduce us to give our speeches.

When he finished, he gave us a gesture that confused both of us. He held his hand toward us palm down and waved to us, bringing his fingers to his palm. Rosemary and I looked at each other wondering what to do because it looked like he was gesturing "Bye." Finally Akane told us to get up. We approached the podium with the audience murmuring humorously at the intercultural miscommunication.

After the banquet was finished, we did a traditional good-luck rhythmic hand-clapping ritual. On cue the audience stood and quickly clapped three times, paused, clapped three more times, paused, clapped three more times, paused, and clapped once more. They repeated this three times.

They wanted to do three *banzai* cheers. Having been raised on a diet of old John Wayne war movies, I did not feel good about joining in. It was strange raising my hands high over my head and shouting "*BANZAI*!!" In the interest of trying to get along I did it once, but I just watched the last two cheers.

To me that cheer is wrapped up very closely with militarism. Afterward, Akane said that the cheer literally means "one thousand years," and during the war with the addition of the words "*Tenno Heika*" (ten no hey ka – Imperial Majesty) it meant "Long live the Emperor." It has no such meaning to the Japanese today. *Banzai* is a cheer shouted on joyous occasions to express unity or to start off a project on the right foot, like the beginning of the semester at a banquet.

Aside from being a great help, Akane is quickly becoming a friend. So the way I have been mispronouncing her name is especially irritating to me. Sometimes I call her *okane* (o ka nay – money) instead of Akane.

She has been instrumental in acclimating me to Hondo. She even recommended the barbershop her brother used before he moved to Kumamoto city. It is a mom-and-pop operation. As with many such small businesses, the owners live in the back of the shop.

The shop has an old-fashioned red-and-white barbers' pole out in front. Inside there are two chairs, and both were occupied when I entered. The radio was tuned to the FM station, which plays mostly American rock and roll. I sat down and flipped through a one-inch-thick Japanese comic book. These are popular with people of all ages, and it is the only way some busy *sarariiman* read the classics: as condensed versions in comic book form. This one, however, was more typical of the comics. It was a story about a big business (complete with the Japanese boss graphically having sex with the *gaijin* woman, who works at the company, which I think is the forbidden-fruit theme).

As I waited, the barber gave a perm to the gray hair of the man in the chair and asked me in equal parts of Japanese and English the typical questions I usually hear: where am I from, what do I do, how old am I, what is my blood type (every man woman and child here knows theirs), how much money do I make, what things do I like about Japan, etc. I have heard these questions enough to be able to answer in barely passable Japanese. Everyone in the shop told me how good my Japanese is. If you butcher their language for a half hour and through sheer weight of the odds, you say something that sounds like a Japanese sentence, they are culturally programmed to make a fuss out of it and say how wonderful your Japanese is.

I am amazed at the things that seem to cross cultural boundaries. Taxi and bus drivers here seem to think they own the road too. Barbers are talkaholics. As I sat down in the chair the questions flowed nonstop. The fact that he and I do not share a common language is apparently not a problem for him as he was totally undeterred by (or maybe oblivious to) my consistent "*Sumimasen, wakarimasen* (sue me ma sen, wa ka ree ma sen – I'm sorry, I don't understand)" answers.

He put some chemical on my hair, cut a little, leaned me forward to a sink that came out of the wall, shampooed my hair, then continued talking and working his scissors so fast that it reminded me of a fast chef chopping veggies. Then his wife took charge of my head.

She reclined the chair back and my feet hit the wall. She giggled as she apologized, saying something which I suspect was "Next time I will take into account the length of *gaijin* legs when I do this." She placed a steaming hot towel on my face, raised me back up and put shaving cream on my chin, cheeks, and upper lip, then on the bridge of my nose, forehead, and, ears. I sat there wondering whether I ever had such a bad hangover that I accidentally put shaving cream on my forehead or ears. In defense of this sweet woman, Japanese men do not have much facial or body hair, but their head hair does seem to sprout out farther down the forehead than that of Western men.

She shaved me all over, then lathered me up and did it again. During the second time she ran the fingers of one hand over my face to seek out any stray hair she had missed the first time. She did so with the intensity of a pilgrim on a mission from God. After more hot towels and another shampoo, she put some cream on my face and gave me a face massage. She was very good at locating the pressure points with her fingers. Next she put a cloth over my face and ran a heat lamp very close to my skin. She followed that with a cool wet towel and gently cleaned my face, paying close attention to my eyes and ears.

When I thought my hair-cutting adventure was done, she massaged my scalp. Then she stood behind me, repeatedly clapping her hands together as if in prayer, each time giving me a gentle double-handed karate chop to the back of the head. The odyssey ended with a shoulder massage.

There was one more thing she wanted to do. She took an eight-inch-long stick with a tiny spoon fashioned on the business end, their equivalent of a Q-tip, and walked toward me. I had already been warned about this. A Japanese wife uses one of these things to clean her husband's ears by scraping the powder that forms in the ear. (The Japanese say they have no ear wax.) It is supposed to show love on the part of the wife and trust on the part of the husband, as one slip and he has a stick stuck in his brain. I am told it happens from time to time. (Divorce is not culturally accepted.) I told her no thanks. The haircut took an hour and fifteen minutes. The cost was $14, which was a discounted rate because the barber said I will be teaching his son this year.

I know you are not adjusted to the idea that I will be teaching. I understand your reasons for thinking that I am crazy to have uprooted myself. Coming to Japan for a year to teach American culture and English to Japanese junior high school students may be the death knell of my legal career. All I can say is you may be right. My seize-the-moment decision may make it impossible to pick up where I left off.

However, after my good friend from high school, Tony, was killed by a drunk driver in February, I decided that it was now or never for my dreams. Two weeks before he was killed, Tony and I talked about his dreams and his plans to marry his girlfriend. Before I had a chance to speak with him again, he had no future, only yesterdays. I may be doing the worst thing I can for my career. As a human who is going to be on the planet only one time, trying to pack in as much living as possible between birth and death, I am doing the right thing. I hope I can pick up where I left off. Even if I cannot, I know I will not regret my decision.

Bye for now.

Dear Lynea,   August 20
After living in Japan for almost a month I concur with the common opinion that the Japanese have an insular feeling about their country. I sense the real purpose of the JET Program is not to teach language but to familiarize the Japanese with people from other cultures by direct contact with *gaijin*. In Tokyo we did not receive much special attention from the locals, but in Hondo (pop. 40,000), far from the usual foreign tourist route, we ALTs are quite the curiosity. The

ALTs living in the surrounding tiny towns and villages are often the only *gaijin* in their community.

I am tired of little kids seeing me on the streets, pointing at me while tugging on their parent's sleeve to get attention and shouting "*GAIJIN*!!" Worse still, the parents also react as if they saw an elephant escaped from the zoo. I tell myself I am being too sensitive, but it is sad that these people are so wrapped up in the Japanese universe that seeing a person who does not have black hair causes such a reaction.

Being great curiosities here, we ALTs are invited to *enkai* (en ka e – drinking party) by civic groups and are not expected to pay for either food or drinks. In an effort to fit in I have been going, but I am tired of all the partying. I suppose they want to beer and sake us to death to show that we are part of the group. The first *enkai* of the evening is obligatory for all group members and lasts on average one or two hours. Then like clockwork that ends and people who want to can go to the *nijikai* (knee gee ka e – second party), which is less formal. There are often *sanjikai* (san gee ka e – third party) and so on to the wee hours of the morning.

During one *nijikai* my crotch was grabbed. By a man! I am not the only man on the program who has had his private parts hand-checked. This springs from the popular myth that all American men are well endowed. Some distinguished-looking, slightly intoxicated gentleman reached over and while smiling grabbed my crotch. For a nanosecond I thought of wasting the guy but then two thoughts occurred to me. First, I thought, "If I knock all his teeth down his throat, he still has his hand on my. . ." Second, in Japan, the renewers say in an altercation between a Japanese and a *gaijin*, it is the *gaijin* who is arrested. So I retaliated in kind. I grabbed his crotch but not in the soft, exploratory way he grabbed me. I also put on my best Let-go-if-you-ever-want-to-use-this-equipment-again look. He immediately let go but I did not. I gave him time to think about whether Americans are the lovers of violence that our movies depict.

They say Japanese men can say and do things under the pretext of inebriation that they otherwise could not, which provides them with an accepted way to blow off steam. I am told that all the people at the previous night's drinking party are expected to go on as if nothing happened. The next day I went to the Board where I go each day because the Japanese summer vacation is not over yet. No one who witnessed the exchange between me and the gray-haired civic leader, whoever he is, said anything.

The women have reported no such problems, although a Japanese man did open his raincoat and flash Patricia, an ALT in Nara,

Japan's ancient capital, while she was leaving the train station at night. Pat is a tall woman with a little meat on her bones. She reacted by swinging her purse at the pervert, who promptly ran. Without thinking, she chased him, swinging her purse at him when in range. He escaped. Now she feels fortunate that he ran. Japanese men are generally smaller of stature than American men, but he could have had a weapon. Although where a flasher would hide a weapon is an interesting question.

I look forward to work each morning. The twenty-five people at the Board have been very easy to get along with. Each has his own desk in the same large communal room. With the exception of the section chiefs, four people each share a telephone placed on a metal arm that swivels. The superintendent has a small office of his own.

The section chiefs all sit next to the windows, with their backs to the windows so they can watch all the underlings. Even the head honchos do not put their feet on the desk. Showing the bottom of the foot is beyond rude in Japan, it is an insult to the sensibilities of everyone in the office (at least that is how they explained it to me when they asked me to remove my feet from my desk).

The desks are arranged in hierarchical order with the lowest peons in the office farthest from the window and closest to the public counter. There are three such desks. The first is the desk of the *OL* (oh a roo – from what they think we call women office workers: *Office Lady*). The *OL* is the woman in every Japanese office who makes the *ocha* and places it on everybody's desk in the morning. She was shocked the other day when I brought in tea bags, made my own tea, and washed my own cup afterward. I have never asked my secretary to be my maid, and I see no reason to lose that habit now. But this woman, determined to do her job, has added my brand of tea to the office's supply and makes it for me in the morning.

The other two peon desks in the office are Rosemary's and mine. Steve, who works at the Board run by the *ken*, has noticed the same pecking order of desks in his office. Although there seems to be an office totem pole with the ALTs at the bottom, all the people are very friendly and willing to help us acclimate to Japan. While teaching me how to use the computer or trying to engage in any sort of communication with me, they rely predominately on high school English with decades of rust. The people who sit within ten feet of our desks have bought dictionaries and are patient when we absolutely butcher their native language. Because we are all motivated to communicate, I think we will be alright.

My college French is rearing its ugly head in my pursuit of Japanese. When I try to say a word in Japanese, a word from French pops into my brain. Other ALTs complain of their college Spanish or German getting in the way of their Japanese. When a Japanese wants to express in body language that he has no clue what I just tried to say, he will tilt his head to one side and say "Hey?" Believe me, I have experienced that a lot in the past couple of weeks.

Somehow our mishmash of English and Japanese allows us to communicate. I have noticed how much we do not even need language. Communication without words is aided when we have an idea of the subject matter and the abilities of the person to whom we are speaking. Today an example of this happened.

A young college student home for the summer named Kyoko has been assigned as our interpreter and is with us during much of our office hours. If Rosemary and I talk at natural speed, Kyoko usually cannot understand. When we speak carefully to her, she does a good job. I asked her to translate for me while I talked to Tsuruta-*san* about the film I had developed at the local camera shop.

From a roll of thirty-six pictures, my camera usually takes thirty-eight pictures, as there is more room on the average roll of film for more than thirty-six prints. When I picked up my first roll of pictures, there were only thirth-six prints but thirty-eight pictures on the negatives. I wanted the store to print the other two. Because Tsuruta-*san* knows the store owner (of course), I also wanted to know if he could tell the owner to check my rolls in the future to make sure that the number of prints match the number of negatives.

I was carefully explaining this to Kyoko in front of him using gestures to help her understand. Before Kyoko could translate, Tsuruta-*san* said, "*Wakarimashita* (wa ka ree ma she ta – I understand). He then talked for a minute or so. While I was watching him talk, I thought about what a results-oriented man he is. I was trying to think of what his words and gestures meant, so when he stopped talking, but before Kyoko began translating, I attempted to tell her what I thought he must have said.

I said, "The machine automatically prints only thirty-six prints, but he will take the negatives back and get the extra prints made. He will tell the owner to set the machine for thirty-eight prints from now on, not thirty-six." Kyoko looked at both of us with disbelief. He and I knew then that we had communicated without one word of a common language being spoken between us. Both of us were proud, I think, that we are taking our background knowledge of human behavior and applying it to someone from a different culture. I think were are both beginning to think that this supposed cultural gap is not such a big deal after all.

One part of the cultural gap I am not becoming accustomed to is the extensive use of bicycles. Even the superintendent rides to work on one. The city has thoughtfully provided me with a bike, which is white and has a wire basket on the front. The bike, the favorite of many adults here, looks like the one Elvira Gulch rode. (She later became the witch in the *Wizard of Oz*.) I sometimes ride down the street shouting "I'll get you my pretty," then give it my best Wicked-Witch-of-the-West cackle. It must make the parents worry about the safety of their kids while at school.

Free bike or not, I will be paid at the end of the month and I am planning to buy a used car. One of the reasons I want a car is that my grocery shopping is limited by how much I can carry on my bicycle and by the heat. I cannot buy anything that will melt before I make it home.

The grocery store is a good example of the difference between Japan and America. Not just the higher prices (for example, even Japanese beer is more expensive in Japan than the same beer in American stores), but fewer choices.

Except for tea, fish and rice varieties, Japanese stores lack variety when compared to American stores. For example, in the States, the stores carry a wide variety of regular, decaf and specialty coffees. In Japan, coffee is coffee. There will be one or two kinds of regular coffee with just a few cans on the shelf. What takes up four shelves and perhaps fifteen linear feet in the States takes up one or two feet of one shelf in Japan. All you need is provided, but choice is not. Just a small thing, perhaps, but something that points out a subtle difference between our cultures. Ours caters to our needs and desires, theirs provides for their needs.

Because I am getting out and meeting people, the community is beginning to know me. Last week I was invited to several homes to celebrate a national holiday called *Obon* (o bone) (from the 14th to 16th of August). Although only three days long, during that week most Japanese go home as we do at Thanksgiving or Christmas. This is one of the designated times when companies permit their employees to take vacation time. Traveling is tough during this holiday. Trains are packed to 150 percent capacity, and employees don white gloves to shove people onto the train so the doors can close. (The Tokyo subway employs men who carefully cram passengers onto trains every rush hour.)

On the national TV news (which is broadcast bilingually) traffic jams under twenty-five *kiro* (about fifteen miles) do not make the news. The longest traffic jam I heard of was one hundred *kiro* (sixty miles). When I say traffic jam, I do not mean slow traffic, I mean cars on the expressway in the traffic lanes with drivers behind the wheel (which in Japan are on the opposite side of the car from ours) sleeping.

The *Obon* holiday is becoming a time when people can go overseas for a week. Airports are crammed wall-to-wall with passengers and their luggage. The already sky-high prices are jacked up at this time, and reservations months in advance are required.

Obon is a time when the spirits of the dead are thought to come back to the house and say howdy. People tell me they believe the spirits really do come back. These people leave food the spirit enjoyed during life on the family shrine. For most, this would include rice. For men, it would include sake. On the last night, there are bonfire and/or lantern festivals in different parts of Japan to light the way back to ghost land.

Just before *Obon* is another kind of event that affects all of the Japanese, the remembrance of the bombings of Hiroshima (August 6) and Nagasaki (August 9). Then there is the anniversary of the end of World War II in the Pacific on August 15 during the middle of *Obon*. No sooner did I arrive in Hondo than these dates came up.

I bring up these topics during quiet moments in my conversations. I simply ask people how they feel about all this and I receive serious responses. People in their late fifties or older have personal memories of that time. One teacher who is almost sixty told me that he and his family saw the mushroom cloud rise over Nagasaki (which is not too far away from here as the crow flies and even closer to the town where he lived then). Some adults speculated it was a volcano (even though the only volcano in that direction is more to the north) or a huge fire.

The consensus of people who were children during that era seems to be that, as horrible as the atomic bombs were, they probably saved Japanese lives (although Truman ordered the bombs dropped solely to save American lives). On Okinawa, the only part of the Japanese islands with a civilian population to be invaded, many tens of thousands more civilians died than American soldiers. Right down to the junior high school level, the Japanese were taught that suicide was preferable to capture because Americans were portrayed as mother-raping, baby-killing, blood-drinking barbarians whose goal was to remove every vestige of Japanese culture from the earth. A memorial was erected to a group of junior high school girls pressed into service as nurses during the invasion by the Japanese army who lived up to the ideal by committing suicide rather than being captured. During the invasion of Okinawa, women and children on the main islands were being trained to defend Japan against the scheduled November 1945 invasion of Kyushu. They were to be armed with nothing more than bamboo sticks with which they were to charge American soldiers and tanks. Hearing stuff like that gives me goose bumps. If there is something to the Japanese belief that Westerners cannot understand the Japanese way of thinking, this might be the example they mean.

People who lived through it remember the hunger they felt toward the end of the war and for a couple of years thereafter. Most mention that they were fortunate to be in a rural area so they could grow their own food. People here think the hunger of the people in the big cities was even worse.

When older people talk about the times immediately after the war, there is a consistent theme: hunger mixed with the initial fear of the American soldiers overcome with the first cup of milk, taste of butter, or piece of chocolate that these people, then youngsters, received from G.I.'s during the Occupation. A couple of people told me that they will never forget that first taste after the war. When they describe the cold milk or butter on a piece of bread, some have a look on their face as if they are caught up in a pleasant flashback. One older Japanese man talked with such tenderness about holding the cup of milk poured from a fifty-five-gallon drum that it seemed more like he was describing the first time he cradled his newborn child.

When they mention chocolate, most of the people chuckle a bit. As kids they saw the goof ball G.I.'s laughing and handing out food and bolted toward them. One candy handout was enough to start to undo the years of propaganda, it was literally overcome by word of mouth. Ironically, the soldiers of the Occupation army must have been the greatest good-will ambassadors America will ever have.

A teacher told me that what he remembers most is when several groups of G.I.'s in Jeeps arrived in his childhood village. He and his parents were flabbergasted that all of the soldiers knew how to drive. At that time, the Japanese felt that a car driver was something like an airplane pilot (I guess because they were so rare then). For me, having been born in Detroit, his observation was poignant as Japan now makes more cars than my hometown.

One thing they do not mention without being specifically asked is how they feel about America, a country that dropped atomic bombs on their homeland. This is a tough question for them to answer. I am curious about this because in watching TV news coverage and reading the newspaper, I get the overwhelming sense that it is politically correct to condemn the bombings but not the bombers; to grieve for the Japanese who suffered but ignore the suffering the Japanese caused; to remember the horrors of war but not to analyze the road that led them to aggression. I will write you more about this later, maybe after the trip to Hiroshima that I am planning.

I look forward to hearing from you again. Bye.

*D*ear Frank,   August 27

  I am glad you and Margaret are getting used to Minnesota and married life. From your letter, it seems you are settling into your new job and will like it even more as time goes on.

  As far as my job in concerned, next week I begin my life as Ken-*sensei* (sen say – teacher). This is how I am addressed by everyone when I visit the schools. I am a little intimidated by the prospect of being a teacher, but I find myself looking forward to it at the same time. The main concern I have is how I will get along with the kids. As a teenager I understood neither myself nor my friends. Now that I am on the other side of the world in a different culture where I do not understand the language, I wonder how I am going to interact with these students.

  My worry has diminished. I have visited all seven schools and met the English teachers. They do not have the summer off, but the six-week vacation period is a slack time for them. At every school there are always some students studying or participating in practice sessions with the tennis club, baseball or soccer team and so on. The poor kids start summer vacation in the last week of July and begin the fall semester in the first week of September. During vacation they are loaded down with homework with the idea of keeping them busy for two hours a day. The cruelest, most heartless thing is that the kids have a big test the first day back after summer vacation. Imagine spending your summer vacation facing a big test!

  When we are at the schools, Rosemary and I have a sort of magnetic quality that attracts a crowd of kids, who are usually friendly. I find myself looking forward to these meetings. I hope that feeling continues once I am in the classroom.

  My real work here does not start until school does, so I spend most of my time at the Board in City Hall, until about 3 P.M. when Tsuruta-*san* usually leans over and whispers in a conspiratorial tone of voice, "Today oba (over) you go home now. Okay?" Or "Miyagawa-*sensei* (our immediate supervisor) say you luke tieyard (look tired), you want go home now?"

I could prepare lesson plans as Rosemary is doing, but I am studying Japanese instead and writing letters. I have asked and no one seems to mind how I am spending my time. I am also trying to figure out the little things that we take for granted at home, like how to use a bank automatic teller machine.

I am amazed how different such an everyday task is here in Japan. The *kashu mashin* (kashoe masheen – cash machine [ATM]) is often placed in the *kashu kona* (kashew co nah – corner, where they usually put a few machines). Both the post office (one of the largest "banks" in the world) and banks issue *kashu kado* (kashoe ka dough – cash card). The Japanese are ahead of us in ATM technology and behind us in utilization of it.

Japanese ATMs are polite. The banks' ATMs feature a screen with an animated figure of a woman who politely welcomes customers. She courteously asks them to wait while the transaction is processed, bows when the transaction is complete, and says, "Thank you very much."

To make a deposit, I key in the amount, then stick the wad of money in the paper-money slot and coins in the other slot. The machine counts all of it, produces a receipt on the spot, and credits my account immediately. A nifty feature is the ability to automatically update my passbook (and use it as a cash card too). I insert the passbook and the machine prints all the times I withdrew (including automatic withdrawals, such as my phone bill) or deposited money. The machine actually turns the pages to continue making entries.

The use of ATMs are restricted, however. Most are placed inside. Once the doors to the building close, my cash card is useless. Others are placed in lobbies that are open a couple of hours after the bank or post office closes. The hours of use are usually from 9 A.M. to 12 P.M. on Saturday and none on Sunday. So in this cash-based economy I have to plan ahead.

I can do that because the limit on daily withdrawals is high, the equivalent of $5,000. This is necessary because the Japanese do not use checks at all. I am paid in cash in an envelope. At stores, people pay for even expensive items, like a TV, in cash instead of by check or credit card. The Japanese are, however, in the process of going from a cash-based economy to a plastic and electronic one, bypassing the use of checks almost completely. Many do not even understand the concept.

They have not quite reached a plastic economy, though. Before coming to Japan, I read that one of the Japanese banks is the largest issuer of Visa cards in the world. You would never know it by shopping in Japan. Credit cards, while known to all, simply are not used much. Off the tourist routes, clerks never ask, "Cash or credit?" Trying to use a credit card away from tourist areas, can throw the clerk into a panic. I bought clothes with my credit card at a local department store. The next day the store manager called the Board explaining that I had to come to the store with cash as they did not accept Visa, just some Japanese credit card. I had wondered why it took so long to complete the transaction that night. Now I know: The clerk sent for authorization to the Twilight Zone.

We have also been undergoing telephone training. I feel childlike when adults try to teach me a simple, everyday task such as using the phone. The last two days my group of teachers has grown to include, at one time or another, everybody in the office except the superintendent. The room where our telephone training is going on is next to the Board's main room. Because the overall office space is small and cramped, the people working away in the main room can hear the giggling and guffawing that is going on in our "classroom." One of my teachers is Miyagawa-*sensei*, a man in his early forties, who stands about five feet three inches tall. A few times he has stood next to me, put his hand at his hip level, which comes up to about one foot short of my hip, then said, "You are tall!" which just about exhausts his English vocabulary. I do not know why he has the title *sensei*. He is not a teacher. I think he was, but he is now apparently the office's golden boy. I like him, and he is Tsuruta-*san*'s good buddy from way back. During the telephone classes when everyone in the room (including me) believed that I am just a hopeless *gaijin* who is never going to learn how to communicate even a simple message over the telephone, he found a way to break the tension. He picked up the phone, did a perfect imitation of me destroying the Japanese language, complete with a mimicking of me slapping my forehead with my palm after realizing I had screwed up again. The way he did it cracked everyone up, including me.

The fact that I have taken such a quick liking to the people in the office surprises me. Before I arrived, I half expected a bunch of dull workaholics who are deathly afraid of losing face. Even though I do not understand the language, from watching the people in the office around me, I see that as much joking gets mixed in with hard work as at any office in the States. There certainly are hard workers here, but man-for-man they do not appear to be the dynamos our press tells us about. I wonder how many of the hours they put in are nonproductive. For example, the people at the office work until 12:45 P.M. on Saturday. At noon they break for lunch till 12:30 and then clean up for fifteen minutes until the chime sounds and they all go home.

The private sector does not appear any different. Housewives tell me their *sarariiman* husbands often come home late because no one can leave before the boss does – even if all the boss is doing is reading the newspaper till nine at night. In my observation, it takes just as many Japanese construction workers to watch the guy with the shovel as it does in the States.

Until their economy turned sour recently, the Japanese had a "labor shortage," and they brought in unskilled laborers from other countries, notably Brazil, where there is a sizable population of Japanese ancestry who immigrated before World War II. I question whether a labor shortage ever existed.

The "labor shortage" was primarily in the manufacturing sector. There are still high-paying, unskilled jobs unfilled because the *san K* jobs are not wanted by today's youth. *San* means three and *K* represents the first letter (when spelled in our alphabet) of the Japanese words *kitsui* (keyt sui–hard), *kitanai* (key ta nai–dirty), and *kurushi* (koo roo shi–backbreaking). Men want to be *sarariiman*, not blue-collar workers because the women look for men with the *san ko*. *Ko* means high or tall. *San ko* refers to high education, high salary, and tall.

Regardless of what we read in the press, instead of the fantastically efficient economy set to blow ours away, I see shockingly - wasteful economic practices. An example is the two-pump gas station, which, to save space, actually has no above-ground pump, only two hoses hanging from an overhead canopy connected to the building. Each customer is greeted by four people. One pumps the gas, one does the windows, one cleans the ash tray and floor mats, and another checks the oil. As the customer leaves, two go into the street to stop traffic, and all bow from the waist as the customer pulls into the street. Four employees here, but at home one or two people run four sets of pumps and a convenience store. To pay for such service the price of gas is about four times the U.S. price.

At the stores it is more of the same. Many are no bigger than a self-respecting walk-in closet, but they will be staffed by three or four employees.

In Japan, the "customer is God." Enter a department store when it opens and the employees will be lined up along the aisle, bowing as you pass and saying *irrashaimase* (e rah shy ma say – welcome). Department stores also seem to have too many employees. With all the time spent wrapping the product, though, maybe they need them. For example, I bought some lunch meat from the meat counter of a department store. (Most have grocery stores in the basement.) The woman wrapped the meat in a plastic sheet. She put that inside a paper wrapper. She put that inside an aluminum foil wrapping. She put that inside a plastic bag. She put that inside a paper bag. She then charged me several times what the price would be in the States. I took no consolation from her bow as she handed my purchase to me.

Now is the time of summer gifts. An ALT in a small town received an elaborately wrapped cantaloupe from someone in her office. Only later did she discover the present cost $100. If the wrapping done at the store is perfect the cost can be ridiculous. We have customs that foreigners think are loony, but this one does seem to take the cake, or cantaloupe.

Speaking of presents, Rosemary has received many, as her birthday was on the fifteenth. Coworkers at the office asked me to help plan a surprise party at my house, complete with twenty-five Japanese people singing "Happy Birthday." We were impressed that they knew that song, until we asked them to sing the Japanese version and they admitted there is none. For their own birthdays they sing "Happy Birthday" in English. Scholars someday will compare the amount of English being sucked into Japanese today to the influx of French into English after the Norman conquest of England.

The highlight of the evening occurred when one of the big bosses in the office, a gray-haired man named Okabe-*kacho* (ka cho – section chief) sang to Rosemary "You are my Sunshine," which he learned in junior high school. I wonder whether any of my students will remember that long anything I teach this year. His voice trembled a bit while singing in a foreign language. We were all still and watched the interplay of his and Rosemary's smiling eyes. When he finished there was a moment of silence. I think everyone was moved by an old man paying a tender courtesy to a woman from another culture.

Although receiving gifts is nice, I am careful about how I respond to the question "Do you like. . .?" Several times I was asked, for example, "Do you like fruit?" only to have that person show up later at the house with a basket of fruit. Like everything else here, fruit is expensive. Apples can be $3 each. Half the cost of the cantaloupe gift was for the fruit.

Because my expenses are low, I decided to buy *mai kaa* (ma e ka – my car). Originally this was a term meaning the dream of one day owning one's own car, but now it simply is another way of saying passenger car.

Hondo is far from the vaunted Japanese mass transportation system and exploring this part of Japan without a car would be hard. I am fortunate to have had my mother hen, Tsuruta-*san*, to take care of the details. He even found a reputable used car dealer, Kyoko's uncle.

Before I bought the car, there were meetings and conferences around the office. Finally, Miyagawa-*sensei*, Tsuruta-*san*, Akane (who acted as the interpreter), a couple other people, and I met in the *tatami*-mat room of City Hall. They began by saying that they did not object to me buying a car. I said, "Thanks, but what are you guys talking about?" They explained that the Board had decided that I could not use the car to drive to and from work. I must have looked at them with a what-in-the-hell-are-you-talking-about look on my face because Miyagawa-*sensei* and Tsuruta-*san* both quickly added that they both voted to let me drive. They explained that if I was in an accident the Board would be responsible and they did not want to risk it. I told them I would reread the contract that evening and talk to them the next day.

As we were leaving, Tsuruta-*san* pulled me aside, held onto my arm and with halting English said, "I [while saying this he pointed a crooked index finger at his nose which is the equivalent of our index finger or thumb tapping our chest to indicate "Me"] berieve [believe], you [pointing at my chest]." "What's the problem," I asked. "You, accident. Yoshi-*san* [the Superintendent] lose joe boo [job]." "Why? I do not understand why." "Eat eezoo [it is] *baka* [bah ka – stupid], but eat eezoo Jaa-pa-knee-zoo [Japanese] way."

In a mixture of baby Japanese and gestures I conveyed that after all those years of driving, I could handle the Japanese road. I said, "*San jyu yon sai desu* (I am 34 years old). *Jyu hachi nen* (18 years)," while using the Japanese gesture of pointing with a crooked finger to my nose and then gestured like I had my hands on the wheel. "I know, I, believe, you." "We should talk more tomorrow." "Okay."

The contract provides that I can drive *except* during school hours. After a long talk with the other ALTs, whose advice was to try to fit in and do things the Japanese way, I decided to give the people at the Board some time to gain confidence in my driving ability before I drive to school. I told the Board, however, that I am tired of riding (and sweating) in my suits on the bike. They offered to have the teachers pick me up in the morning. After talking with the teachers I agreed. By picking me up they are excused from some morning and evening chores, and they are also happy to have the chance to practice their English in a private setting.

Buying the car gave me a more in-depth lesson concerning the *hanko* (han co) system. The Japanese have personal seals, called *hanko*, which are made of wood, are about three inches long, and no fatter around than a dime. The *hanko* has the owner's family and first name written in *kanji* (khan gee – Chinese characters with which the Japanese write).

My *hanko* has my name written in a phonetic alphabet called *katakana* (ka ta khana). The Japanese use *katakana* for foreign words and names, which is how my *hanko* ends up proudly proclaiming me as a boy partially named Sue. Using *katakana,* instead of my first and last name, there is only room for Kenneth. When the Japanese say it using *katakana* as a pronunciation guide it comes out sounding more like "kay knee sue."

My office could not issue my pay envelope until I "signed" for it, and I could "sign" for it only with my *hanko.* So I had one made and had it registered with City Hall. The Japanese *hanko* system results in buyers not signing for major purchases such as a car or house. I was told to guard my *hanko* closely because if someone gets hold of it, they can make contracts in my name for which I will be responsible. I wonder how true that is in my case. I mean, there cannot be too many Japanese named Kenneth.

In the car lot office, Tsuruta-*san* took my *hanko* and affixed it to this paper, then that paper, then the next one and so on. I trust Tsuruta-*san* was not *hanko*ing my life away. He even had to put his *hanko* on one of the forms as guarantee. Why? I have no clue.

I will not pick up the car for about two weeks because of *shaken* (sha ken), which is a government enforced inspection of all used cars. Every car on the road goes through this, beginning when the car is three years old. Mine is ten years old and will be due again in two years and then yearly inspections. *Shaken,* which costs about $1,000.00, is why there are few older cars on the road. That is just for the inspection; if they find anything wrong, repair is extra.

I had to prove to the police that I have a place to park before they would issue a *nambapureto* (numba poo ray toe – number plate). Because my house was only two weeks old when I moved in, one of the forms Tsuruta-*san hanko*ed was to request the police to measure the house's parking area to ensure it is large enough to accommodate the car. The landlord also had to provide a document granting me permission to park the car in front of the house. All this in a rural area. I can only guess at what the restrictions are in the megalopolises.

So that is where it stands now. I bought a car that I will use only after work. When I will start driving to work I do not know, but I am going to be as reasonable as I can. These people have been great and I do not want to thumb my nose at their concerns, even though I think their worries are groundless – well mostly.

After I bought the car, but before I could pick it up due to *shaken,* Tsuruta-*san* wanted to give me some experience on Japanese roads while he was with me. On the appointed day, he picked me up and handed me the keys to his car. It is a stick shift, but as the steering wheel is on what would be our passenger side, the stick shift was on my left.

The pedal arrangement is the same. Neither the pedals nor the stick shift caused me any problems. I put the car in gear and pushed the turn signal up to indicate a right turn out of the parking area; the wipers went on. That was my first clue that the wiper and turn signal indicator stalks are on the opposite sides from ours.

I pulled onto the steep road in front of my house, heading downhill toward the T-intersection at the high school about 150 yards away. The two-way road was about a foot wider than the car. I had gone about fifty yards when a car came around the corner and up the hill. I thought "Ahhhhhhhhh!!!!"

I pointed the car toward a gravel pullout to which Tsuruta-*san* gestured in a way which revealed his please-God-don't-let-him-dent-my-car concern. At the far end of that area was the woman who bears a striking resemblance to Granny of the *Beverly Hillbillies*. She always sits there on her stool next to the cow shed where her one stinking (in the smelly sense) cow is kept.

As he passed, the other driver lightly tooted his horn and bowed slightly. I waved. Granny waved back. So I waved again. We made it past Granny, past the T-intersection and all the way to the bottom of the hill where there is a big curved mirror on a pole at the corner. In Japan mirrors often are placed at intersections, because many are built up right to the corner. Without these mirrors my car would be in the middle of the intersection before I could see if there was oncoming traffic. Without this particular mirror the traffic on my right (which in Japan makes it the oncoming lane of traffic) would be blocked by the high school's stone fence. I turned onto the slightly wider road in front of the high school and Tsuruta-*san* used a pushing gesture to tell me that I was on the wrong side of the road. I moved over and saw oncoming traffic approaching around the next corner. I thought, "Ahhhhh!!"

The traffic to the school was heavy. I edged as close as I could to the side of the road without falling three feet into the rice paddy on that side. An oncoming car splashed water from a puddle. I tried to engage the wipers only to find I signaled a turn into the rice paddy. I was as frustrated with the signal/wiper problem as a golfer is with a putter which refuses to shoot straight. I finally turned the wipers on.

The road narrowed to one lane again, and kids on bicycles were passing on either side of the two oncoming cars. Tsuruta-*san* motioned for me to back up to the gravel pullout we just passed. As I backed up and angled toward it, the kids passed on either side of me. I could not help laughing to myself when I considered that the students had no idea how much danger they were in. Tsuruta-*san* nervously laughed too, I guess hoping he would not have to explain how the *gaijin* nailed one of

Hondo's youngsters while driving his car.

Approximately 200 yards before the intersection with the big street that would take us to City Hall, we came up behind an elderly woman pushing a wheelbarrow. Until the intersection, we cruised down the road at wheelbarrow speed. But I was making better time than the traffic facing me, which had to back up and pull over to make way for her, the wheelbarrow and us.

We finally made it to City Hall. Tsuruta-*san* got out and dramatically wiped his brow while saying "Whew," in Japanese. Then he put his hand inside his shirt at chest level and pantomimed a madly beating heart. I could not help laughing.

As I observe Japanese driving etiquette, I am learning that, as with so many of the rules in this country, the rules of the road are both written and unwritten. The unwritten ones are just as important as any of those on the books to the safety on the road. My experience of driving on narrow, twisty dirt mountain roads in the outback in Arizona has prepared me well for the unwritten rules of who has to yield to whom on narrow stretches.

I am trying to learn the rules of the Japanese classroom too. Classes will start in just a few days. I will write again shortly after that. Bye now.

*D*ear Barb,   September 5
Monday was my first day as a teacher in Japan. I am more settled in now that school has started. For the first time in years, I am getting chalk on my hands (and usually on my pants too). So far I am really enjoying the experience of being Ken-*sensei*. It was raining off and on most of Monday, as it seems to do every other day here in Japan. The result was a *mushi atsui* (moo she a tsu e – hot and muggy) day. After being in Japan a month, I am firmly convinced the phrase *mushi atsui* is permanently scorched into my brain.

Although it was my first day of the year, it was not for the students or the teachers. The Japanese school year begins in April. I started the year at Honmachi-*chu gakko*, where Akane teaches. Honmachi (hone ma chee) is the name of the school, *chu* (chew) means middle and *gakko* (ga ko) means school. I was overwhelmed a couple of weeks ago with all the new people, the new places and all the names to go with them. For some reason I could not remember Honmachi's name so I called it Akane-*chu*. Now when the people at the Board talk to me about this school they refer to it as Akane-*chu*.

Classes are 50 minutes long and I usually will have three classes a day. The first day after summer vacation, the students took their big test.

Before 8 A.M. I walked into the teachers' entrance (all schools have separate entrances for the students and teachers), and began the ritual in the school's *genkan* that I will be performing every school day. I took my shoes off, put them in my pigeonhole and stepped into my slippers. It took awhile but finally I found a pair of slippers that I can wear without having my heels drag along the ground.

I was met at the *genkan* by Honda-*sensei* (which is what I call Akane in school). As we made our way to the teachers' room, the students bowed and said good morning in very polite Japanese. I said "Howdy." As at the other schools, the teachers' room is also the school's business office, where the vice principal has her desk, next to the principal's. In Japan the vice principal is the person who actually runs the school.

I walked to their desks and we exchanged bows. The principal's bow, like that of the other people with whom I exchange bows, was deeper and looked nicer than mine. I decided early on that yes, it would not kill me to bow to people here. But I decided that my bow would be a Western bow. By that I mean that I have an all-purpose bow. Never deeper, never shallower. Because bowing is not our custom, the Japanese understand that few Westerners learn to bow properly and in the appropriate situation. So with my all-purpose bow they probably just consider me a *gaijin* who does not understand the technique of bowing. The Japanese, on the other hand, always have to know to whom they are bowing so they know how low to bow, how long to hold it and who goes first. Considering the social rules of Japan–the socially "inferior" person bows first and deeper–I do not like the idea of bowing to another person. Soon after my arrival, however, I found a practical reason to prefer bowing over shaking hands. Few Japanese public rest rooms, including those in schools and train stations, have either soap or towels. People carry handkerchiefs to dry their hands, but they just pass on the soap.

As I sat in the teachers' room listening to the morning meeting without understanding, I thought about how much fun Akane is to be with. I already like her quite a bit. If today's classes are any indication, I think I am going to have fun in her classes.

She is a pretty, intelligent, likable Japanese woman. I have known her only a month, but she is just as much a sponge trying to soak up the world I come from as I am in my effort to absorb her culture. Our conversations have ranged as far as her vocabulary can take them.

She wants a transfer to Kumamoto city where there are attractions such as movie theaters, and eligible men. She has been trying for over ten years and there seems less and less chance of a transfer happening.

The-practically-devoid-of-eligible-young-men Hondo is ninety miles from the "big city." Without knowing about Japanese geography and Japanese roads, you might think that on the weekends she could zip up to Kumamoto for shopping or entertainment. The problems include the snail's pace, two-lane road between Hondo and Kumamoto and the several islands in between. The drive, behind someone else's slow-moving car every foot of the way, usually takes three hours, or two and a half when the roads are clear. The roads gave one elementary student the impression that Japan is a big country. He told me Japan is the biggest country in the world because you can drive for hours between cities.

Akane liked her first assignment in Hondo, an elementary school, but she was transferred to junior high and made an English teacher, which fortunately she also loves. However, she teaches not only English but girls gym as well.

She hates the gym class, but in Japan, teachers are often assigned to teach classes or coach teams that they have no expertise or interest in. The boys' soccer coach, who started in April, never played it at any school he attended and is quick to say that he likes baseball (a sport he played) much better. The disregard of teachers' skills and prefer-ences is only half of it.

Family pressures mount on a woman Akane's age to find a husband. It is common for women in their late 20s (and intensifying in their early 30s) to be driven to distraction by mothers who want them married off. Men start feeling the same pressures in their early 30s.

Those who do not find a spouse on their own are pushed to find a mate through *omiai* (o me eye, literally see and meet: the Japanese form of matchmaking). The people who arranges the meetings are known as *nakodo* (na ko dough). There are both professional and busybody *nakodo*. Usually they present pictures and a résumé of the prospective spouse. The least objectionable are invited to the house for a meeting in the presence of the *nakodo*.

There is a cute TV commercial for heartburn medicine incorporating *omiai*. A young lady on a structured date with a guy she is meeting through *omiai* needs the company's medicine. The way the *shiemu* (she emmu, meaning commercial, which they abbreviate to CM) portrays the tense and awkward moments in the meeting it is funny even to a one-month veteran of Japan.

When the chime sounded for the first class, Honda-*sensei* and I walked down the all wooden hallway toward the *ninensei* (knee nen say) classroom. *Ninensei* literally means second-year student, but is equivalent to eighth graders. The halls were deserted but the classrooms were noisy. During the ten-minute break between classes, all the teachers are in the teachers' room, leaving the children seemingly totally unsupervised. They, however, are very regulated.

Girls wear white sailor blouses with blue trim and pleated white skirts with blue trim. The boys wear black pants and white shirts. Outside school the uniform includes a black short-brimmed hat, which they tip while bowing as they greet teachers at or on the way to school. Because the schools have neither lockers, nor showers, the kids have to wear all the clothes they need for the day (such as gym wear) when they leave home, in both sweltering summer and freezing winter.

The kids attend class six days a week. My job is five days a week. The kids are in uniform at school, and some schools require them to wear their uniforms any time they leave the house during the school year – even on Sunday! I have seen my students in this young semester in uniform at virtually any time of the day or evening. Girls' hair is not regulated, but they cannot wear jewelry of any kind. Boys all have short cropped hair cuts. Students cannot wear watches.

Even how they go home is regulated. If they live a certain distance from the school, the students must walk to school. A little farther from the school and they may bicycle. Under almost no circumstances may a student be driven to school by a parent – even if the parent is a teacher at the same school and it is raining cats and dogs.

We entered the classroom and one of the students shouted *kiritsu* (key reets). The students all stood next to their desks. Akane walked to the center of the front of the room. When she faced the class, the student leader said *rei* (ray). The students bowed while saying *onegai shimasu* (oh nay guy she maas), which the dictionary defines as "I ask (beg, request of) you." But they use it for many more meanings than that. In fact, in this context, even the Japanese teachers are not sure what it means except that it is a polite way to begin the class by telling the teacher, in effect, nothing more than "Please." She bowed and the kids sat. The girls put their hands on the back of their skirts and brought their hands down and out to make sure theirs would not be wrinkled. The first part of the class was like the next 100 or so are going to be. I gave my self introduction. We learned in the seminars things the children are curious about so I have my introduction planned out, complete with a map of the U.S. During my introduction, pointing to the map I had taped to the blackboard (although in Japan they are green), I told them I was born in this state (pointing to Michigan) and that my father still lives there. I asked if anyone can tell me the name of the state. The rush to volunteer was totally underwhelming. Finally a girl raised her hand. She is the first student I called on as Ken-*sensei*. She stood up and said *mishigan* (me she ghan – Michigan). As was suggested at the seminars, I gave her a stamp that I had taken off of a letter from home. The kids seem to treasure them. The next time I asked a question the response was more enthusiastic.

I talked about Arizona and although the kids have heard of it and a couple even know that the Grand Canyon is located there, no one knew where it is. I cannot blame them. When I was a kid, the pairs of Arizona/New Mexico, Nebraska/Kansas and Vermont/New Hampshire confused me. After my first day of class, it is obvious that Japanese students, and their teachers for that matter, can identify on a map the states of California, Florida, Michigan, Hawaii and Alaska, although they can name several more. During my introduction I pointed to Ohio and asked if anyone knew the name of that state. No response. I told them the name and then had the class repeat it after me. After they said "Ohio," I said "Good morning" and half the class laughed. In Japanese, the sound "ohio" is a way of saying good morning. Okay, I agree Robin Williams has nothing to worry about from me.

This class was a little shy but I thought it went well. Certainly part of the lethargy is caused by the heat. None of the classrooms in Kumamoto-*ken* schools is air-conditioned.

After the first class Akane said she hoped that I would be intimate with all of her students. "I beg your pardon?" I questioned. When she repeated it, I gave her a "Huh?" look as she pulled out her dictionary to show me the Japanese word that had "intimate" as the first definition. The third definition was the one she wanted, "become acquainted with." This exchange shows how much people who are trying to communicate in another language are at the mercy of the dictionaries. Buy a bad one and you sound as if you are inviting criminal sexual conduct.

Her mistake is indicative of a bigger problem. The teachers' English ability is barely enough to carry on a conversation. Of the teachers I work with, Akane's English is the best. But even she cannot watch an American movie and understand it. Until this program began the emphasis in English was on the written, not the spoken, word. Consequently many of the teachers have a spoken vocabulary not much bigger than what they need to teach their classes. As do many of the ALTs, I catch myself sometimes picturing my high school French teacher standing in front of the class. I wonder if she really could speak French.

My second class as KEN-*SENSEI*!!! It was an *ichinensei* (e chee nen say – literally first-grade student, but it translates into seventh graders) class.

They are the very definition of the Japanese word *genki* (gain key). I have grown quite fond of the word. It has a breadth of meaning that escapes any direct translation in English. It means energetic and lively but can also mean, for example, effervescent or a real go-getter when describing someone's personality. It is also a one-word greeting/conversation. ("Genki?" [How are you doing?] "Genki" [I'm fine]. "Genki?" [And you?] "Genki" [I'm fine too.]) It is a word that you learn quickly when studying Japanese and one that all of the ALTs use now, even when talking to fellow ALTs. It ought to be adopted into English.

Well, these kids were *genki* alright. We are told about how sedate and well mannered Japanese kids are, but no one told that myth to this class. They were hooting, hollering and just plain loud and noisy. They had a good time with the *gaijin* – even my Ohio joke was hilarious. I may have found a second career as a stand-up comic for Japanese teenagers.

The boys raised their hands so far in the air there was a danger of dislocated shoulders. Their butts were barely brushing their seats while they shouted the Japanese equivalent of "Ooh ooh me me, teacher call on me!!!" Girls were giggling and covering their mouths with their hands.

Today, however, was a triple bummer day for the students. First, the test. Second, the heat. I had sweat pouring down my back and the kids found anything they could to fan themselves. After lunch it was worse because there is a play period before classes resume. During the break the students go outside to play and work up a sweat, then return to the hot classroom. All the windows in the classroom, its doors, and the hallway windows were open. When we felt a breeze, we were all grateful. Third, they were let out of class early so they could do extra *soji* (so gee – clean).

In Japanese schools there are no janitors. I have been introduced to women who are described as janitors, but only because every Japanese dictionary mistranslates a Japanese word into that in English. These women do not use brooms or do anything else that we associate with a janitor's role. Their position is really the "school *OL*." Their first job in the morning, before the teachers' meeting, is to serve the teachers' *ocha*. They also serve the teachers' meals (the daily shipment of lunches everyone, from principal to students, is required to buy from the Board), wash the dishes and are in charge of the copy room.

There being no "custodial engineers," everyone at the school – students, teachers, the vice principal and the principal – every day cleans the school. Today was a heavy-duty dose of *soji* so everyone changed into sweat pants and were out pulling weeds or pushing brooms. Everyone except me, that is. No one seems to mind that I walk around harassing the kids instead.

There was good old-fashioned rock-and-roll blasting out of the school's loudspeakers, picked by the student in charge of audio-visual. It was quite a contrast to the classical music we were treated to during lunch. Over the course of the couple of hours we were out there, I walked up to several groups of students who were diligently watching to ensure that work was getting done. The student body was definitely creating more noise than doing away with dirt or weeds.

I figured if they were not working, they could converse with me in English. One girl was down on her haunches pulling out weeds at such a rate that the species she was attacking would never have to worry about a declining replacement rate. Seeing me she suddenly became too busy to talk. But I dragged some things out of her. "Which do you like more English or TV?" "TV." "Which do you like more, English or *soji*." "*Soji?*" "Which do you like more, talking to me or pulling weeds?" "Pulling weeds." Who says these kids refuse to speak their minds!

I returned to the teachers' room to type this letter. I chose the teachers' room instead of the computer room, because this room has air-conditioning. I found a boy on his hands and knees wiping the floor with a wet cloth. Another student was nearby with a two-foot-long broom made of horse-hair bristles. He was sweeping dust onto the just-cleaned floor. I guess all of this indicates why 100 students are needed to replace a crew that in America would number three or four.

The vice principal, who is the only female vice principal in Hondo, came in and we "conversed" in Japanese. Toward the end of our rather limited conversation she said something I did not understand. I asked her to say it again and when I still did not understand it, she repeated it a third time. When I smiled, shrugged my shoulders and said I was sorry but I still did not understand, she said it in English, "Your Japanese is very good." She saw no inconsistency whatsoever in being forced to tell me in English how wonderful my Japanese is. Normally people say my less-than-survival Japanese skills are *jozu* (joe's ooh – skilled, or good), but the vice principal said "*Umai* (ooh ma e)," which I now know means the same thing.

This is a typical trait of the Japanese. They praise Westerners for their pathetic "mastery" of Japanese; for using *hashi* and for other things thought to be hardcore Japanese. But this praise is getting real old. I know my Japanese is light-years away from being *jozu*, and it is irritating to be praised for something I know I cannot do. Unfortunately, this form of politeness is drilled into every last Japanese.

After the vice principal left the teachers' room, I was doing the best I could to talk with an eighth-grade girl when the phone rang. We both looked around and suddenly realized that we were the only ones in the room. I casually motioned for her to answer it. She crossed her hands in front of her chest making an X, which is a gesture the Japanese use for all sorts of negative meanings.

I tried again to have her answer it because I admit, I am intimidated by the phone here. The sweet little teenager gave me the no-way-José gesture. With my limited telephone training in Japanese, I do not relish the thought of picking up the phone in front of one of my students and sounding like a five-year-old. Maybe its stupid, but that is how I feel. So I tried to reassure *her* that there was nothing to worry about in answering the phone.

She was hopping up and down by then to emphasize her total inability to do what I asked. She was probably thinking "Ken-*sensei*, I am just a student. Who am I to answer the phone? That's for the teachers to do, like you." The phone stopped ringing. We went back to our conversation and by the time another teacher walked in the room no one was the wiser about our 20-second dilemma.

Although the weather cooperated during *soji*, I am at home now riding out another typhoon. It has been raining off and on for most of the time I have been here. I am convinced that the Japanese have weathermen on TV only because they see that all the other industrialized nations have weathermen on TV. Unless Japanese weathermen predict rain, they do as accurate a job of predicting the weather as those unbalanced souls who predict the end of the world.

I arrived in Hondo during the middle of the typhoon season. Here typhoons are numbered and we are up to number 25. They all start in the Pacific and head toward China. They run into what I think is a big meteorology-type sign in the ocean when they are in a line between Japan proper and Okinawa. The sign says "All typhoons must turn right." At that exact spot they make a right (to the north) and turn their homing radar frequency to the electronic signal that I am convinced is emitted by my house.

A week after my arrival there was a power outage throughout Hondo due to a typhoon. At the high school down the street from my house, at seven thirty in the evening, there were kids practicing volleyball in the school gym with the main lights out. Emergency lights were on, but they illuminated the area like the TV does when your eyes are already accustomed to the dark. Not enough light to play by – unless you are in Japan.

Ten days ago another typhoon hit. Within a 60-mile radius of my house electricity was knocked out but quickly restored. In parts of Kumamoto city electricity was out for several days. As I sit here now in the kitchen writing in my notebook, it is early evening and I am riding out another typhoon. It is expected to be worse than the last one. The good part is that the worst is supposed to be over before dark so if the electricity goes off, I still may get the air-conditioning back before I go to bed.

My house has three rooms with big sliding windows that open to create a very airy feeling on a calm Saturday afternoon or evening. But during a typhoon all that glass will result in too airy a feeling if one of the windows break. Fortunately, the Japanese have long experience with building houses in typhoon alley.

The house comes equipped with six-foot-high metal storm shutters on rollers that, when deployed, can button up the house to the point it feels like living in a submarine. The shutters are stored in a housing attached to the side of the house next to each bank of windows. To use the shutters, I have to open the window, put my hand inside the housing and pull them out. I do not like doing that as the shutter housings are favorite spider hangouts and every time I use the shutters (I put them up when I travel on the weekends just in case) spiders spill out. Even with the shutters in place there is still a band of windows about eight inches high just above the big windows that remain uncovered. As strong as the wind is, I am concerned that it will propel the objects it picks up right through those windows.

This typhoon is turning out to be strong one. The door lock is struggling mightily to keep the door shut against the force of the relentless wind. The wind hitting the house makes it feel as if the house is being rammed by trucks. The gusts are strong enough to shake the house, making the wind chimes attached to the kitchen ceiling jiggle slightly as if moved by a gentle spring breeze.

It is now 8:45 P.M. and the worst of the typhoon is over, the electricity never went out and the rain has almost stopped. I opened the windows to cool the house off, and the breeze reminds me of sitting on a cool beach after sunset. I can hear the crickets and other bugs shouting out their calls.

I do not get it. This country is prone to typhoons, earthquakes, landslides, volcanos and, do not forget, tidal waves. Yet the Japanese think they are blessed with the best land on earth. I, for one, however, am not going to miss the excitement when I return home. Bye for now.

*D*ear Lynea,   September 13
Thanks for your letter. It was great to hear from you. I am writing this by candlelight because the forecasted typhoon rolled in just after 4 A.M. I awoke when something whacked against the house with a terrific smashing sound. With the racket outside, I cannot fall back to sleep. After fidgeting in my futon and trying to read, I am passing time by writing a running commentary of the storm.

The electricity is going on and off on an average of one minute on and fifteen minutes off. I know this because I turned the TV on for info and it has been shutting itself on and off on that schedule. (All the channels display the time daily until about 9 A.M.) Only a chart of the storm appears on the screen with a note as to when the next live broadcast will be; they are a half hour apart.

It is 5:30 A.M. now. The wind is trying to force its way into the house through any crack it can. The wind is howling and rattling everything it smacks. It has abated only once since it so rudely woke me up. It seems as if the front door, which is a not-very-sturdy looking sliding door, is straining to get a closer look at the hallway floor.

To know what a typhoon feels like, imagine sitting five feet away from a freight train passing by at 60 mph. That would probably give you the right feel for it.

There was a sudden calm not long ago. It was just an intermission. Then the typhoon geared up for round two and again smashed debris into the house. The sky is starting to lighten and the wind is abating. I wonder what sort of destruction the storm has caused.

It is now 8:30 A.M. I have been outside looking at the mess.

Tiles are missing from the roof next door. My carport is smashed but the car is undamaged. A neighbor said a tree fell on a car a few blocks away. Leaves are glued to the sides of houses. Other leaves wiggled their way through the crack between my door and the door jamb into the *genkan*.

I pieced together what the big crash was. Tiles from the house next door slammed into my storm doors, leaving a big dent. The neighbors and I decided that without the storm doors, the tiles would have crashed through the windows and probably hit me in the head or chest.

Except for the excitement of the occasional typhoon, I am settling into a routine. I rotate on a daily basis among the seven junior high schools in Hondo, which have a total of 1,932 students. The biggest school is Hondo-*chu*, which has 936 students and 5 English teachers. Miyajidake-*chu* (me ya gee da kay), the smallest school, has 34 students and one English teacher. Over the course of the year I will be in the classroom of every junior high school student in Hondo.

Although I will be primarily teaching at junior high schools, last week I spent a day at Minami-*sho gakko* (me na me – south; show gakko – elementary school). They want me to teach at elementary schools once a month or so, but after this one, unlike General MacArthur, I am not so sure I shall return.

The day was a disaster. I wondered if they purposely threw me a hardcore sanity test. I should have known it was not going to be a normal day. As I walked up to the school the rooster running loose on the playground crowed, the chicken in the courtyard was being chased by the rabbit, and as I stepped into the *genkan* the parrot said hello in Japanese. I pulled my slippers out of the plastic bag in my briefcase and was escorted to the principal's office for introductions. There I was asked to take off my slippers. The principal's office is carpeted and slippers are not allowed on carpet. I will never get this shoe, slippers and stocking-feet stuff right.

I introduced myself in Japanese, which launched the principal into a stream of Japanese that left me in his linguistic wake. He introduced me to all the teachers. They introduced themselves in English, including what they taught, their marital status and their hobbies. I imagine they practiced their short speeches as long as I practiced mine.

I was handed a glass of *mugicha* (moo ghee cha – barley tea). When I tried it some weeks ago, I did not like it, but I find myself growing fond of it. It has a light brown color, a musky smell and stark taste that I am learning to appreciate because my favorite cold drink, water, is not popular here. Whenever I ask for it they pass something else off on me. I assume they know more about the purity of their unboiled water than I do, and consequently *mugicha* constitutes a part of my daily liquids.

From my previous letters, you may be catching on that the Japanese have a real love of English. In a Japanese business or office, the door usually has the words "Push" or "Pull" on it instead of the Japanese word. In the elevators "B" is for basement, not the Japanese word *chika* (chee ka). The Japanese love English so much they love it even when it is not English.

My glass with *mugicha* had typical Japanese non-English written on it. It said "Tapir (then in bold colors and capitalized) G, Y, R, B, and O. Happy Presenter. . . Tapir! Happy colors give our Tapir friend a colorful transformation. Whenever he is near we feel happy. After all he's a Happy Presenter." This kind of nonsense English is rife all through Japan. An advertisement for some sort of cold remedy has a picture of a smiling face and the words "My Wellness!!"

The hands-down worst offender, though, is Japanese T-shirt English. From the ALTs' perspective, the non-English that scores the most points is text that uses recognizable nouns, adjectives, verbs and so on, in grammatically proper sequence (if possible), but still ends up making perfect nonsense. So far this one is my favorite: "Yes, the idea. A flower, a kitten. Oh I am happy day and that is my friend. Shall we?" Another T-shirt suggested in big bold letters: "Oh let's pee." Singapore bans the import of T-shirts made in Japan because they do not want their children learning Japanese T-shirt English. Who can blame them?

While sipping on my *mugicha* in my "Happy Presenter" glass, the teacher with whom I worked that day "translated" for some other teachers who wanted to "talk" with me. I say "translated" because if I had not been here over a month and listened daily to what the Japanese consider English, I would not have understood the translator either.

For example, Japanese typically pronounce words with the "th" sound as an "s" or "z," as in za car, zoez carzoo, zeesu car, or zeez carzoo. *"But it not just pronunciation, it also word and other thing they don't say to make understand defee coo roo toe (difficult)."*

I am not trying to make fun. I make plenty of funny mistakes when I butcher – I mean try to speak – Japanese. My Japanese causes people to politely yet valiantly try to stop from breaking out in unrestrained belly laughs. We do not share a common language. What we share is some overlapping vocabulary, an uncertain grasp of parts of the other's native grammar and a sincere desire to learn the other's language. I am sure that listening to me speak Japanese is as much hard work for them as me listening to their Ing goo ree shoe (English).

My first class was with the second grade. They knew their ABCs and from one to ten in English. They introduced themselves with a molasses-in-January speed saying, "My name is," followed by their names, which they said so quietly and fast that I could not understand. My Ohio joke was such a hit that I made a disturbing observation. It appears the younger my audience, the wittier I am perceived.

The students and I engaged in such intellectual activities as the hokey pokey and musical chairs. One time the music stopped and I was still standing. Two boys and one girl pointed to the empty chair for me. They wore such genuine God-I-have-to-help-him-cause-he-can't-see-it expressions that I acted startled and rushed *gaijin* rear end to wooden seat with as much excitement as I could feign. The class breathed a huge sigh of relief that I had made it to the next round. The competition among the kids was as fierce as the rush for the door from a burning building. The biggest boy walked around the circle dragging his chair with him. When the music stopped three boys jumped on that chair anyway. The chair finally fell over with the boys all holding onto various parts.

The teacher settled the dispute in a very traditional way. She made the boys *jyan ken pon* (john ken pone) for it. This is the paper, scissors, rock game. It is a sure-fire, no-doubt-about-it, fast, reliable way to end disputes in Japan. When the teacher said *jyan ken pon*, the boys were lying in a pile on the floor jockeying for position and grabbing desperately to the chair as football players do to a fumble, shouting things that probably meant "ME ME ME I WAS FIRST" or "GET OFF OF MY LEG, LARDASS." As the teacher shouted those magic words, the boys instantaneously leapt to their feet and formed a circle.

They put their right hands behind their backs and one boy shouted "*Gu choki pa* (goo cho key pa)!" The class struggled to see what the result of this momentous event would be. What *gu choki pa* means and especially how that kid was chosen without a word to do that part of *jyan ken pon* would take either a million-dollar anthropology grant from the federal government or growing up in Japan. At the leader's command the boys' hands flashed into the circle like bolts of lightning seeking the ground. Before it even registered in my brain that their hands were all in the circle, they whipped them behind their backs again. "*Gu choki pa!*" and hands flew out again.

Just as fast they were behind their backs again except for one boy who turned away from the circle with a look on his face like he just lost his puppy. How he lost I have no idea, and how they could process all that action so fast I could not figure out either. Quickly the whole matter was decided. "*Jyan ken pon,*" I thought "Better put that one in my bag of teacher tricks for use on a rainy day."

With the chime for lunch came my first movie-star-type moment of fame. The teacher headed back to the teachers' room just as kids from the other classes came pouring in. They wanted to shake my hand, and shouting *sain* (sa een – from "sign"), they begged me to sign books, hats, hands, anything. Walking down the hall to the teachers' room without the authority figure of a Japanese teacher present, the kids all wanted to touch any part of me they could. The dirt on their hands merged with the sweat on my back to form little smudged handprints on most of the back of my shirt.

As I walked down the hallway, my groupies (consisting of several boys) walked parallel to me jumping up and down, with heads turned toward me, trying to see how far up they could jump in relation to my height. They put their palms on their noses and pulled them away as if their nose was growing like Pinocchio's. To them our Western noses seem big, because theirs are flatter, more pushed back against the face, and this difference fascinates the children.

At the door to the teachers' room, one of the students asked me to eat lunch with them and those still hanging onto my arms and hands and belt screamed their delight when I said Okay. I did not really want to, not just because I wanted to escape my adoring fans, but because I wanted to eat in the air-conditioned teachers' room. But they seemed to want it so much, I agreed.

We went back to the class where the students arranged their desks in groups. A dispute quickly developed as to which group I would be gracing with my royal *gaijin* presence. Having studied the decision-making process of young Japanese (not enough for a dissertation, but enough for a wing at a real-life trial run), I shouted *"jyan ken pon."* Somebody shouted, "*Gu choki pa.*" Hands flashed and *voilà*, way faster than either you or I can say *gu choki pa*, I was grabbed by a couple of kids and escorted to another group where my lunch awaited.

After lunch I went to the gym to shoot some hoops and about 80 kids surrounded me, insisting that I teach them basketball. I tried to explain that I am no good, but they did not believe me. When I agreed, the kids turned and bolted for the storage room and about 30 balls appeared. I lined the students up to teach them how to do layups on the nine-foot rims. One boy threw the ball straight up in the air several times, so I finally picked him up and he dunked the ball. I am counting that as a partial dunk for me too.

When classes began in the afternoon the students were told that they were going to use the school's outdoor, slightly algae-green pool that hour. "Like these kids are not already *genki* enough," I thought. The boys and girls were seven and eight years old and changed into their bathing suits in the classroom. One boy had trouble putting his trunks on.

The teacher pulled up his trunks. He immediately thanked her by pulling them half-way down and mooning her. She giggled and turned away while covering her mouth with her hand as Japanese women do when they laugh in public. The boy ran around the class with a perfect crescent showing. The children squealed with delight. Boys started to pull each others' pants down. Oh, elementary school child, *genki* is thy name. I thought about yelling *jyan ken pon* because I did not know what else to do, when the teacher blew her whistle and shouted something that, from their reaction, must have meant: "Anyone with their pants still not on in two seconds stays in the classroom."

In one of the rare quiet moments of the day, the teacher and I talked for a few minutes in the teachers' room about her college days. She went to school at the University of Kyoto which is one of the better ones in Japan. She learned that the U.S. did not bomb Kyoto or Nara in World War II because of the cultural treasures in those cities. She said, "I think America has a big heart."

When I left school that day, I was a tired man wearing a tiny-fingerprint-patterned, formerly white dress shirt. The kids waved at me while hanging out of windows. One boy ran out of school and right up to me. He pointed at my crotch and shouted, "Penis!!" Everyone within the sound of his voice was laughing. By this time I was beyond wondering "Where did he learn that word?" He was hustled back in the school by teachers offering apologies and no doubt dying to go home to relate how the *gaijin* was abused by the kids.

There are two things that I am sure of after this day. First, I respect that classroom teacher. That sweet little woman is a master of managing human interactions. She so skillfully manages, manipulates and deflects the students' enormous overflowing energy that she can sometimes even teach that wide-eyed, never-say-"slow down"-gang of deceptively cherubic-looking kids. Second, the next time I am scheduled to be at this school, I will call in with the flu.

After the day at the elementary school, I had a three-day stopover at Hondo-*chu*. I taught my first class there with a middle-aged man named Sakai-*sensei*, who is the head English teacher. I met him at school during summer vacation. His most striking attributes are his silver-rimmed teeth and the world's worst breath.

At first I was uncomfortable around him. I thought he was too caught up in the traditional roles the Japanese assign themselves. I wondered if working with him would be a chore, resulting in me not liking teaching with him or at the school. In the halting English typical of Japanese teachers of English he began our first conversation by telling me that each morning I would be required to go to the principal's desk and bow. He suggested that I practice bowing to the principal's empty desk at that very moment. He offered to correct any errors in my bow before I did it wrong in front of the principal. I managed to steer the conversation away from bowing to empty desks.

When I come to school, I first head to the principal's and vice principal's desks in the teachers' room. Long before I ever get into "bowing range" myself, they are out of their chairs bowing. I respectfully return theirs.

Sakai-*sensei* has not said any more about bowing so I assume that issue is over. And my feeling of uneasiness around him is over too. I was overly concerned about what I considered his hardcore attitude toward strictly following the requirements of Japanese culture. For a while my feelings about him even changed to sympathy.

In class the kids snicker to themselves when they think he cannot hear. During a lesson in which we asked the children what they want to be as adults, Sakai-*sensei* offered that as a child he wanted to be a farmer. The students did not attempt to restrain their guffaws. In their eyes, Sakai-*sensei* is light-years behind the times and is hopelessly doomed to the life of a nerd.

While helping me with my Japanese between classes he confessed he does not like classes with me. They cause him more work and he knows the students see his English shortcomings when we have trouble communicating. Miscommunications in the classroom happen a lot, not just with him, but with many of the teachers. I try my best to figure out what they are saying, but many times I simply cannot. I know there are teachers who do not like the idea of a *gaijin* in class and avoid classes with ALTs, probably for this reason. I cannot say I blame them. An ALT in another town does not even have any classes because the teachers simply refuse to teach with an ALT in the classroom.

In spite of Sakai-*sensei*'s feelings, I have had more classes with him than with all the other teachers at Hondo-*chu* combined. I asked him why, as the English department head, he schedules so many classes with me. He said having *gaijin* in class is good for the kids, not only to improve their English skills, but also to expose them to different customs and ways of thinking.

His philosophy is that his job and goal in life is to teach the young. He puts his children first and his own fears of a bruised ego second. All this when he knows the kids are not-so-secretly making fun of him. So my opinion about Sakai-*sensei* is continuing to change. Now I respect this man. I even find myself laughing and joking with him much more than I thought he would find "proper." Though I have not had any great classes with him yet I think the kids have benefitted from them.

My first day at Hondo-*chu* was the first day for an Australian high school girl on a two-week exchange program. Her name is Katie although she pronounced it more like "Kigh (which rhythms with high) tee." Sakai-*sensei* asked her a question and when he did not understand the answer, he asked me what she said. Her thick Tasmanian accent left me clueless too. Sakai-*sensei* was beaming when he realized that I had trouble with her English.

I cannot end my at-school report without mentioning the continuing fascination of the Japanese students with touching, grabbing and poking me. While I was in the hall a boy poked me in the rear with his thumb. I was only partially able to engage my brain before reacting. Instead of handling the matter properly, I asked him if he liked boys. His friends pointed at him and said *homo*, which is one frequently used way the Japanese express the idea of "homosexual." I did not handle the situation professionally, but the Tokyo seminars did not cover how to respond to students grabbing one's private parts.

When I am helping individual students, they invariably ask me questions in Japanese. Because the lessons are uniform throughout the city, I hear the same questions from students at all of the schools. In this way I develop a specialized Japanese vocabulary concerning the lessons we are doing. If they ask the questions in Japanese, we usually end up communicating, sometimes only because a few kids sitting around the child who posed the question pitch in to help. I have decided that the students should not hear Japanese from me. I will be at each school only a short time each month, and throughout their academic careers they will have very few opportunities to speak with a native speaker. I will, however, respond to their questions posed in Japanese if they cannot manage the question in English.

I cannot really describe the feeling I have while kneeling in the midst of kids leaning in their chairs to form a circle around me. It is a thrill to be engaged in a joint effort to share information with students whose English is as rudimentary as is my Japanese. I feel they and I are somehow making the world a little smaller and better place.

Much of my job is to read model sentences. A student is usually singled out to repeat after me. When called on, the students stand next to their desks. They are reluctant to stand in front of their classmates because I must correct their pronunciation several times until they get it right. The kids understandably just want to sit down and forget the whole thing. I encourage them to keep trying and, painful as it is for them, most get the words out of their mouths. When they do, I walk over to them and give them a "high five" along with a slap on the back while saying "Good job." When I do someone invariably asks the teacher what "good job" means. (High five most know from Japanese pro baseball.)

For those who give up and sit down without answering, I go to them, put them in a head lock and give them "nuggies." I raise them to their feet while doing this and have them try to finish the assignment. Now that the kids are laughing at the goofy teacher, the student usually has enough confidence to try again. Almost all of those kids make it through the assignment, and I give them a high five.

When a very shy student makes it through something like that, I usually ask the teacher to translate a short speech for me, which I keep simple for both teacher and student. I tell the kids not to worry about making mistakes and explain that everybody makes mistakes, even teachers. I end this speech by pointing to and praising the student who reluctantly answered. My hope is that next time the students will be less inhibited. I gave this speech in Akane's class and she pointed to herself in mock amazement in response to my statement that even teachers make mistakes. "Me?" she asked. I used gestures to indicate a volcano overflowing. The kids loved it. Akane is not cut from the mold of the myths we know about Japanese teachers having an iron control of the class, which sits there stone silent.

Just when I think I am a teacher and not a walking tape recorder, valuable only for my native English ability, a student will raise his or her hand and say "*Sensei!*" They do it in a singsong kind of way that you have to hear everyday to know how sweet the sound is. I walk over to answer the student's question only to see the student cover his giggle while having a no-I-meant-the-real-teacher look on his face.

Well, this letter is really finished. As the Japanese say, "Bye bye." No kidding, I hear that all over the place and hardly ever hear *sayonara*. Except for formal occasions, "Bye bye" has almost supplanted "Sayonara" among Japanese people under 50.

*D*ear Dad,   September 22

    I am glad the weather in Detroit is good and the coffee at Kay's Kitchen is hot. My second time teaching at Miyajidake-*chu* was on Monday, the 17ᵗʰ. It is my favorite school.

I visited several times before the semester working on lesson plans and have a high opinion of the school's English teacher, Tahara-*sensei*. Her teaching ability is outstanding, and she is a pleasure to work with. I respect her both for her dedication to her students and for her desire to continue to learn. Most of the teachers I teach with live the motto "I learned English in college so I know enough for my needs," but not Tahara-*sensei*. She is a regular at the Thursday-night English conversation classes at Amakusa High School where ALTs volunteer as conversation partners for the Japanese who teach English. Of Hondo's 13 English teachers, she is the only one to use an English-only dictionary. Her English is the best after Akane's. Tahara-*sensei* encourages my study of Japanese. She finds time during each visit to help me, and she has come to the house to tutor me as well.

    Tahara-*sensei* is a middle-aged woman whose physique is typically Japanese: short and thin. She has a pleasant personality, but she tends to be very formal in public, using polite Japanese. If she ever met the emperor, he might think that she was overdoing the politeness thing. There are still some very formal-minded Japanese who will, depending on the occasion, thank people by kneeling and bowing so low that their forehead touches the floor. Tahara-*sensei* is definitely one of those people. When we are in the car together, she is almost as goofy as Akane. I think Tahara-*sensei* was destined to be a more open, spontaneous woman but was bitten by the formality bug. Or maybe she bowed to the pressures of Japanese mores and allowed her public persona to be molded by it. I feel her inner self is the girls-just-wanna-have-fun woman that she shows at times.

    We talked last time in her car on the way to school about protests. I started chanting "We want bigger roads and we want them now!" Tahara-*sensei* and I both cracked up as we rode down the narrow street shouting to each other "What do we want?" "Bigger roads!" "When do we want them?" "Now!" Of course, her conservative Japanese upbringing would not permit her actually to roll down the window so someone other than I could hear her protest.

I enjoy the ride to school with her, not just because of the conversation and language learning. The scenery we pass is normally pretty and often eerily beautiful. Hondo is on a tiny island called Shimoshima with Miyajidake in its highlands. Those facts combine with the salt air from the Ariake and South China Seas to form misty fog banks on the two-lane road we take to school. It changes the feel of the low, steep mountains almost every time.

There is one more enjoyable part of the trip. On the way we pass Kamegawa-*chu*, where I have taught several times. At the traffic signal in front of school, the faces of students crossing the street light up when they see me in the car and wave while shouting "Hi, Ken-*sensei*." I realize that they are not reacting solely to me as an individual but to a rare species of creature known, in these parts, as *gaijin*. My ego, however, has convinced me that though the natural inquisitiveness of the children in this town makes them predisposed to accept an American, I am the person they have come to know and like. Speaking for myself and, I believe, for the majority of the ALTs, we find ourselves falling for our students lock, stock and barrel.

The ride on Monday was a bit of a learning experience. You cannot get away from English in Japan by driving in the countryside. As we drove through the manmade hole in the mountain, Tahara-*sensei* responded to my question telling me in Japanese it is a *toneru* (toe nay roo – a tunnel). Down the road the big concrete wall in front of the large body of water is called a *damu* (da moo – a dam). Because Tahara-*sensei*'s tiny golf-cart-wheeled car does not have air-conditioning, I put my arm on the door with my elbow slightly sticking out of the window. In a panic, Tahara-*sensei* asked me to bring my elbow completely within the car. I looked around at the other cars on the road. Although many people had their car windows rolled down, no one had an elbow sticking out. With the narrow roads and the constant near misses, I realized that in this country, I am well advised to follow Tahara-*sensei*'s advice.

Another reason I like Miyajidake-*chu* is because of its setting. The school is located off a narrow, quiet country road. To the left the school's long driveway is a small dilapidated shack used for husking rice. Despite its age the building probably cannot fall over, because it is being held up by a pyramid-shaped pile of golden-brown rice husks.

The white, wooden school stands out against the lush green hill that rises steeply immediately behind it. Outside every window is a flower box bursting with colorful flowers. As we drive past the school to the gravel parking lot, wide-eyed kids lean out of the windows to see the new *gaijin* teacher.

At the far end of the parking lot there is a tiny, unpainted house, which is owned by the city and is currently the home of the vice principal. Many last minute transferees, like the vice principal, end up in temporary housing supplied by the city.

Looking to the right as you walk back down the driveway to the main entrance, the bright flowers planted on the far side of the driveway help frame the small, rustic valley. A tiny creek runs in front of the school, and past several terraced rice fields and four or five scattered, ivy-covered, unpainted, weatherbeaten black barns so brown with age they shout out how ancient the place is.

The view from the homeroom of the ninth-grade class is the prettiest in Japan. On Monday the windows were open, which let in the warm breeze and the sounds of bird songs. The windows are painted, but the nicks and gouges give ample proof that this truly is Hondo's oldest school. Looking out, you can see the flower boxes hanging on the outside window sill are full of flowers in bloom and that the tiny valley reaches up the thickly forested hill. The mist around the top of the hill seemed to make this valley its own small world.

Every Monday principals haul students into the gym and give them a speech. At this school, with its 34 students, they sit in the hall on the floor in *seiza* (say za), which means sitting on the floor with the legs, from the knee to foot, in contact with the floor. Their behinds rest on the back of their ankles. You have probably seen people participating in martial arts sitting that way.

The principal gave a short speech, then everyone sang the school song. I predict one day scientists will take the essence of this song, distill it and stuff it into a gas canister. It would make an effective antiterrorist knockout gas from which not even a gas mask will afford protection.

After the assembly, the teachers conducted the daily meeting in the teachers' room. It was hot enough for the air-conditioning to be on there, but school rules prohibit it before 11 A.M. An up side to keeping the air conditioning off is that the occasional butterfly floats through the open windows.

In the first class we taught seventh graders how to order at a fast-food store. I was the "friendly" clerk. Tahara-*sensei*'s props included play money and fake food. We practiced reciting the script in the book until the kids could, without looking, order a hamburger and orange juice. I called on the students who were to do the skit with me.

Although I have been a teacher only a few weeks, it is easy to spot the *genki* kids who are not likely to be intimidated by being in front of the class. With the first student, I did not use the script and ventured into territory he was not expecting. He ordered the hamburger and juice as he was supposed to, but that was the last time he had the safety of the book to rely on. In the fast-food context the students already know a variety of English words. (Although they have Japanese words for most such words, English is "cool" enough to muscle out native words.) At *macudonarudo* (ma coo dow new roo dough – McDonald's) and Mos Burger (which has a great chili burger) they use words such as: *hambaga* (hah moo ba ga – hamburger); *kechapu* (kay cha poo – ketchup); *chizu* (chee zoo – cheese); *saizu* (sigh zoo – size); *sheku* (shay coo – shake), *sutoroberi* (sto raw bay ree – strawberry), *banira* (ba knee ra – vanilla: our words with Vs in them are pronounced like Bs in Japanese because they have difficulty with the "V" sound) and *chocoreto* (cho co ray toe – chocolate); *apuru pai* (ah poo roo – apple; pa e – pie); drinks and *poteto furai* (po tay toe – potato; foo ra e – fry: french fries) come in *esu, emu,* and *eru* (eh sue, eh moo, eh roo) size, which is the Japanese pronunciation of "s," "m," and "l," (*s*mall, *m*edium and *l*arge).

I asked him what size juice he wanted. His dumbstruck look said, "Ken-*sensei*, I have no clue what you are talking about. Please follow the book so I do not look stupid." His entire self-worth was on the line so he could not think. The other students cupped their hands to their mouths and shouted to him in hushed whispers *"Saizu!, Saizu!"* Finally a spark of recognition crossed his face. He said, "*Erusaizu.*"

When I pretended not to know what *eru saizu* meant, students whisper/shouted, "*Raji*" (rah gee – large). He smiled and said, "*Raji!*" I corrected his pronunciation.

"Cheese on your hamburger?" "Yes, pureezoo" (which is the closest to "please" most of my students can come). "Will that be all?" He responded with fervent hope, "*Hai!*" "Huh?" asked the clerk. "Yes!" cascaded from the class. He was the only one who did not realize that he had answered in Japanese. "Yes," he shouted.

"For one large orange juice and one regular hamburger that will be four billion yen (about $30,00,000,000)." He handed me the 720 yen in play money Tahara-*sensei* had given him. I looked at the money, shaking my head with what I hoped was a this-is-not-enough look on my face. I gestured with my hand for more money. This time the other students could not help him because they could not understand the word "billion." Clutching the 720 yen and telling him "More, more," I wrote the amount in numbers on the board. Index fingers around the room counted the number of zeros and giggles spread. I mentioned earlier that this boy is *genki*, and what he did next convinces me that if he were dropped out of a spaceship upside down on Mars without a spacesuit, he would still end up owning half the planet.

He picked up the orange juice and asked how much would the total be if he bought a small. "Three billion," said the pain-in-the-rear clerk. How much if the hamburger were a small? "Two billion." How much without the ketchup? Without pickles? The class shouted other ways to reduce the total. Finally, he pointed to the picture of one sesame seed on the fake hamburger and asked, "How much?" I said, "Seven hundred twenty yen." "I'll take it."

With applause for him still filling the air, I called on the *genki*est girl. She squealed and pumped her feet up and down while hiding her face with her book. The other kids were yelling at her, and I assume they were saying "Glad it ain't me," or "Go ahead, it's not so bad." To her I said we did not sell orange juice and we were out of hamburgers. I threw roadblock after roadblock in her way. After what she probably felt was an eternity, she ended up ordering fish and popcorn. (No, they do not sell that stuff at McDonald's here, which is another reason her effort was so commendable.)

I tried to pocket some of her change. She pointed to my pocket and said, "My money!!" As I worked my way from the *genki*est to the shyest kids in the class, they realized that there was no way to prepare for the skit with Ken-*sensei*. Because everyone was being abused by the *gaijin*, there was really no way to be any more embarrassed than anyone else. I thoroughly enjoyed the class and they seemed to also.

At lunch the students asked if I would eat with them. They will never know what an act of devotion that was. There are no cafeterias at school so the children eat in their homerooms. There I was sweating in the classroom again when I could have been in the only air-conditioned room, the teachers' room.

The two class-appointed captains don white caps (covering every bit of their hair), chef jackets and white gloves. The children arrange their desks into small groups. The captains dish out their classmates' gourmet food from metal vats. The other children line up to have the five-star food plopped on their army-style tin trays.

When all are seated, they bring their hands together as if in prayer. The class leader then says "*Itadakimasu*," (e ta da key ma sue). It is a very polite word and literally means "I (or we) receive." It has no religious meaning, but it is a habit that people carry with them throughout their lives. Once this ritual is over the children eat. Captains clean the room after lunch and return the used tin pots and dishes to the "janitor" who takes them to the loading dock.

While my students are saying *itadakimasu,* the same ritual is being carried out in classrooms all over Japan. Conformity in the system is so well orchestrated that when I talk on the phone with ALTs in other parts of Japan, they are on virtually the same page in the lesson book as we are.

Sports Day is another example of this uniformity. For ten days before Sports Day, the Japanese school system has classes only half days. The students used the time off to prepare the school grounds and practice.

I was at last Sunday's Sports Day at Akane's school. Students, parents and faculty gather for a day of a few dangerous and some goofy competitions wrapped around traditional track and field events. The ceremonies begin with the goose-stepping students, in the fashion of Nazi troops, turning their eyes to look at the principal on the reviewing stand. They smartly saluted him with right hands outstretched before them in the fashion of the *Heil* Hitler salute. All I could think was "Scotty, beam me up. NOW!" I wonder whose idea it was to use those military motifs. Even worse, no one there seemed to think anything was wrong with teaching marching and saluting techniques so closely associated with Imperial Japan's old ally, Nazi Germany.

During the opening ceremonies I was asked to introduce myself. I was prepared for it because I know *gaijin* are an exotic species of animal and if you have one you certainly want to impress the neighbors by showing it off.

I recited my really poorly pronounced three-sentence Japanese self-introduction, which I can by now say in my sleep. The crowd applauded. Not a polite applause, but so forceful as to make me feel they wanted an encore. The Japanese have a way to go before they accept *gaijin* as people too. I felt more like a critter called *gaijin* than a person.

The games began. The first was the human pyramid in which only boys participated. They took the field and formed three groups. In each group ten boys formed a circle on their hands and knees. Then another group climbed on their backs. This continued with the smallest boy in each group climbing to the top of the human pyramid. One pyramid collapsed before it was finished. The others collapsed the same way after being completed. What this was supposed to prove I have no clue. I later saw on the TV news that at a school somewhere in Japan such a pyramid collapsed, killing a boy.

The next event made the human pyramid seem tame. The boys put on team-colored bandanas and took off their shirts. They divided into two teams with one at each end of the athletic field. Each raised a ten-inch round bamboo pole taller than the one-story school. Each group formed into two subgroups, one defending their team's pole and the other attackers of the opposing team's pole.

The attackers charged across the field. When the attackers reached their goal, they leapt onto the defenders, forcing their first row to fall. The next wave of attackers flung themselves onto the second row of defenders. The last group of attackers reached the circle of boys holding the pole. Throughout the ordeal bodies slapped together with plenty of pushing, shoving and elbowing thrown in. Each attacker aimed to climb the pole, making it too heavy for the defending boys to keep upright. When the losers' pole tumbled down, many of the boys walked from the field rubbing various body parts.

Afterward the goofy yet not dangerous events began. I raced with one of my favorite students in a three-legged race. Then I was drafted into an event in which contestants used a croquet mallet to roll a softball 50 yards to a stake, around the stake and back to the starting line. I came in next to last but received the same prize everyone else did, a blue plastic pail. Later I was dragged by students into the tug of war. Parents and teachers then raced against each other in an event that could have been called the Tuckered and Puffing 200 meters. Finally came traditional track and field events for the students: dashes, relays and hurdles. It was fun watching young athletes having a great time giving it their all.

I ate lunch with the principal and the *PTA* (pea tea a – PTA, honest, that's what they call it). We sat on the floor of the teachers' room. After eating, the beer flowed, as it usually does when two or more Japanese men get together. The thing I was not expecting was to take part in one of the Japanese bonding rituals. Though I had been initiated before, I thought I had devised a sure-fire antidote. I was wrong.

The ritual consists of a Japanese man chugging his beer glass dry, then handing it to the other person, in this case me. At the same time, I am to drain my own glass and hand it to the other guy. (This is strictly a guy thing.) Then I refill for him the glass I just handed him and he refills for me the one he just gave me. We both chug the glass the other just drank from without wiping off the rim.

The first time I went through this ritual I tried to avoid looking at the other guy's black teeth held together with silver and gold dental work. I have observed that Japanese men drink primarily *ocha*, coffee or beer, but almost never drink soda pop. After my initiation in the spittle-bonding ritual, I decided that to deter others from desiring to bond with me, I would drink pop. Older Japanese seek out pop as children seek out a second helping of vegetables.

To my relief having pop in my glass seemed to act on their desire to bond with me as agent orange wilts foliage. My budding

Japanese cultural survival skills, however, failed me this time. An earnest-looking man drained his glass and held it out to me. I showed him my glass with what a look I hoped conveyed, "Gosh, I do not know what to say, I have <u>POP</u> in my glass." His glance at my glass said, "Whoa, what is THAT?!?." He thought it over for a moment, then saddened me with his resolute intent to make the *gaijin* feel like part of the group.

The others, seeing that pop would neither kill nor maim, lined up and sadly my saliva-laden bonding days recommenced. As soon as I felt it would not look simply like an exit strategy I excused myself to use the rest room and never returned.

Speaking of bonding, I feel like I am doing that with the kids. I find the time I spend in the classroom not work at all. Occasionally time drags during writing assignments, but most classes are fun. Before I arrived I wondered how I was going to interact with teenagers with whom I do not share a common language. Now I find that I enjoy this job more than any I have ever had. When a student's face lights up with that sudden spark of comprehension I get a wonderful feeling that is difficult to describe in words.

Teaching with Ezaki-*sensei*, the main English teacher at Kamegawa-*chu*, is one of life's little pleasures and one of the reasons I enjoy this job so much. She overschedules classes for me, sometime six in a day, which is hard work.

Ezaki-*sensei* is almost five feet tall and maybe 95 pounds. Yet this gray-haired bundle of energy bicycles to school most days, and when the chime sounds she hustles to class at the velocity of the leading edge of an exploding fireball. I admire this woman for her teaching skills and her constant effort to improve her English.

For all her enthusiasm, and as hard as Rosemary, the city's other ALT, and I work to understand what she and the other teachers are saying, miscommunications, even with Ezaki-*sensei*, happen. She has a good command of grammar, but her spoken English is not very good. We had been in Hondo for two weeks when Rosemary and I were sitting with Ezaki-*sensei* at school. She asked me what we thought was "Have you used a Japanese bus yet?" I told her no, that I used my bike or was driven around town by Akane. She had a quizzical look on her face, as if to say "What is he talking about?" She asked the question again and I said no. She asked it yet again, this time using gestures as if she were washing herself. For a split second I began to wonder if she had lost her senses. Finally we all figured it out. The Japanese adopted the English words *bus* and *bath* and both are pronounced "basue" in Japanese.

Now that she has access to native speakers, she takes advantage of the opportunity. She is so intensely focused on improving that she lets nothing stop her, not even showing her inadequacies to her students. I was shocked the first time she practiced pronunciation after me right along with the kids. She always has questions about English when I come to school, and she is a regular at the Thursday-night conversation classes. I have told her that her desire to improve her skills inspires me when studying Japanese. She then confided that a happy frequent dream of hers is when she speaks in English in her dreams. Only then is she able to understand everything that is said to her by native speakers and she can express herself as she, well, dreams of doing.

From conversations with ALTs across the country, I gather that most Japanese teachers of English are in about the same boat. Until the JET program started, these teachers infrequently, if ever, had occasion to speak with native English speakers. The older teachers like Ezaki-*sensei* doubt whether their own teachers ever saw a *gaijin* during their lifetimes, except maybe on some battlefield.

We hear that classrooms in the States can resemble battlefields but that in Japan students are strictly controlled and unquestioningly obey authority. Forget that. The fact is, like students anywhere, the students respect some teachers and abuse others. It seems beyond Ezaki-*sensei*'s ability, however, to conceive of a student not studying attentively during class. She is so wrapped up in her mission that when a student interrupts her efforts, the disbelief on her face is visible. She would not say it this way, but she is a dedicated teacher who views her profession not as a job but as a sacred trust of passing on information the students will need in life. When this grandma walks into class, you can sense her businesslike air.

One of yesterday's classes proved the exception. Ezaki-*sensei* asked me to use a phone as a prop for a conversation. I was to "telephone" a student and have a two-minute conversation necessary to leave a message for someone to call back. The first boy I "called" put the earpiece to his forehead, causing a ripple-effect laugh around the class. I said if that is how one answers the phone in Japan, I would do it too. My sorry attempt at humor only encouraged his antics. He answered, "No," we do not answer the phone that way, and placed the phone over his rear end. As he did that, I set a bad example by laughing. Ultimately the phone was a hit. Kids who are usually too shy to talk suddenly found the courage to do so when they were talking into a phone receiver instead of directly to the teacher.

As Ezaki-*sensei* and I were leaving the classroom, the boy who placed a call to his derriere came into her smacking range. She let loose with a patented Ezaki-*sensei* swing to the back of the head. From the seminars, I knew that corporal punishment is still taken for granted in Japan. Although it is not prevalent, I have seen teachers strike children here.

I was surprised such a sweet woman had that whack in her. It gave me pause to consider whether I had misread this seemingly nice woman and good teacher. After thinking about it, I believe the Ezaki-*sensei* swing is used as an attention getter, not to inflict pain. I would not want to receive one, but it is an acceptable part of a Japanese teacher's methods to maintain control.

As I write this and think of her, I have an image in my mind of a frail little woman in a Marine Corps green blouse, skirt and one of those wide-brimmed hats drill sergeants wear, smartly marching big Marines around the parade grounds. Because she has taught for so long, she has ex-students who are grown men with junior high age children. I can imagine that, to this day, some men remember the quiet resolve with which Ezaki-*sensei* kept order in her class. When they think of her, I wonder how many involuntarily gently rub the back of their heads.

When Ezaki-*sensei* recalls her childhood, she remembers the violence she lived through during World War II. She shared with the Thursday-night group a memory from the war. Toward its end, she was an elementary school girl living in Fukuoka (the largest city on Kyushu). Air raid sirens regularly warned the people of the coming of the planes they called B-*san* (Mr. B), the B-29 bombers. With the Japanese air force virtually nonexistent, the B-29s flew almost at will over the country raining bombs. In one night fire-bombing raid in March 1945 over Tokyo (with most of its buildings made of wood), it is estimated 100,000 people were killed by the incendiary bombs and the conflagrations they created. The wood houses burned instantly. The smoke was so thick in the air that the B-29s, flying thousands of feet up, returned to base with a covering of soot on their underbellies. So when just a couple B-29s showed up over Hiroshima and later at Nagasaki, the Japanese air force did not even bother sending any fighters up. Even today, every Japanese school teaches what the B-29s looked like and what they did. Ironically there are two American-made planes, both Boeings, that all Japanese know, the B-29 and the 747. I guess that is progress; the former was used in war and the latter helps bridge the two cultures.

There being nothing the Japanese could do to stop the B-29s, Ezaki-*sensei*, like the other people in her town, headed to the air raid shelter during the bombings. One day she left the shelter to watch the planes drop the bombs. She was fascinated with the colors, shapes and sounds of the explosions. The people in the shelter went to look for her, and she was punished for her foolish action. Yet the beauty of the exploding bombs stayed with her. Later, when she was old enough to realize that with every "beautiful" explosion, her fellow townspeople were dying, she reflected back on the little girl so happy to see the bombings and felt a deep sense of sadness.

She can never forgive America for what it did to her country, regardless of who started what. But, like so many Japanese, she admittedly admires America. From my perspective, her childhood memories do not seem to be an impediment to our budding friendship.

Bye for now.

*D*ear Frank,   October 8
Summer is officially over but it is still warm. Fall offers Japan's best weather, and the cooler weather will be welcome. Life in Japan is regulated by the seasons more than is ours. On October 1 the seasons, as far as the Board is concerned, changed. The children changed to their winter uniforms. Girls now wear dark blue sailor's skirts and blouses, complete with a sailor's bow around the collar. Boys have the same uniform as summer's except a black suit coat with brass buttons has been added. Women's uniforms at the Board changed too. (Men do not wear uniforms.) The drinks of summer, such as cold *mugicha*, also vanished that day.

Today was another *mushi atsui* day. Because I was at Hondo-*chu*, only a five-minute bike ride away, I went by bike. In those five minutes I still sweat so much I hated putting my tie on at school. Soon I am going to drive my car to work as my contract provides. In every other respect these people have been considerate to me so I am trying to be as reasonable as possible. I would like them to recognize that I am a careful driver and invite me to use the car to drive to work. Failing that, I will say enough is enough and just do it. One of those two things is going to happen before winter comes.

For now, I use the car only after work. I began exploring the mountain roads. Most of Japan consists of low-lying, steep mountains, and my island is no exception. While the mountains act to cram the Japanese together, they give me the chance to get away from people. The mountain back roads, unlike Arizona's, are all paved. They are almost all two-way although they are all about as wide as the width of one car. Getting around is easier than you might think, with pullouts strategically placed and big curved mirrors positioned at blind corners.

I enjoy driving these roads and finding villages consisting of a couple of houses, a general store and a *pachinko* (pah cheen ko) parlor. *Pachinko* is a machine and a game of chance to which the Japanese seem addicted. *Pachinko* machines look like upright pinball machines with steel balls that are released from the top. As they fall down the face, the player tries to maneuver the ball into the hole with the most points. *Pachinko* is said to have been developed in Detroit in the 1930s. Brought to Japan, it flourished.

Gambling is illegal in Japan. To avoid that law, winners are given prizes that they redeem at the nearby store, which obligingly pays cash for those same prizes. In an open "secret" *pachinko* is run primarily by the *yakuza* (yah coo za – the equivalent of the Mafia). My friends say *yakuza* are easy to spot. They drive big black "gangster" cars and have parts of fingers missing, cut off to prove loyalty or for mob oopsies.

Pachinko is woven into the fabric of Japanese culture so deeply that villages too small for a temple, a restaurant or even a bar are big enough for a *pachinko* parlor. They are brightly lit, noisy, packed with machines, mirrors, a blue hazy cloud of cigarette smoke and people throwing their money away. The stories are legendary of savings being wiped out by *pachinko*. People I know who are opposed to gambling enjoy *pachinko* because it is not "gambling." When I ask what *pachinko* is if not gambling, they change the subject.

As I drove in the mountains, I decided that a mountain bike would be a good way to explore them. I called a recommended private mountain-bike dealer who sent a catalog. He called a few days later. I told him I was not ready to buy but the blue one on page eight looked nice. When it arrived, I called and told him I was not sure I wanted it. He said use it and if I like it, pay him for it. If not, send it back. I ended up buying it. I have called the "Benz" dealership (they do not say "Mercedes") several times and told them their cars look nice, but so far no Benz has shown up. My transportation consists of a ten-year-old jalopy, a blue mountain bike and a white Wicked-Witch-of-the-West bike.

A pleasant part of today's bike ride to Hondo-*chu* is that I traveled with a group of students. I enjoy this extracurricular contact. Whenever I go out, a student or two will greet me and maybe stop to chat. At noon on Saturday, I was leaving the *Gintengai* (gheen ten guy), which is a three-block long shopping area converted into a pedestrian shopping mall. Twenty-five elementary kids on the other side of the street on their way home from school shouted *HARO!* (ha row – hello). They crossed the street en masse, surrounded me, started shaking my hand and touching me. After a few minutes I tried to leave, but a couple of kids grabbed my shirt and said, "Donto go!!" (don't go). I finally managed to escape my adoring fans.

While riding our bikes to school, even high school students (whom I do not teach) exchange greetings and bows with me. The police and I exchange bows and pleasantries at two intersections as they go about the business of directing morning traffic. As I enter Hondo-*chu*'s school gate, there is a teacher in charge of greeting the students and teachers. We exchange morning pleasantries and bows too. Bowing from the seat of a bike, what a concept!

Hondo-*chu* has three floors. For a structure made with such liberal use of glass, it is one ugly building. What is not glass is poured gray unpainted cement, which looks as if it were decades old. This gray poured cement must have been popular for many years as buildings in every part of Japan are made of it. Americans are familiar with the myth how the Japanese love nature and make their architecture in harmony with it. As I see it, much of this architecture is in harmony only with the concept of dividends to cement company shareholders. You never want to see such emotionally cold buildings.

I enter the school through the teachers' entrance. As I make my way to the teachers' room, I exchange greetings and bows with students, teachers and staff members. The children, female teachers and female staff members say the formal *ohayo gozaimasu* (ohio go zai maas – good morning). Males who consider themselves socially inferior to me say that too. Men who consider me their social equals say *ohayo*. Men who consider me their social inferior say something that sounds more like *oosuu*. If I speak first, I say *ohayo gozaimasu*. When someone else greets me first, I respond the same way. I have been told that I should not say *oosuu* to the principal. I respond that it cannot be rude if the principal says it. One of the things I am having trouble adjusting to is that Japanese culture dictates that one has conversations with an equal only infrequently.

A freshman must use polite Japanese when speaking to an upperclassman, but the upperclassman is under no such obligation. If those two people meet 30 years from now at a school reunion, they will jump back into the same posture. Both of them must use what is called *sonkeigo* (saun kay go – respectful language), which has its own vocabulary, when talking to the principal. The Japanese use far less profanity they we do. In Japanese, if you want to insult someone, you speak to him either as your social equal if, according to Japanese mores, he is not. Or speak to him as your social inferior if he is your social equal. For the Japanese it is natural. To me, it seems that if segregation is enforced inside your brain through the language with which you communicate to the world, a logical consequence is that other kinds of segregation will naturally follow.

The segregation spills over into the workplace. For example, there are no female principals. When I ask teachers, administrators and people in the Board why this is true, they inevitably reply with the Japanese equivalent of "Gosh I do not know, it is just the way things are I guess." All the teachers recognize that a woman becoming a principal is not likely in Hondo.

The principal's position points out one of the quirks of the Japanese social system. Even though the principal is the most honored man in the school, he has little to do on a daily basis. The vice principal carries out the real work of the school. Probably the principal's most important real job is to represent the school at all public functions, especially at PTA meetings. He is supposed to have a dignified demeanor, and the ones in Hondo fit the bill. The teachers often giggle softly during the day when they see principals doing their most famous chore: tending to the garden. How this situation can exist is beyond me, but it does.

Today, two periods before lunch, the "janitor" and I were trying to communicate in the teachers' room when a teacher came in and made an announcement I did not understand. All but one of the eight teachers in the room scattered. A minute later, students wearing white chef hats, surgical masks, white aprons and white gloves came in carrying food on trays. I had a sinking feeling it could only mean one thing: They were looking for guinea pigs to test the concoctions made in cooking class.

Two students approached me, one holding a tray. The main course was spaghetti with a sauce on which was sprinkled dried chips of brown fish flakes. The fish was so thinly sliced that the heat from the spaghetti made the penny-sized slivers of fish gyrate as if there were a school of live landlubbering fish. I have seen this topping on pizza here. Under normal circumstances I would have passed, but I knew what was for lunch and this looked like a better bet. The dried fish added a bad taste to an otherwise tasteless sauce.

The most disagreeable part of the meal was listening to the other teacher in the room make a slurping sound while sucking up his spaghet-ti. This slurping noise is typical when the Japanese eat noodles such as ramen or *soba* (sow ba – buckwheat noodles). They consider it rude to omit the sucking sound while vacuuming up noodles. Usually they will not complain that we Westerners quietly eat our noodles, but cooks are a little let down that we do not slurp our food. They think eating quietly takes away from the taste of the food. I cannot bring myself to suck my noodles or make sound effects.

I admit to cultural prejudice on this score. It is one of their habits that irritates me. I tell myself that it is simply their custom. However, I am so used to the idea that it is rude to eat aloud that I tolerate it unwillingly. When the slurping in the teachers' room stopped, the children picked up the trays and asked how the food was. I told them: "As good as Mom used to make." They smiled. Good thing I did not have to explain what that means.

When the chime sounded for the next class period, the entire school did *shodo* (show dough – calligraphy), which is the art of writing *kanji* with a brush. The principal thought the students might be happy to see me take an interest so he asked me to visit each classroom. As I walked into the first class, I was shown three *kanji* and asked to choose the prettiest. Being a Japanese cultural veteran of over two months, I knew what that meant. I have been asked questions before such as "Do you like. . .?" and "Which is prettier?" These questions are often their way of asking me "Do you want. . .?" I assumed that whichever one I chose would be the one used as a model. I further assumed there was a 50-50 chance I would be asked to take part in the exercise. I decided the simpler, the prettier.

Sure enough, I was presented with a brush and a piece of paper and we all begin using the *kanji* I had picked out. I walked to the back of the class, where I hoped I would be inconspicuous, trying my hand at *shodo* for the first time. A salivating fox in a henhouse had as much chance of being inconspicuous. The students stayed at their seats but turned around to watch me. Those near me stood up. Those behind them stood on their chairs to see the *gaijin* do *shodo*.

There is a very definite stroke order to follow when writing *kanji*. Just as we would think it strange for someone to write the right side of a "B" first, so too the Japanese watch with interest and amusement when a *gaijin* is trying his hand at *kanji*.

I picked up the brush, wet its bristles in the ink bottle and directed brush to paper. I was about to start the first stroke going up from the bottom, when my self-appointed coaches said in unison "ah ah." I took the hint and started the stroke from the top. My mentors oohed and ahhed approvingly. After I finished, the teacher held up my effort before the applauding students. I felt pretty stupid. Afterward I walked around the class to see the students' *shodo*, but the girls were all shy and covered their papers.

From that class, the teacher and I toured all six classes at the school. My *shodo* was displayed to all the students, with the same reaction. I saved that *shodo* to see what I would think about it with the passage of time and the end of my studies in Japanese.

When the chime sounded, the lunch period began. Imagine how yummy food is when shipped in huge tin canisters from a central kitchen. Today's lunch featured a fish I have seen too many times already. We each received a bowl of straight-pin-size fish plopped down in front of us. Because the fish are so tiny, the entire fish is fried and served as is. They come hundreds in a bowl. The worst part is that their beady eyes fall off and line the bottom of the bowl. Once accustomed to them, I am told these fish are crunchy and tasty. I guarantee that I will never know from firsthand experience. Hardcore traditional Japanese food prepared en masse, served on a tin plate, eaten with *hashi* – is it any wonder that I do not look forward to lunch?

After lunch the students and teachers pull out their toothbrushes and toothpaste to brush their teeth. To rinse, the teachers use the sink in the teachers' lunchroom. School brushing etiquette does not preclude teachers from walking about the teachers' room holding whole conversations while brushing. Students use the concrete sinks in the hallway. With such an emphasis on dental hygiene, it is nothing short of amazing how many mouths filled with bad teeth there are here. Not just crooked teeth, but tartar plastered on golden smiles and bridges holding teeth in. I have not seen one set of braces. After seeing the teeth of the Japanese I concluded I would ask for toothpaste to be included in my care packages from home.

Entering class after lunch, for a second I wondered how far these kids would go to keep cool. The girls were in their gray top and bottom underwear and the boys were changing in the room with them. They had just come in from the practice field, where they are getting ready for some kind of track meet. After they put all their clothes on, they fanned themselves with fans, notebooks, anything they could find. Because of the heat, these students were definitely not *genki*. Morbid or near death would be more descriptive. The sweat started to roll down my back and legs too. Throughout class I continually thought about TV commercials that feature lakes, cool mountain streams and ice-cold beer.

After my last class, I went the teachers' *tatami*-mat room. Located just off the hallway, it overlooks the courtyard. One after another male teacher came to change into sweat pants for *soji*. Some of them closed the door to the hallway, some closed the curtain, some both, some neither. I figured I was in the way there so I went back to the teachers' room. As I sat down, a teacher reached his desk, dropped his trousers and changed into this sweat pants right there. I guess I am the only one not ready to get naked at school.

The students in charge of broadcasting music over the school's loudspeakers chose the theme from the movie *Top Gun* as *BGM* (bee gee emu – background music). During *soji* I stay in the teachers' room to keep my buddy the air-conditioner company. Seeing only the *gaijin* in the teachers' room, the kids decided to have *soji* time trials.

These cleaning races started with the boys clearing the chairs from the long center area of the room. Two boys at a time lined up to race, with another boy holding the stopwatch. Wet cleaning cloths were put on the floor. The boys bent over them, leaving their butts high in the air. The object of the race was to go to the other side of the room leaving a wet trail behind and return to the starting point. The boys found a starter's gun, which they used by saying "*Ban!*" (the equivalent of our bang).

Except for two girls who came in during races, no work was being done. Aside from the students at the smallest school, Miyajidake, who clean like they are on a mission from God, the children at all the schools clean like the ones at Hondo-*chu*. The 30 or so students at Miyajidake make the school's one hallway shine so bright you can see your reflection in it, despite the fact that nothing besides wet rags and elbow grease are ever applied to it. But Hondo-*chu*'s 900 students are allergic to cleaning dirt and dust.

Finally I told the boys that either they had to work or speak English with me. To my everlasting surprise they decided to talk to me in English instead of doing *soji*.

Well, I have to clean up my desk, having ended this letter just as the "work" day ended. Hope to hear from you soon.

*D*ear Uncle Chet and Aunt Dottie,   October 15
        My laptop computer arrived. I bought it mail order from
New York. Even with the telephone calls, shipping fees and import duties, I saved over $1,000 on what the same computer would cost here.

I knew about Japanese prices before I came. I have seen the Japanese camera I bought in the States for up to 50 percent more here. When I ask why prices for Japanese goods are cheaper in the States than in Japan the Japanese say either "I do not know" or "I wonder why" I am going to have to learn how to say in Japanese, "Because you are being robbed by your big companies."

Having the computer delivered was an educational experience. Last Friday at 6 P.M. the phone rang. The caller spoke in what I am sure was polite, grammatically correct Japanese but which was largely unintelligible to me. I was going to wait for him to catch his breath, then tell him that he had the wrong number when I picked out familiar sounds, such as "pa soun cone" (perso[nal] com[puter]) and "rah poo toe poo" (laptop). I mustered together my feeble Japanese and said "Mine?" From that he must have constructed the complete sentence "Are you calling about the computer I ordered from the States?" because he said, "*Hai*!" followed by reading my address to me. Then he asked for directions from downtown, which, fortunately, I can handle in Japanese.

I now know that street addresses are largely useless except to the post office. Only a couple cities name their streets. I have a long and elaborate address, which I thought made it simple for anyone to find my house. Part of my address includes a house number, 602, which means that my house was the 602nd house built in this neighborhood. The house two doors down is number 57. Having the exact address gave the delivery company only a general idea of where my house is, so they called for directions.

People who have invited me to their house or told me about a shop or restaurant have drawn detailed maps for me. I had assumed these maps were for my benefit as a *gaijin*. But for other Japanese, too, they have to draw maps because addresses are useless. This explains why I have met so many accomplished mapmakers here.

I asked why they do not use named streets with sequentially numbered buildings. The two most frequent answers were: (1) "*Shirimasen* (she ree ma sen – I do not know)"; and (2) the practice was started in the hope of confusing ancient invading armies. Great. I am happy to know that in the event an ancient army invades, I am safe. In the meantime, I wonder how many of my packages may not be delivered.

I am enjoying my "Japan" experience partly because the city goes out of its way to make me feel welcome and comfortable. The initial visits by coworkers with fruits, used appliances, dishes and the like have stopped, but the city has started piling on the money. Since I wrote last, I met with the mayor in a *tatami* mat room for my official contract-signing ceremonies. Being on *tatami*, I had to take off my shoes, even in City Hall, which revealed the hole in my sock. I found out the hard way that in Japan you never know when you might have to take your shoes off.

Near the end of the largely (to me) incomprehensible meeting, Tsuruta-*san* took me aside to explain that the city had allocated more money for my trip from Los Angeles to Hondo than it had cost. He handed me an envelope with the equivalent of $500 in cash. He said I would be going on a trip at the city's expense for a three-day seminar. Assuring him I would be staying at the home of an Australian couple who are ALTs and did not need money for accommodations made no difference. Tsuruta-*san* insisted regulations required the city to pay me. All I had to show them was a quote from a hotel, not a receipt. I did nothing. When I returned he handed me the amount he concluded the city owed me. I gave up and pocketed the equivalent of $150. What a rough life.

For the Japanese at the Board life is not so cushy. My coworkers at the Board are expected to work from 8:00 A.M. to 5:30 P.M.. During the middle of sweltering summer, the air conditioning was on only from 8:30 to 5:00. In winter the same is true for the heat. The workers are being toughened up, but for what I do not know.

The good news about the weather is the typhoon season is over. (I'll take their word for it.) If I understood correctly, the one we had just this week was moving at 80 *kiro* per hour and with winds up to 200 *kiro* per hour (about 135 mph – a record for this part of Japan). Five people were killed and about 100 were injured. Two million houses in Kumamoto-*ken* lost electricity. Mine was out for three or four hours and went out several more times for a couple minutes each. The typhoons usually do not last long – maybe five hours altogether, including a one-and-a-half hour buildup and the same for wind-down with the main brunt of the storm in between. The day following a storm is often beautiful.

It is unfortunate the storm did not hit yesterday evening. It would have extinguished the fire I witnessed. Instead, I watched Japanese firemen in action as I ate pizza (with a favorite Japanese topping, corn) at a restaurant next to the river. Soon after the fire started nine red fires trucks arrived. They were all converted small pickups, with a complement of three firemen each.

The firemen threw hoses with filters at the ends into the river. The other end of each was attached to a pump on a truck. A hose was then connected to the "out" spigot on the truck. The fireman flung 10 to 50 feet lengths of rolled hose in such a way that they unfurled like red carpets. They put lengths of hose on their shoulders and ran to the end of the just-unfurled hose, unrolled the second roll in the same way and then connected the two hoses. Other firemen were running to the end of the just connected hose to repeat the process.

They ran in a most distinctive way. Imagine running as fast as you can with leg irons clasped to your ankles. This would give you the appearance of waddling like a duck or running like a Japanese fireman. They were concentrating on their jobs and did not notice that I was getting a big kick out of their running style. Finally they connected the last hose a block away from the river. By then the building was a total loss.

This morning I was at City Hall, which is across the driveway from the fire department's main station. Every morning between 8:00 and 8:30 firemen in the courtyard do calisthenics to blaring music that makes elevator music sound emotionally moving. Watching them, I saw one of the firemen whom I know from the private gym where I work out. At lunch I walked over and "talked" to him (which really means I went with my dictionary and prayed for communication). He explained that they did not use the big truck whose bumper we were sitting on because the fire was on a road where it would not fit. The small fire trucks enable them to reach more fires. If yesterday's fire was representative, by the time they get set up, they may just as well bring along hot dogs and marshmallows.

At school, the classrooms are less toasty. Of all the great times I have had since arriving here, the best ones have been at school.

After the *sannensei* (san nen say – ninth grade) class at Kamegawa-*chu*, during my last visit there two ninth-grade girls approached my desk trying to speak but could only manage to giggle while covering their mouths. They shifted their weight from foot to foot and finally spoke a few English words. They were giddy with happiness when I understood. It was as if they believed their words were some sort of magic incantation. I have the same "magic incantation" feeling about Japanese. When I learn a new word, I think of it more as a sound than a word that conveys meaning. When I repeat it to a native speaker I expect a "Huh?" look back. When the person responds exactly as I hoped, I have a "Wow, it worked" feeling.

The *gaijin* desk is a people magnet. After the girls left an older teacher asked me how to ask a question in English. Armed with the question, he asked me to explain "son of a bitch." When the teacher was a little boy he heard American soldiers say that a lot and he always wondered what it meant.

When Ezaki-*sensei* and I taught the last class of the day, the seventh grade, it was a little bit out of control, even though she parceled out the patented Ezaki swing. She is a tiny woman but she has perfected a touch that has earned the respect of even the biggest boys in class. She also whacks the board with the chalk so hard to emphasize her points I think she might one day put a hole in the board.

The class was rowdy in large part because I was in a goofy mood and it showed. We were teaching them how to use words like "on, in, under," etc. I asked one of the smaller boys to come to the front of the other students. We both faced the class. I stood behind the boy, grabbed his right leg at the ankle and lifted his foot out of his slipper up to his waist level.

I pointed to his sock and asked the class, "What is this?" "Eat eezoo a so coo (it is a sock)." Then I said, "There is a sock on his foot." As the class was repeating after me, the boy had difficultly with this balance and hopped two times on his left foot. I hopped two times toward him and the class broke up. Then I grabbed his other foot, and with most of his weight on my hip (he was upside down and his feet at my chest level), I pointed with my free hand while I said "What is this?" "Eat eezoo two so coos." Close enough, I figured.

I put the boy back on his feet and gave him a high five. I led the class in applauding his help. Boys then held their feet up in the air begging in Japanese "Do me, do me!!" Instead, one insistent boy felt the Ezaki swing. I gave out nuggies freely. Another boy made a funny noise while Ezaki-*sensei* and I had our backs to the class. I turned around to see his friends pointing him out with one hand, rubbing their heads with the knuckles of their other hand and shouting "Nuggies!"

Ezaki-*sensei* asked me to teach the students some American gestures. Well, that turned out to be a mistake too. I taught them some useless gestures such as "Okay," and the like. But I also left them with important ones, such as the Vulcan gesture for "Live long and prosper."

Then it happened. One boy with a big smile on his face in the front of the class flipped me the bird (or is it called the "finger"?). His friend next to him said with mock surprise in his voice, "Oh my Go dough!" (This is how they pronounce "Oh my God," which for some reason is an expression all the students know.) I thought I would let the boy know he had gotten his message across. I walked over to him and became serious. I spoke to him angrily. Even though I knew the students could not understand my words, with my expression and the way I said it, the point was made, I hope, that he should never do that again. I told the class that using the gesture in America could cause a fight or worse. (I did not bother to tell them about roadway drive-by shootings.) I hope it was a vivid lesson for all the students that gestures that mean nothing to them can be emotionally power packed to people from other cultures.

I know the boy intended a joke. Japanese kids use the "finger" when they make a good play in sports, or games, or find the answer while working together on homework and the like. So it now has a Japanese meaning too, kind of "Hey, ain't I great!"

Getting the "finger" is not so bad. It beats classes in which I have been pinched, poked or handled by the students. They are naturally curious about adults anyway, but that is probably even more true of a real-live *gaijin*.

Girls ask to put their palm against mine to compare sizes. They also like to check out my foot size. One lunchtime I decided to take a short walk outside but could not find my shoes in the locker. A couple of girls had taken them outside to take turns walking in them. At another school when I was leaving the men's room I expected to see my slippers where I had left them so I could change out of the toilet slippers. All I saw were a pair of mismatched girl's slippers. About 20 feet away, I saw a group of girls testing out how small their feet were in my slippers.

When I was kneeling at a boy's desk, another ran his hand along my arm to feel the hair. Then I felt something against my slipper. A boy was measuring his foot against mine. I am often asked to "Make a muscle" and receive frequent invitations to arm wrestle. I guess boys will be boys no matter where you are.

This afternoon I was at Miyajidake where I added to my collection of non-English. On the door of the refrigerator in the tiny kitchen connected to the teachers' room I saw this: "Lisa Jean at A.M. cobalt hour." Manufacturers obviously know that English enhances their product's marketing strength, but the stuff they throw on makes me wonder whether these guys have a quality control department.

As I walked from the kitchen I stopped to admire the view of the tiny valley studded with rice paddies and realized why October is Japan's best month for weather. The skies seem bluer every day now that the typhoons are over. The weather was so pleasant that day that the vice principal walked around in his bare feet. (A violation of regulations no doubt but no one seemed to care.)

I had a good class with the eighth graders. We discussed the color of the sun. Whenever a Japanese kid draws the sun, he will color it red. They were surprised American children draw the sun yellow. During this discussion, one boy looked outside shouting "Hey, it's yellow!" They decided they draw red suns because the Japanese flag has a red disk in the center.

We discussed other small cultural differences, such as how animal sounds are represented in our languages. In Japanese, a duck says: *ga ga*; a dog: *wan wan*; a cat: *nyao nyao*; a pig: *boo boo*; a chicken: *co co co*; a cow: *mow mow*; and a rooster: *co kay co co*. The whole class broke into hysterics when I did a cockle-doodle-doo rooster call for them. By popular demand I repeated it a few times. Each time the class broke up. I wondered whether what they really wanted was to go home and tell their families about the weird noises they coaxed the *gaijin* to make.

They said English is definitely wrong about ducks. In the opinion of the entire eighth-grade class, a duck definitely does not say quack quack. To me it is interesting that they actually believe the vocalizations they use to represent the sounds the animals make are close to being authentic. On the other hand, they were amused that I actually believe "woof woof" is closer to the sound a dog makes than "wan wan."

The thought came to me that even more than we realize, in big things and small, language and culture shape how we see things and how we hear them too. I told the students I was glad to be learning Japanese to broaden my view of the world. Perhaps because we were in English class and they are learning a second language, several kids said: "Me too!" I think we all left wondering whether either language is closer to the truth. Who knows whether any student took anything from the classroom that will stick more than a day or two. Nevertheless, I know *I* left class thinking "Hey, I learned something today."

The day was not, however, without unpleasantry. I hesitate to bring this up but do so in keeping with my original decision to portray Japan to you as I see it, even the warts. During class, I walked toward a boy in the front-row seat next to the hallway. His head rested in his right palm. He had a hang-dog look on his face as if someone told him he could not play outside after school for two months. I approached with the idea of kneeling in front of his desk and asking him quietly what was wrong.

As I reached him, I was hit by a terrific stink. I thought, "I'll help solve the kid's problem, but after that smell clears." I walked to the center of the class. The stink followed me. I walked to the back of the room next to the windows. The stink still followed me. By then I realized the smell was not from the boy. Oddly, no one else in the class reacted at all. A green truck, about the size of a pickup, with an oval-shaped tank, came from the back of the school. As it headed for the main road, the smell dissipated. Tahara-*sensei* later explained it is a pump truck, which vacuums the tanks beneath the toilets.

I became curious about the toilets. They are outside and "outdoors." A wooden roof covers the " rest room," and there is a wooden divider between the men's and women's areas, but it does not go all the way to the ground. The men's half has no doors except on the stalls to the toilets. So the entire "urinal" is easily visible as female teachers and students pass by on their way to the women's side. I put urinal in quotes because it is simply a raised step for the men to stand on, a concrete wall to aim at, and a cement trough sloped down to the stalls. Seeing that, I lost my courage of discovery and did not and have no intention of venturing into the stalls.

Being in a downturned state of mind, I thought other sad thoughts. It is obvious that schools teach reading and arithmetic, but the more important lesson is how to thrive in the Japanese universe. Schools give students a sense of one nation, and as far as humanly possible they give each student the same experience. On any given day, from one end of the country to the other each student in each grade is studying virtually the same page in the same book.

I try to teach the students about the world outside of Japan. But to them, the rest of the world is less real than the next test they have to pass. The Japanese tradeoff personal dreams for doing what is expected of them much more than we do. They seem to be satisfied with the trade off. If my students live the Japanese dream, many will become *sarariiman* and will be called upon to spend the early part of life in study and the postcollege part of life working long hours. They will see their family only late at night or on the weekends.

They are conditioned to accept this as they learn through trial and error and the exhortations of parents what it takes to succeed in school and by extension in Japanese life. In school the number of winners is set even before the semester starts.

Grading of the students is done in a thoroughly Japanese way. In every class across the nation, it is decided that a final grade of 5, or A, will be given to a certain number of students, let's say five. If the test results show six students have done well enough to qualify for the top grade, instead of giving an A to all six students, the teacher will look over the qualifications of each student. If one did not study hard, in spite of doing well, that student's grade will be dropped to the next rank. Or perhaps they all studied hard but five of the students were active in school activities. The one who was not will get the next notch down.

As in later life, the race does not go to the smartest. It goes to the smartest who has lived up to the expectations of the system. School teaches students not just to read and write but how to keep their opinions to themselves, their heads down and their sights focused on the next rung of the ladder. In essence, the emphasis is not on being the best student but the best Japanese.

They give their lives to the system and it provides them the highest standard of living in Asia – a standard that I can adjust to knowing that I will be going back to the States. And it gives them the opportunity to boast that Japan is a rich country. Never mind that the system here has perfected the trickle-down theory of economics to such an extent that schools have gravity toilets and no heat.

I just lost my morose attitude. As I finished the preceding paragraph, I heard screaming and a commotion coming from the science room. A snake from the surrounding hills had found its way into the school and a boy was sticking it in the face of anyone who showed any fear. Kids will be kids! I decided to enjoy the rest of the day.

In my last class a girl had difficulty pronouncing words with the "th" sound. I am told that English is one of the few languages that has this sound. I know it is exceeding difficult for Japanese to master. I knelt next to the girl so she could look at my mouth as I pronounced "the" and imitate me. The Japanese never touch their teeth with their tongue when speaking, so it is hard to explain the technique short of demonstrating it. I must overemphasize the tongue sticking out underneath the top teeth, or they have no clue what I mean. When I exaggerate this way, I look like I am sticking out my tongue.

Trying to follow my example, she was overcome by giggles. I waited until the attack passed and asked her again to try. Same result. She did her best to regain control of herself. She grabbed her desk with both hands, took a deep breath and tried again. By this time her laughter had infected the other students. I finally gave up when I caught myself chuckling too.

At the end of class, the students, as required in Hondo, stood and thanked Tahara-*sensei* for the class. They turned to me and instead of the usual "Thank you, Ken-*sensei*," they said, "See you later, dude." Tahara-*sensei* leaned to me and whispered, "Rosemary taught them this." I decided to load the students' brains with the salutation "*Ciao* baby!" to tell Rosemary at the end of her next visit.

When I left school the kids were all still there studying or taking part in sport club activities. About half the student body leaned out of the windows as Tahara-*sensei* and I passed. Some said good-bye in Japanese, some "See you later, dude!" and a few yelled, "*Ciao*, baby!"

Please write soon.

*D*ear Lynea,   November 2

Hondo celebrated, in a way, Halloween for the first time in history. I bought candy and as the 31st approached I handed it out in class. On the 29th, I was at Hondo-*chu*. The first class started with the teacher handing tests papers back, with the top right corner of each paper folded to hide the grade. The students lined up with the girls holding out both hands, cupped slightly, to receive their tests. Some of the boys took the paper with one hand. Each student raised the paper slightly after receiving it in a sign of respect they also use when receiving presents and will use later in life when receiving business cards and the like. As the kids returned to their seats, they put the paper on their desks and a pencil case or eraser over the score, even a good score.

After reviewing the test material, I told the kids about Halloween and asked if they wanted candy in exchange for saying "Trick or treat." They shouted "Money!!" Their accent was not bad either. They came up one by one, held out their hands the same way they did for the test, said the magic words, received a candy and thanked me. A couple of the boys thanked me only after being gently whacked in the back of the head by the teacher.

On the 31st at Higashi-*chu* I asked if the students liked Halloween. One boy said no because he does not like pumpkin. Because he dared to be different, I walked to his seat and gave him a piece of candy. I dropped a piece returning to the front of class and two boys scrambled for it.

Between classes in the hallway, several girls said, "Trick or treat," so I gave them candy. A small incentive to encourage them to ask for what they want without being shy about it, which is different from the norm here. Prompting them not be shy, however, proved a little touchy. Out of the blue one girl asked if all Japanese people look alike to me. I suppressed a laugh as I thought of class after class of girls and boys in identical uniforms, with hair cut no longer than permitted for each gender. I told her in September I had a hard time distinguishing the students in their uniforms, but now I see them as individuals.

Entering the teachers' room, the thought occurred to me that everyone ought to live in a different culture for a year. If my experience is typical, living abroad gives one a different perspective. Broadening one's viewpoint can end up in nothing more sinister than understanding.

The teachers are preparing for another PTA meeting tonight, so the kids were let out early. From my vantage point in the computer room where I am writing this, I can see the children putting their extra free time to use. Some are playing tennis on the school's courts and others are playing baseball on the school field. Another game of baseball has sprung up on the dry, harvested rice paddies. Rice-paddy baseball no doubt calls for appropriate modification to the rules, as did alley ball when I was growing up. Rice-paddy baseball uses four paddies: one is the infield, one is right field and so on. Ground balls are brutal on fielders because remnants of rice plants stick up a few inches, slowing the ball and altering its trajectory. The base path is the two-foot-wide, one-foot-high mound of earth that separates the paddies. It acts as a fifth infielder preventing grounders from rolling out of the infield.

This baseball game is good training for driving on Japanese roads with their many moving and stationary obstacles. Before I arrived, I thought mass transportation was Japan's preferred mode of people moving. The truth is Japan has a deep and abiding love affair with the car that rivals (or considering the difficulties and cost of driving the Japanese road, perhaps surpasses) America's. This passion, coupled with cramped quarters, results in overcrowded roads.

We are told the Japanese drive on the left side of the road, or the opposite from us. It is more accurate to say that there is a legal preference for cars to drive on the left, but daily road and traffic conditions make driving practically anywhere acceptable.

Their expressways (similar to ours) are an exception to the chaotic Japanese roadway. They are scarcer than ours, with the nearest to my home a two-hour drive. They are the fastest way to drive between cities. Posted top speeds are 80 *kiro* (48 mph) but police generally do not stop cars going less than 100 *kiro* (60 mph). (My car has a chime that sounds incessantly when the car reaches 103 *kiro*.) The expressways are fast but expensive toll roads. A three hour trip can cost $40 in tolls.

To reach the expressway, I travel on "National Roads," which are two-laners barely wide enough in spaces for one car and often no wider than a driveway for a two-car garage. Uncovered three-feet-deep and two-feet-wide concrete drainage channels are dug next to the white line on the "shoulder" of the road. Cross-country trips take forever on these roads. Between villages traffic can crank it up to about 50 mph, but often an old farmer driving a wheelbarrow-size pickup and going about as fast that slows everyone down.

The city is where driving in Japan becomes an art form. The main city roads, two or three lanes in each direction, are virtually identical to ours and adequate most of the time. You have never been, however, in *rashu awa* (rah shoe ah wa – rush hour) traffic until you have been in a Japanese big-city traffic jam where to pass the time people bring reading material or watch dashboard-mounted televisions. The traffic does not flow so much as ooze.

In non–rush hour traffic the national mania for illegal parking (caused by a scarcity of parking lots) results in the lanes painted in the road becoming only suggestions. Cars traveling in the curb lane glide into the next lane (crossing the center line if necessary) to avoid the illegally parked cars then glide back. Stiff parking fines (up to $90) are not effective. Cops seem resigned to illegal parking. One day I saw a cop get off his motorcycle to close the door on an illegally parked car. His good deed done for the day, he proceeded on his way.

All of this on the good-sized roads. Many city roads, however, even in the biggest city, are too narrow for sidewalks and are full of pedestrians, making near misses a daily part of the commute. Without sidewalks, often one's first step out of a house or store is directly into the street. Space on these roads is so tight, there are times when passing cars nick my shopping bag, making me worry for the safety of my toes. The intrepid pedestrian or driver has to be vigilant.

Concrete telephone and electric poles are planted right in the roadway. The only concession traffic engineers make to the exposed and brave pedestrian is a "sidewalk" created by painting a white line three feet from the curb within the "safe haven" created by the poles. With parks rare, children use the shelter created by utility poles to play in the streets. People walk primarily in the designated area, but wander all over the road if shops line both sides.

Pedestrians who want to stay on the "sidewalk" often cannot because store owners display goods there. Japan is also the vending machine capital of the world. Many are set on the "sidewalk," exposing the customer's rear end to traffic during the purchase.

Not all pedestrians scurry about fearful of collisions. Perhaps as a silent protest for their too-little reward after a lifetime of hard work helping Japan become what it is today, elderly women move for no one. They chat away walking two abreast pushing baby carriage-like carts for support. Many of these women have backs so bent over their chests are parallel to the street, and they walk looking at their feet. Drivers recognize the women's intractability and never honk, instead resigning themselves to wait for the opportunity to go around them.

Not all people in the roadway move at all. Driving on a fairly major Hondo road, I came upon a storekeeper squatting on his haunches about a third of the way into the road. Lazily squirting the street in front of his shop with a garden hose (shopkeepers nationwide share his passion for a clean street), he looked at my car but did not move.

On the side streets, people of all ages ride bicycles predominately on the "sidewalk" but, like pedestrians, all over the road. Students break the law and ride two to a bicycle. Passengers stand precariously with feet on either side of the rear axle with their hands on the driver's shoulders for balance. Perhaps based on their belief that they are bulletproof, these teenagers dart in and out of traffic. Adding to the danger on rainy days, the passenger holds the umbrella (which are illegal on bicycles – another universally ignored law).

Motorcycles and motor scooters zip in and out of traffic, using the "sidewalk" as an additional lane. Cars, too, drive on the "sidewalk." Illegal parking on these streets makes cars look like snow skiers as they slalom past the cars parked on both sides of the street.

When you add to all these obstacles a good-sized truck negotiating one of these narrow arteries, you have a viewing experience. Going "straight" down these streets is a tight squeeze for these trucks, but turning at postage-stamp-size intersections is a manual dexterity and spatial perception test we ought to require of our fighter pilots. Drivers begin the turn, back up, continue the turn, back up, and continue the turn again. They watch closely as the truck's protruding side mirror edges nearer to the inconveniently placed concrete utility pole. If the driver thinks the mirror will only gently kiss the pole, he will inch the truck forward, slowing brushing the mirror against the pole. If he anticipates a less congenial encounter he will grab the mirror from the inside and pull it in. If all else fails, he gets out to push the mirror against the side of the truck. After clearing the intersection, he pulls the mirror back out. Due to these roadway gymnastics, it is faster to take a bicycle than a car during peak time.

Compared to Japan's truck drivers, *takushi* (ta coo she – taxi) drivers are Japan's version of terrorist hit squads. Some speculate they are either Kamikaze school dropouts, or were trained by them. To make up for their dodge-'em-car style of driving, they wear white gloves (as do older Japanese women when driving) and throw doilies on the seats. Back doors open only by remote control from the driver's seat. If you do not pay, you do not leave. There is, however, no tipping – and at the rates they charge, they better not expect tips! One reason for the high costs may be because many taxis run on propane gas (The propane tank takes up half of the trunk.)

Taxis are used more here than in the States. Driving with more than a trace amount of alcohol in your system is against the law. Most Japanese men are responsible about not drinking and driving, preferring to take a taxi to and from the bar. The cost is prohibitive, but it is less costly than being arrested, which is reason enough for a *saraiiman* to lose his job.

I have been stopped at a drunk-driver's roadblock. On a street near my house there is a technical school's student dorm. The all-male residents have a reputation for drinking, so the police periodically set up roadblocks. I did not understand what the cop was saying, but it appeared he wanted me to breathe into his face. After a few minutes of noncommunication, he popped his head into the car, put his hat in front of my face and gestured with his hand for me to breathe in face. I did. He said Okay and waved me on. Whatever his salary, he deserves a raise.

This and other aspects of driving in Japan take some getting used to, but I am. It took several attempts of inadvertently pulling into the oncoming lane of traffic to get it through my thick skull which side of the road I am supposed to drive on. I also no longer scream to myself when I pull onto a tiny road and see a big truck approaching from the opposite direction. Well, Okay, I still do that. I must be improving, though, because bicyclists no longer scurry for cover when they see me coming.

I have managed to figure out some of the more obvious unwritten rules of the road, such as who has the duty to back up and where to pull into. (The driveways of private homes are considered safe havens when faced with a truck the size of a bus or when faced with a bus, for that matter.) I no longer think it is strange to see drivers turn off their headlights at night when stopped at red lights (to reduce the glare to drivers stopped on the other side of the intersection). I have even perfected the light toot of the horn and the bow as I pass the cars that pull over for me. The unwritten rules, however, steadfastly hold that it is impolite to sound the horn to warn the driver encroaching in your lane to get back into his. Instead, when I see the other car begin to glide into my lane, I am supposed to slow or glide into the lane next to me. I have to be constantly aware of the fluidity of the traffic around me, because no one gives any warning of their intended actions.

As an example, as I approached the shopkeeper in the street I mentioned earlier the other drivers and I mentally calculated who would arrive there first. In an ESP kind of way, we calculated that I would arrive before the oncoming traffic. Along with the cars behind me, I pulled around the shopkeeper. The oncoming traffic patiently stopped and waited until the line of cars I led went around. If we had all mentally calculated that the oncoming traffic would arrive first, I, and all the cars behind me, would have stopped and patiently waited for the oncoming traffic to clear. Still other times, in a Zen-like approach to driving that one has to learn through experience, the later part of the line of cars going around will stop as the oncoming traffic nears and continue again when the oncoming traffic has passed.

To be cast in this choreographed iron-and-steel ballet, Japanese drivers have to pass both a written and a driving test. These tests are a much more serious endeavor than ours. To sit for the test, one has to have a certificate of passing a driving course. As with everything in Japan, the driving lessons are expensive (between $2,000 and $4,000).

The official rules of the road offer some measure of protection against *rukii* (roo key – rookie) drivers. Drivers holding a license less than a year have to display a symbol in their cars that lets the rest of the driving public know that they are rookies. I do not have to do that nor do I have a Japanese license. Japan and America have entered into an agreement whereby licensed drivers in each country are permitted to drive in the other so long as they obtain an international license before arrival. It would have been impossible for me to pass a driving test here. I cannot tell you the number of important driving laws I have learned by being honked at (for example, what their one-way signs and their no-left-turn signs look like). I think it would cause a stink in the international community here, but I for one would not object to a distinctive colored flashing light displayed on the top of cars driven by *gaijin* for their first year in Japan. After all, I want to get out of this alive too.

I am, however, getting used to parking. Even legal parking is a bit of a challenge. In Hondo, many people park in front of their homes. Drivers park in any space big enough to permit traffic to still flow on the street. Cars are squeezed within inches of the house, and *saido mira* (sa e dough – side; me rah – mirror) are for that reason made retractable, either manually or electronically. Houses with garages exist, but those built for the tiny Japanese cars of the 1970s cannot accommodate the snoots of today's longer cars, which stick out of the front with the garage door lightly resting against the windshield. Still other homeowners concrete over tiny front or side yards for the car.

In big cities many homes and apartments have no space for parking. Owners pay nonrefundable deposits of $500 to $2,000 in central neighborhoods to park in a lot or a *gareji* (ga ray gee – garage), which is what they call parking structures. Either way monthly rates vary from $50 to up to $150 to $250 per month. People who live close to where they park their car walk. Others bicycle or even take the subway from their home.

Store lots have narrow spaces that force people to squeeze out of cars. Nevertheless, the tight spaces do not result in car doors with dings in them because people are careful to avoid banging other cars. The fact that most people are slim helps too. My car has a range finder when backing up; it beeps louder and louder until I am within a foot of an obstruction, when it becomes a steady tone. With all the tight fits here, I like this feature.

What I have written may have given you the false impression that driving in Japan is a more anxiety-raising experience than in the States. Surprisingly, my anxiety level is lower here. The reality is, amid all this confusion, a traffic flow emerges that results in about 10,000 traffic deaths a year compared to about 40,000 on American roads. In my experience, Japanese roads are safer than U.S. roads. I have not seen an accident caused by the obstacles built into the roadway.

Traffic moves because drivers are more courteous than in the States. People here have a different approach to driving. Instead of being upset when they are slowed down, they are excited when they can drive without having to back up. Maybe it is a function of their culture or maybe it is because they have more thorough training than we. I think they recognize that with this many cars and such tiny spaces, it is cooperate or nobody moves. "Cooperation" is the most important unwritten rule of the road, and one in which I happily participate. I hope to take Japanese-style road manners home with me.

Another consequence of the small city streets is the small-town feel they give to even the biggest city when you are off the main thoroughfares. There are no cars blasting down the road, and during the evenings most side streets are almost deserted.

Of course, no discussion about driving would be complete without talking about English. Cars are another area where the Japanese love affair with English manifests itself. The gauges and gadgets are in English. The car names are English too. They seem to love using names they cannot pronounce: Corolla comes out *ko ro ra*; Silvia comes out *she'll be a*. There is a class of car called *saloon*, which conjures up the image of a tobacco-spitting, rot-gut-drinking cowpoke, but the Japanese think of a fine family sedan. Words derived from English abound around the car – such as *waipa* (why pa – wiper), *taiya* (tie ya – tire), *oiru cheinji* (oh e roo change e – oil change). Some words that are derived from English are not used in the States, such as their word for stall, which is *ensto* (en stow – *engine stop*).

Well, the chime is signaling the end of school. I bow to you and thank you very much for reading this letter. I had better print this and wrap up another hard day at the office. Bye for now.

*D*ear Barb,   November 16
        Last Friday I went on a hiking trip to a rain-forested island called Yakushima. After school I grabbed my gear and hit the road for the other end of Kyushu to catch a ferry. A camping group of five ALTs was cut to two by the forecast for rain over the entire long weekend. (Monday was a holiday.)

Whitney, from North Carolina, and I decided to brave the elements. She lives in Kuratake, which is a town of a few thousand and is a thirty minute car ride from my house on a winding and sometimes single-lane, two-way road. Whitney is a devout Christian, a pleasant person and a short bundle of energy who jogs several miles a day.

The ferry is 250 miles from my house, but with road construction and getting lost umpteen times and the trip took six and a half hours. After dark we made our first stop for directions, at a store near where we thought the expressway should be. The storekeeper drew an elaborate map for us. We made the first turn the map indicated and were lost again.

Then we bought gas and asked for directions. The attendant drew a map and we found the expressway. After an hour the road, still under construction, thinned out into an alley-sized national road with confusing construction detours. We stopped at another gas station, where three men gave two different sets of directions. Laughing we pulled out of the gas station, knowing we would soon be lost again.

Ending up on a pitch-black, tiny road, we saw an eighteen-wheeler. Big semis are rare so we guessed he was looking for the toll road too. He led us to Kagoshima, a city famous for Sakurajima, a continually smoldering volcano that makes for beautiful sunsets (and deposits ash on everything in town).

We stopped at another gas station for directions to the youth hostel. It was surprisingly busy for that time of night and there were only two attendants. Although we protested, one dropped what he was doing to pull out a huge book full of detailed street-by-street maps that listed all the buildings in Kagoshima. To keep up with the customers, the other attendant was running from one car to the next pumping gas and taking the money. Our attendant drew us a map, ran out into the street to stop traffic and bowed as we left.

We found the street but did not see anything on it. Frustrated with our inability to understand foreign-language directions in the early-morning hours, we stayed at a hotel we stumbled upon. The 6:30 A.M. wake-up call startled Whitney. Springing out of her bed to answer the phone, she head-butted the TV and, half asleep, apologized to it.

After breakfasting at the only restaurant we could find, Mr. Donuts, we made our way to the ferry and were escorted to our cheap "seats." Located as far belowdecks as one could go without being attacked by sharks, our "seats" were a big *tatami*-mat room we shared with 50 others. Men were smoking and drinking beer, but most passengers were snoozing. We walked down the aisle, took off our shoes and stepped up one foot to the *tatami* area.

Once under way, we went topside. Dolphins crossed the ship's bow, which Whitney declared a good omen. Birds circled over them, looking for leftovers. Through the morning mist a short plume of steam rose from Sakurajima before gently wafting away, disappearing into the overcast sky. The waves were choppy but bearable for the two hours we plowed through the bay. Our guide book says the Japanese Imperial Navy practiced the bombing of Pearl Harbor here. As beautiful as the day was, it was hard to believe the place had a connection to such a violent day.

The open sea was rough. I felt queasy and returned to the *tatami* area. Looking out of the porthole, one minute I saw nothing but sky, the next nothing but sea. Added to this side-to-side motion was a bow-to-stern up-and-down motion, complete with spray from the bow smashing into the waves. Most of the Japanese in the room were lying on their backs. I decided to try it and immediately felt better. Whitney left, which I thought was brave, because I knew if I did, I would be on my knees at the porcelain wishing well. Soon the steady pulse of the powerful engines and the rocking motions of the boat hit my sleep button and I dozed off.

The ruckus made by drinkers heading upstairs woke me up. One gray-haired man staggered with the motion of the ship in the center aisle with his arms out for balance. He made it to the stairs. A woman who tried it fell onto the *tatami* area, rolling into a sleeping man. She stood and immediately sank to the floor. Laughing uncontrollably, she covered her mouth with her handkerchief. She made it to the stairs doing a less-than elegant, on-all-fours crawl.

I decided to look for Whitney. As I put my shoes on, another drunk pointed upstairs and made a throwing-up motion. I answered with the Japanese gesture indicating he was wrong. I put my hand in front of my face with fingers together pointing up, then waved back and forth in front of my face in quick shallow movements. No way was I about to upchuck.

I walked the aisle to the stairs as the first drunk did. Whitney was sitting at the head of the stairs next to the rest room. Her head was resting on the railing, cushioned by her hands. She had tossed her cookies. Back at the *tatami* area, she tried my accidentally discovered anti-vomiting strategy, which worked for her too.

At the port, we had a good view of the island's forest, which the books describe as "enchanted." For once they were right. Luxuriant green ferns sprout everywhere. The trail follows the bed of a fast-moving clear stream. We made it to the rustic (as in barely maintained) mountain hut and heard some noises from inside that sounded like two people on their honeymoon. We hiked up the trail about 30 yards and waited for the rumpus to end before we knocked on the door.

As we entered, I said the typical polite Japanese word used when entering a room, "*Sumimasen.*" For once I really meant it because I thought our presence would end the party. The hut had all the amenities of a typical Japanese junior high school: indoor (gravity-only) toilets (separated from the main area by a short hall), running water (cold only) and no heat.

During a candlelit dinner of beef jerky, bread and some kind of Japanese snack that tasted like fish garnished with seaweed, we "talked" in a mixture of Japanese and English with the couple. As it was November in the mountains, the unheated hut was cold but my sleeping bag was warm. Whitney and I slept in the hut's other room on bunk beds made of *tatami* mats. Not long after we turned in the rumpus in the other room resumed. It was almost as entertaining as radio, though more graphic.

The next day we hiked eight hours along a beautiful trail with few but great views of the mountainous island and the Pacific Ocean. Staying on the proper trail was hard as the age-faded signs are marked in *kanji* that barely resemble the *kanji* on the maps. We had to be careful to match the two up, because some of the *kanji* of the various trails closely resemble each other. As a result, we had some long stops at these trail-head signs.

Our destination, Wilson Tree (named after an American botanist who came here in 1914), is the remains of one of the centuries-old, gigantic cedars that grow on the island. All that is left of the tree is a huge hollowed-out stump that our guide book says "was cut by seven men in 1586. . . ."

The stump is about 12 feet high, with a diameter of about 40 feet or so. The interior is empty except for a *Shinto* (sheen toe – literally the way of the gods) shrine (*Shinto* is the Japanese home-grown religion). The shrine is about four feet high with small mirrors on it (a *Shinto* motif) and loose change on the small altar. A spring starts inside the tree near the shrine.

We used its water to boil lunch and ate inside the tree. On the way back we came across our hut mates. They were hiking to a different hut. We spent the night alone and missed our noisy neighbors.

As we returned to the port, we hiked to a small road that led us directly into the town. We passed a construction crew with elderly women pushing wheelbarrows. They wore typical woman's outdoor work hats: big bonnets with brims that stick out several inches in front and on the side of their faces, resembling blinders.

On the trip home, Whitney told me about something that happened in August. She was in the teachers' room of Kuratake's only junior high school when a few big shots from the district's Board stopped by.

The principal glanced around the nearly empty room looking for something. Finally he looked at Whitney and asked her to make *ocha* for the visitors. Guests at schools or businesses are presented something to drink without regard to what, or whether, they want to drink. She immediately knew what he had been looking for: a woman to make the tea. She was incensed. Not, she says, because making tea or pitching in is below her. The thought that the principal would not have dreamed of asking one of the male teachers to make the tea, and that the principal decided that she, as a woman (albeit a *gaijin* woman), was the next best thing to a "janitor," made her blood boil.

She played dumb. She asked the principal where the tea was. When he told her where it was, she smiled and shrugged her shoulders. He walked her over to the tea. She put the tea leaves into the cups, which she knew was wrong. The principal politely threw out the tea leaves in the cups and put some in the teapot, which has a strainer built into the spout. Whitney then pretended that she had not learned how to use the *potto* (poe toe – a Thermos-like container and about as big). The *potto* is kept upright. Pushing down on the big button on the top forces the hot water out through the spout. She grabbed the *potto* and held the spout over the cups. Feigning shock that the water did not flow out, she held the *potto* up and looked up at the spout as if there were something wrong with it. The principal put the water in the teapot. This went on for a few minutes. The guests were served with the principal doing as much of the actual work as Whitney felt she could get him to do without making her feigned ignorance totally unbelievable.

After the tea episode she excused herself and went to the school's front door, where street shoes are kept. She walked to the *tatami*-mat room where she knew the principal takes a short nap every afternoon. She put her street shoes on and, stomping around the room silently, screamed to herself while holding her hands over her head as if that would add more weight to her 100-pound frame. She finished, put her street shoes away, walked back into the teachers room and smiled to the principal.

Before I put my walking shoes on and wrap up another "hard day at the office," I will share with you another example of the kind of "English" the Japanese love to put on products. It is *exactly* as it appeared on a tissue box I saw at Hondo Higashi-*chu*:

> Early American Style – It's a heritage of New England.
> Main which became the first colony at the beginning
> the North East comprising six states
> are called "New England"
> Primouth, Maine-the first town
> of May Flower crew as a
> pioneer is one of the high light.
> Half of the border is
> faced on Canada.
>
> Beautiful shore line of
> Atlantic ocean at South East, dotted bays'
> colonial house you can dream of on the ocean
> view hill are there, and scenic port
> depicted in Mervill's novel as well.
> You can savor the seacoast
> ambiance to New England,
> Especially lobsters and clams
> are superb not to mention live
> shell bake and lobster
> bake on the shore,
> It's satisfying for
> every gourmet.

Take it easy, and I hope to hear from you soon.

$\mathcal{D}$ear Dad,   November 29
Happy Thanksgiving! We ALTs and guests celebrated Thanksgiving Day on Sunday. (We could not get Thursday off.) Our goals were to enjoy ourselves and to show our Japanese colleagues what a Thanksgiving Day dinner is. ALTs and Japanese teachers of English within an hour or two of here were invited.

We found an 8.8-pound turkey in Kumamoto for $35. Tsuruta-*san* found a local farmer who provided one of about the same size for the same price. We bought the food with donations from those attending. Most people also brought homemade dishes, and there was an unspoken faith among us all that Tsuruta-*san* would bring the beer. We were not disappointed.

The group totaled about 40. Rosemary and I arrived at Honmachi-*chu*'s kitchen classroom at 9 A.M. to start the dinner. I brought my *minicompo* and my Christmas music. A few minutes later a group of eighth graders came in and asked what we were doing. We asked them what *THEY* were doing at school (in uniform of course) on a Sunday morning. They came to practice for an upcoming concert. Mostly they hung around picking up everything in sight asking "What's this?" until the Japanese teachers showed up.

We ALTs wanted to do the cooking ourselves to thank the teachers for their kindness. Some of the Japanese women insisted on helping. I told them that any Japanese woman who came into the kitchen would be tied to a chair immediately. That proved to be an idle threat. Keeping a Japanese woman from helping in the kitchen would be as hard as coaxing an American man out of a recliner during a football game to help clean the dishes. Some of the Japanese men helped cook, much to the surprise of everyone, especially the Japanese women.

Ovens big enough to cook our eight-pound turkeys are unknown in this town. So we cut them in half and cooked them in four small microwaves brought by volunteers. We cooked until 1:30 P.M. and had a great time: god-awful music wafting in from the girls' choir down the hall mixed with Bing Crosby Christmas carols; people busy mashing this here, chopping that there; voices chirping away in English, Japanese and our best common language, laughter; some people taking pictures; and Tsuruta-*san* testing to make sure the beer was of an acceptable vintage.

Outside the blue sky reminded me of Arizona. There were a few hawks in the air too. Arizona has more hawks than anyplace I know of in the States, but Arizona's hawk population is no more than ten percent of Amakusa's (the name of the area in which Hondo is located). Arizona's soar better, probably because the air thermals are better there. Just as I did at the party, I have to pull myself out of this digression to finish what I started.

When the feast was ready, we hauled it across the farm road to the Buddhist temple, which we rented. (One of the teachers is the brother-in-law of the priest who owns the temple.) There were banners outside the temple which, I thought were a nice touch, until someone explained that they were for a funeral the next day.

The feast included turkey, potatoes (mashed and scalloped), *mikan* (me khan – a tangerine), homemade stuffing, corn, green beans, cauliflower, *kaki* (ka key – persimmon, a Japanese favorite), salad, cranberry sauce (which was as hard to find as *natto* in the States – what's *natto*? – smelly, sticky-oozy fermented soy bean), pumpkin pie, cookies, apple cobbler, wine, beer, pop, coffee, *ocha* and chips. Everyone brought their own knife and fork because we did not have enough. (Japanese each own a few of them and use them at home occasionally.)

We ate in a 40 *tatami*-mat room at long, two-foot high tables formed into two long rows. I gave a short prepared speech in English, which Ezaki-*sensei* gave in Japanese. In the speech I said that for the ALTs this was similar to the first Thanksgiving. We had journeyed across an ocean. Like the Indians and settlers, there had been rough times between our peoples in the past. We ALTs had met and had been helped by new friends. And we all sat down together to enjoy each other's company and to give thanks for the friendship between us.

Joe, an ALT who teaches in Hondo senior high schools, shouted, "Are you done yet? I'm hungry." Sensing the natives and their new friends were looking at me with hostile intent, I canned the rest of the speech and proceeded directly to the obligatory "*Kampai*!!" (kaam pie –– bottoms up). It is something said before Japanese in a group will drink alcohol.

Everyone liked the turkey. Only two Japanese said they had eaten it before. At $35 for eight pounds and the fact that we could not find any in Hondo's stores, I can understand why.

After dinner, we had planned to watch a football game on the school's TV. Several of the American men had asked relatives to send a tape of a football game, but that plan was ruined when no tape came. We thought about playing volleyball in the school's gym, but the girls' team was practicing (as usual from 1 to 5:30 on Sunday). In the end, we sat around and talked until we decided to clean up.

We washed the dishes in the temple's kitchen. While working some sang what I thought were traditional Japanese songs. As I listened, I realized they were singing Christmas carols translated into Japanese. I know the junior high students of today learn the same ones we do, but I now know that it is not at all unusual for Japanese of all ages to know them. It seems as if each Japanese person has memorized about the same number of carols as the average American has.

After the cleaning was done some people headed home, but most of us did not want the evening to end. We decided to go back to my house and watch a *bideo* (be day oh – video). We rented Japanese-subtitled tapes of *The Wizard of Oz* and *It's a Wonderful Life*. (Most rental movies are American with Japanese subtitles.) A group of about 35 crammed into my living room intent on drinking the last of the wine. People were lying wherever they could find floor space with some using parts of other people as pillows. When everyone was situated so they could see the screen through the maze of feet, hips and heads, we turned off the lights, lit the candles and fired up the video.

We watched *The Wizard of Oz* first. Someone started to sing the first song along with Dorothy and we all joined in. From then on everyone sang. Most people had never seen the movie before, but all soon became adept at singing the "We're off to see the Wizard. . ." part. At the end of the next video, *It's a Wonderful Life*, when Clarence got his wings, there was not a dry eye in the house. The worst part of the evening was that it had to end.

Bye.

*D*ear Frank,   December 6
        I thought I would tell you about the small "gym" (which is actually a converted shed) where I work out. It is the only gym in town and owned by a man who runs a small grocery store. The few men who use it are all acquaintances of the owner, who does not want to work out by himself. I met him through Tsuruta-*san*. As I said before, if Tsuruta-*san* does not know you, you do not live in Hondo.

The equipment is a mishmash he has picked up over the years. (The chin-up bar is a metal pipe hung from the ceiling by ropes.) The necessaries are there and the men who use it are friendly. Entering the gym, I put slippers on.

Most of the men are not very big. (Bench press 180 pounds and your name is engraved on a wall plaque.) The average Japanese man is not only shorter than the average American, he is also thinner. If a Japanese man is as tall as I, he is usually 20 or more pounds lighter. Many Japanese ask me why this is so. I have as little clue as they do, but I tell them what I think: They eat too much rice and fish and not enough meat.

Although we do not share a common language, it does not dampen one iota the zeal of these men to communicate. They are typical in this and in their inability to master the variety of sounds English depends upon but which are unknown to the Japanese language. Their vocabulary is limited too. A college-educated Japanese will have had at least six mandatory years of English (in junior and senior high) and most take four more in college. For all that study however, we need dictionaries to "talk."

The emphasis in their studies was on the written word. So when I say things like "I'mina," they have no clue what I am saying. What's that? You do not either? Sure you do. For example: I'mina study for an hour. Then I'mina watch TV. Then I'mina go to sleep. I never realized I condensed "I am going to" into "I'mina" until Akane asked what it meant. She said I use it often but she could not find it in her dictionary.

Since then I have learned I use English words such as "jawanna," "woodja," "whatsa" and "whoja."

We "talk" using bits of English, Japanese, gesture language and drawing on a small chalkboard. As with so many of the people I meet, they see me as a window to the world. I feel like a vacuum cleaner hose is attached to my brain when we talk. I have to concentrate as hard to speak Japanese as I do to understand their English so there are times I come home feeling tired even after a light workout.

Because the gym has no showers, I shower at home, which is becoming more difficult as the weather becomes colder. Actually, I am not sure what I do is "showering." In Japanese fashion, I bathe next to, *not in*, the tub. As at the *ryokan*, I use the shower hose while sitting on the short plastic stool on the tile floor.

Because the bathroom has no heat, I have developed a process I may patent. I carry the *toyu stobu* (toe you – kerosene; stow boo – stove: portable kerosene heater) through the kitchen into the tiny laundry room, which is my only entrance to the bathroom. I close the sliding plastic door shutting the laundry room off from the kitchen. I put my clean clothes and towel on top of the washing machine in the order I will use them. I enter the bathroom fully dressed.

I turn the hot water on full blast, which quickly steams up the postage-stamp bathroom. Half the room is tub; the other half is tile floor where I wash. The laundry room is now warm enough for me to undress. Reentering the bathroom, I spray the tile floor and plastic stool with hot water to heat them. With the room thoroughly filled with steam, I turn the water temperature down, sit on the stool and shower. Sometimes I have to interrupt my shower to heat up the room again with steam.

Only after washing and rinsing do the Japanese soak in the tub of hot water. Because the cost of energy in Japan is much higher than in the States, after soaking in the tub, they *DO NOT* empty it. The water is left in the tub and a collapsible plastic cover is placed over it. A Japanese family uses the tub water for a day or two, then the women pump the water into the washing machine. (Otherwise Japanese women use only cold water for washing.)

Cold-weather drying and dressing takes a bit of forethought. I grab my towel from the laundry room and dry off in the bathroom. Next I go into the by-now-toasty laundry room to dress. The Japanese just bathe and go from the steamy hot bath into the unheated adjoining room to dress, which explains the advice Japanese doctors give to their patients: Do not take a bath when you have a cold.

New houses have baths and many older houses have had them added, but houses without baths still are not uncommon. Even people with baths, however, use the *sento* (sen toe – public baths) for a change of pace. *Sento* are public baths with men's and women's bathing areas. Each is a big, open room similar to the baths at the *ryokan*.

As in any city, *sento* are scattered throughout Hondo's neighborhoods. They can cost about 400 yen per person (a little more than $3). Most of the ticket takers are *obasan* (oh ba san – older women) who are strategically placed to view both areas. Every evening in virtually every neighborhood, in rain, sleet or hail, the same scene is played out. People walk to the *sento* with a towel draped over their shoulder and carry a shallow plastic bowl in which they place their toiletries. The Japanese bathe in the evening to wash the days' grime off and do not understand why we bathe in the morning. I tell them that if I shower in the evening I wake up with poof-head hair. They take care of that by washing their hair in the morning, known as *asa shan* (ah sah – morning; shan – from shampoo).

I may have the convenience of a bath but I have offsetting inconveniences. After my shower I carry the *toyu stobu* from the laundry room to the "bathroom" sink, which is in the unheated hallway. I am careful as I move the heater because it is designed to shut itself off if it is shaken or knocked over (a useful safety device in a country plagued with earthquakes and abundantly supplied with wood homes).

As you can appreciate, it is sometimes a chore trying to stay warm in a Japanese house. As much as I like the *tatami*-mat floor, the cold weather has revealed the short-comings of this unique flooring material. Between the floors and the dirt under the house is nothing but two feet of air. A grate on the side of the house provides for air circulation. In the summer the *tatami* was fine, but in the winter, the charm of having a *tatami* floor is overcome by the winter drafts come right through it. The typical Japanese house in winter is definitely colder than the typical American house.

To counteract chilly drafts, Japanese place area rugs over the *tatami*. Many Japanese have *denki kapeto* (dain key – electricity; ka pet toe – from "carpet"). *Denki kapeto* are warm and comfortable to sit on which is important because most Japanese sit on the floor. If the room is small, as so many in Japan are, a *denki kapeto* can go a long way toward heating the entire room. A *denki kapeto* under the futon makes for a warm night (alternatively, they could use an electric blanket I suppose). You would think your backside could get well done in the process, but it is in no danger of becoming charcoal.

The traditional (and still most popular) way the Japanese counteract the *tatami* chills is by using a *kotatsu* (co tat tsu). It combines the idea of a rug, a blanket, a coffee table and an electric stove. It is the knee-high coffee table I talked about, which has more uses than I suspected last July. Veteran ALTs tell me living in a Japanese house in winter leaves fond memories of the *kotatsu*.

Recently I spread out the *kotatsu*'s thick, soft, bottom cloth, which covers most of the *tatami*. After that, I lifted the removable portion of the tabletop. I laid a blanket about as big as the bottom cloth on the nonremovable plywood portion of the table. I then reattached the tabletop. Underneath the plywood is a small electric heating unit. On my *kotatsu*, this consists of what looks like a simple red light bulb surrounded by wire mesh. I use the *kotatsu* by sliding underneath the top blanket. Within a few minutes of flipping the switch my feet, legs and lap are warm. Depending on how I sit, I can even warm my chest.

On winter nights whole families cozy up under the *kotatsu*. For millions of Japanese, the *kotatsu* is the only source of heat in the whole house. The American picture of a couch potato is a father in a recliner with his feet up, a beer on the coffee table and his snoring competing with the TV. The Japanese equivalent is a father with his head on a rice pillow, his head the only part of his body sticking out from under the *kotatsu*, a beer on top of it and his snoring competing with the TV.

At bedtime, I push the *kotatsu* to the side of the room to make room for my futon. Though visiting at a friend's house for the weekend is is nice, there is nothing like sleeping on your own floor.

I turn the heat off because the electricity is expensive and my comforter is plenty warm – but I am dreading February, the coldest month here. I already see my breath in the house in the mornings. As soon as I get up I dash to the kitchen and grab a match to light the *toyu stobu*.

By the time I start cooking, the kitchen usually has warmed to the point where I cannot see my breath anymore. But some days even with the heat on full blast, the room is still cold and the stove's heating element seems as if it gives off no more heat than a red light bulb in a metal casing. Those days I cuddle up to it while cradling a hot cup of tea and try to stop my jaws' involuntarily chattering. During the recent cold snap, mornings were so bad I wore my down jacket too.

After reading my letters, perhaps you can understand my disbelief with the assertion that the Japanese are more "in tune" with nature than Americans. I have no idea how that rumor started (in cities there is an occasional tree, but it is outnumbered by rows of ugly, gray, poured-concrete buildings.) I would wager there is not a people on earth who live farther from nature than the Japanese. The truth is that they live closer to the *elements*.

At school they are closer to elements too. Central heating is unknown to Hondo schools, as in most of Japan. No classrooms in Hondo are heated except under certain conditions at Miyajidake-*chu*. (It is in the highlands and therefore colder than the rest of Hondo.) There the *toyu stobu* may be used in the morning if the outside temperature is below 45 degrees (but never in the afternoon). What is more, during the ten-minute breaks between classes, stoves are turned off and windows opened, to dissipate kerosene fumes. The total effect seems to be that once the room gets warm, it is time to cool it off again.

My last visit at Miyajidake-*chu* was a cold day. Sure enough, just as the room became toasty, the class captain turned off the classroom stove and opened the windows. I was wearing a thick undershirt, a shirt, a wool sweater and two pairs of socks yet I was still cold with the heat off. Tahara-*sensei* explained that it is against school rules to relight the stove until the next class, so I asked a student to bring my suit coat from the teachers' room.

To warm up I shoot hoops after lunch in the gym during the kids' play period. I like the opportunity to mingle with the kids outside class. As an American, I am assumed to be a decent player. I may miss ten in a row but when the eleventh shot goes in, they applaud and say "*Nice shooto*" (nice; shoe toe). Shoot has an "o" on the end because they add an "o" to the end of any English word that ends in a "t" or "d." *Nice shooto* is now a Japanese phrase, like so many English words having to do with basketball.

Any English speaker can almost have a conversation in Japanese about basketball. They use *basuketo boru* (ba sue kay toe bow roo – basketball), *pasu* (pa sue – pass), *reboundo boru* (ree bown dough bow roo – rebound), *man tsu man defensu* (mahn tsu mhan de feign sue – man-to-man defense), *doriburu* (doe re boo roo – dribble), *tsu pointa* (tsu po een ta – two pointer), *suree pointa* (sue ree po een ta – three pointer), *suree pointo rain* (sue ree po een toe rah en – three point line), *zon* (zoe – zone), *pasonaru fauru* (pa sone na roo fa ooh roo – personal foul), *tekunikaru fauru* (tay ku knee ka roo – technical foul) and so on.

Unfortunately, the word *misu* (me sue – miss) is a big part of my basketball vocabulary. Fortunately, I never have to chase after my *misu*. Students throw me their balls and take off after mine. Trying to get them to stop doing that is proving to be an impossible task. Alright, I confess, I am not trying *THAT* hard.

The other Hondo ALT, Rosemary, warned me that I should be more careful about what I say when I clang a brick off the rim. The day after I visited a school she heard the children say "Oh, shit" when they missed their shots. While I will not deny being a bad influence on them in terms of basketball skill, I think what she heard was *oshi* (o she), which means something like "regrettable." They say it after a miss, a word I hear a lot.

In one way, I am a big disappointment to the kids. To them, my six foot frame is tall so when they see me with a basketball they shout, "*dunku shooto*," which, when they say it, sounds to my ear more like down shoot. At every school, every day, from somewhere in the gym I will hear a kid shout, "*DUNKU SHOOTO*!!!" I explain that I cannot, but none gives up easily. When they finally realize that I am not just being modest, they give me a What-a-waste-of-all-that-height look.

While writing this at 2 P.M. on the computer in the teachers' room, the principal asked me if I was cold. (My down jacket may have been a clue.) When I said yes he surprised me by turning the heat on. I had watched him shiver and I think he reached the point where he could not stand the cold but decided to make it look like he was trying to take care of the poor *gaijin*. Whatever he was up to I had no qualms about being considered a wimp. I was happy for the heat.

I took off my jacket in a few minutes. After 20 minutes, I took off my wool sweater. Apparently another teacher decided it was too warm, however, for he turned the stove off and opened the window. "To exchange air. Healthy!" the teacher said. I made a mental note; next time "Keep the sweater on as long as possible."

My last class of the day was with the seventh grade. Because it was also my last day here before Christmas, we sang "White Christmas" and "Silent Night." From the music class down the hall, I heard the same songs being sung by another class, but in Japanese.

Our lesson included the use of a prop phone. I called Santa. He asked what the students wanted for Christmas. Their gifts of choice ranged from a bicycle (a blue mountain bike – "just like Ken- *sensei*'s," one boy said), to a novel featuring a little girl in a big adventure (a girl's wish), a radio-controlled car (the hope of the boy who said he wants to be a race car driver), a Barbie doll (blond dolls are popular here too) and a house as big as the school, with a gym.

One boy asked me where Santa lives. I said the North Pole. He asked me whether Santa was real. I stumbled through that question by saying that some believe in him and some do not. I said that if you are good all year, write him a letter. (At the boy's request, I wrote Santa's address on the board.) If you receive what you ask for, that would be your answer. It was a terrible answer, but looking at the kids' hopeful faces, I just could not be the one to burst their bubble. Then the dam broke with kids asking questions like: "Do I have to write in English or can Santa read Japanese?" "What does Santa do in the summer?" I told Tahara-*sensei* it was time to move on and she saved me by skillfully changing the subject.

I have come to rely on Tahara-*sensei* for more than just her classroom skills. Since I wrote last, I was knocked down by a vicious flu bug. I called Tahara-*sensei* to cancel a tutoring session. Instead she came by in full Florence Nightingale mode. Although too young for the job by many years, she has assumed the role of my mom away from home. She came with the Japanese version of chicken soup complete with roots, berries, and other floating things, which I felt it was better to eat without asking her to identify. I have found that eating first and asking questions later or not at all is the better policy. I may never know what was in it, but it was delicious.

She also brought over an assortment of Japanese medicines. I was a five-year-old in a man's body. She had to explain how to take Japanese medicine. They prefer powder form to capsule or pill. They also firmly believe that medicine that tastes good or is at least palatable cannot be effective. But they are not thrilled about tasting disgusting medicine either. As a result they have a unique way to take medicine. You fill your mouth with water, pour the powdery medicine onto the water sloshing around in your mouth, then quickly swallow the whole thing. Whether it was her home remedy or the medicine, I felt as if I had turned the corner within a few hours. By the next morning, I was feeling much better.

As much as some teachers enjoy classes with me, others consider it worse than a case of the plague, such as the teachers at Higashi-*chu*. I have one maybe two classes each visit. The teachers there do not speak English well, but it is not too far below the average for the teachers with whom I work.

Many Japanese make mistakes for which I cannot understand the basis. Some of the mistakes are things like "My wife, he . . ." or "My husband, she. . .." Japanese has pronouns for he and she so why they make this mistake in English is baffling. At least their usual failure to use the articles "a" or "the" is understandable. In Japanese there is no real counterpart for them and nouns do not become plural. Many Japanese therefore take sentence A and say it as in the sentence B.

> A. My wife has two hats. She likes the red one more than the white one.
>
> B. My wife has two hat. He like red one more than white one.

Here is another example of the average level of the teachers. A teacher whipped up a quick conversation that he wanted to have the students practice:

> A: Excuse me.
> B: Yes.

A: I'm stranger here. I want to go to the city library.
Will you tell me the way to the city library?
B: All right. You ask me to go to the city library?
A: Yes. I ask you to go to the city library.

It is a bit of a battle to steer between avoiding embarrassing the teacher in front of the students and not teaching the students gobbledygook. I believe it is better to teach something that is wrong and then consult with the teachers after class to have them correct the mistake in their own way.

To avoid problems, I go over everything carefully with the teachers before class. I use words I will use later in class, so, when the students hear our interchanges, they will assume their teacher can converse in English. Progress in these meetings is often slow, and once or twice I have ended up with a headache.

Sometimes my hard work is fruitless. The other day at Higashi-*chu*, the teacher did not understand what I said in class, in spite of my preparation with him. I covered for him as best I could, but the students knew I could not understand his English and he could not understand mine. It became uncomfortable when the students started snickering. After class I told him the miscommunication was my fault, but he acted as if nothing unusual happened in class. He is a man near retirement, and is seems obvious that he is going to avoid such embarrassment in the future not through renewed vigorous study but by avoiding any more classes with the *gaijin*.

Bye for now.

*D*ear Lynea,   December 16
Let the parties begin! On Friday I attended an office *bon enkai* (bone en ka e – Forget the Year Party). It is a traditional end-of-the-year party that businesses and government offices have before New Years. Board workers were invited as well as selected teachers and school administrators. The party started at 5:30 P.M.

When an event is scheduled to start at a certain time in Japan, it not only begins exactly on time, but everyone arrives on time too. The concept of being fashionably late absolutely does not exist in this country. When the teachers I work with say they will be at my house at a certain time, if my watch shows that they arrived a few minutes late, I reset my watch because it must be fast. They do not say "I will pick you up at quarter to seven or thereabouts." They say, "I will pick you up at 7:43." And they will show up exactly at 7:43, not 7:42, not 7:44 and certainly not 7:50, at least not without an endless stream of apologies. Being late reflects badly on you or whatever group you are representing and those are things a Japanese will avoid if possible.

I spoke with a Japanese judge in Tokyo who gave a speech at one of the seminars. He thought that every wristwatch and clock in the city is probably no more than a minute or two off from all the rest. In his house every clock on the wall, microwave, TV, VCR – *everything* shows the exact same time. He said it was imperative for everyone to have the same time in order to be on time. For that reason, the national TV gives the time every morning and every evening. Since then I have noted that the clocks have been all been synchronized in every school and every home I have been in. Except, of course, for my house which has clocks within a few minutes of each other.

The party began on time in a hotel's big *tatami*-mat room. The tables' legs were two feet high, so we sat on cushions. In some respects it was typical of the *enkai* I have been to: no spouses were invited; there was plenty of food and beer; and they sang too much karaoke (ka rah oh kay). As with all *enkai*, the party officially started with everyone raising their glasses and shouting "*Kampai!*"

A female kindergarten teacher whom I had never met sat next to me and took it upon herself to pamper me. She took my plate and put food on it. When that was gone, she did it again. I made a halfhearted effort to stop her, but I have been up against these unrelenting domestic types in Japan before. If a woman has decided to take me under her wing, there is little point in arguing.

Sitting next to her was like sitting next to any other Japanese I have just met. I introduced myself and she exclaimed, *"Jozu DESU NE!!* (Oh dear me, your Japanese is very good isn't it!)" Then she asked my age and blood type. As I ate she commented, *"Hashi ga jozu desu ne!* (My you are good with chopsticks, aren't you!). I wanted to shout "If I was not *jozu* with my *hashi* by now I would be dead!" But I knew that she could not help herself. She could not appreciate that I have heard the same thing thousands of times already. She was simply saying the things Japanese are somehow somewhere taught to say to a *gaijin* they have just met. I took her comments as conversation starters and set aside the urge to scream.

As the resident guest *gaijin*, I was invited politely but unrelentingly to sing karaoke. The place had a very elaborate system with a couple of TVs scattered around the room, a digital video disc player, a couple of mikes and plenty of speakers. When a disc is inserted a scene with the words to the song is shown on the bottom of the screen. I chose "Jingle Bells." A winter scene of people riding through a forest in a horse-drawn carriage accompanied the music. As the music reached the point in the song where I was to sing, instead of a bouncing ball, the words changed from white to blue.

Many people in the room sang along in the Japanese version. Mercifully they were satisfied with the *gaijin* singing two songs. Unfortunately, then the Japanese took over. Karaoke is a strange cultural phenomenon. When we think of the Japanese we envision people who are shy in public. With karaoke, however, that myth goes right out the window. Some of the most god-awful singers immediately volunteered to "sing." I use the quotes because it was more like using their voices as weapons of aural violence. Of all the times I have survived karaoke, I have never seen anyone throw fruit, or laugh. The audience, almost without exception, listens politely and applauds warmly when it is over. It is a part of the culture to accept someone who gives his best, even when his best is awful.

When the karaoke began, the *enkai* began a slow, gentle turn into the twilight zone. It started innocently enough with a guy using a cushion as a veil on the small stage. He did a slow dance with plenty of hip action. It looked like he was pretending to be a woman doing a traditional Japanese dance. At the end he slapped the floor. Everyone got a big kick out of it.

The next man completed the turn from normal social restraint to the land of "Anything Goes." He jumped on stage, undid his belt and zipper, and lay on the floor. He grabbed the kimono of one of the middle-aged waitresses passing by, and she happily hopped on stage. This 50ish woman, who probably was no beauty at the height of her attractiveness, stood over him, straddling his groin. Then she bent over to grab his pants, I thought to pull them up. But he grabbed her arms and pulled her down on top of him.

She giggled as he pulled a sash off her kimono. She sat up and the audience squealed as she rotated her hips over his crotch. The men in the audience especially were howling. The women were holding their hands over their mouths as they laughed. Before leaving, she grabbed his pants again and pulled them down around his ankles.

Another man grabbed a second kimono-clad waitress and

danced with her. Within seconds he tried to pull up the kimono to put his hand under it. She continued to dance with him but expertly fended off his efforts. By this time the first woman was on the floor near the stage with two guys who were trying to kiss her. It seemed like everyone in the place thought it was high entertainment.

It comforted me to know that the party would end as punctually as it began. Toward the end, I was invited to go to a *nijikai* at a local bar. With the natives so obviously restless, I passed. If this was how they were acting in the presence of the big bosses, I did not want to see what they would do at the progressively less formal *nijikai* and *sanjikai*.

I was saying good night to an attractive coworker in her middle 30s when a man from the office staggered up. Putting his hand around her, resting his wrist on her shoulder, he said he was going to the *nijikai*. Suddenly his hand made a beeline for her right breast. It was one of those moments when everything seems to happen in slow motion. It took her until his hand was almost on target to react, but when she did it looked as if she had had plenty of practice. She squatted and rotated toward him with the result that his arm fell off her shoulder.

When she completed the maneuver, she was again facing me and still next to him but well out of fondling range. She had on a big smile, trying, I thought, to act as much as possible as if nothing had happened. He looked at his hand and said, "Oh, baa do! (bad)" while slapping it with his other hand. She then slapped his hand too and wagged a finger at him while saying "Bay ri baa do (very bad)." True to the rules of Japanese culture, I imagine the breast-grabbing attempt will never be brought up again.

Later that night, long after I was in bed, the totally blasted Tsuruta-*san* and Miyagawa-*sensei* stopped by the house. They shouted my name and banged on the door until I realized that my plan of pretending not to hear them was not working. When I opened the door I saw they had a taxi waiting. They grabbed me and said that they knew a bar that was still open.

As I pulled away from them, one said something that I presume was "Of course he can't go to the bar, he's in his underwear." And the other must have responded, "Okay let's drink here." Tsuruta-*san* said to me, "U a ho su, we co mu (your house, we come)." I said, "Your house, you go." After a few more minutes of negotiating, we decided that I would go back to sleep and they could do anything they wanted except bang on my door again that night. I cannot blame them for being over exuberant. Their culture, which stifles most outward expressions of emotion, relaxes its grip at this time of year.

We are getting a kind of break too. Tomorrow we ALTs go to a city called Miyazaki for a conference with all the ALTs on the main island of Kyushu. I am looking forward to it because we have decided to take a back way over mountain roads. (My car has become the local ALT Transportation Company.) Though it is winter, the mountain roads will not be dangerous. On Kyushu, except for a couple of high mountains that we will not drive near, there is no snow.

The conference we are going to is called a Block Conference and is designed to give the ALTs a few days to exchange ideas now that we have a few months' experience under our belts. As usual the city will be overreimbursing me for my costs by one or two hundred dollars. I think I finally understand the rationale behind it: to buy *omiage* (o me ah gay).

Omiage is the custom of purchasing gifts for friends and coworkers any time you go to another part of Japan. It usually consist of some variation of the traditional Japanese pastry called *omonjyu* (oh mohn jew). With its soft bun, *omonjyu* looks tasty, but the Japanese do not have much of a sweet tooth. *Omonjyu* stuffing is a thick, oozy, bland bean paste. I think the stuff is awful, but the Japanese love it. As with everything else here, it is more expensive than it ought to be.

The hotel, the Phoenix, is Western-style. Everyone is looking forward to central heating, showers in the bathroom (instead of down the hall) and honest-to-gosh beds again. I hear it is complete with palm trees, so during the conference I ought to feel right at home.

I will be back in Hondo before *Oshogatsu* (oh show ga tsu – New Year's). *Oshogatsu* is traditionally one of the most important Japanese holidays. At this time of year, families come together. The men smoke, drink and talk: the children play; the women clean the house and cook the meals. It is also the time of year to exchange "*Oshogatsu*" cards. The accepted form is a postcard with your own best calligraphy on one side and a lottery number at the bottom. The winning lottery numbers are announced in the first week of the new year.

The average Japanese celebrates Christmas too, at least the gift-giving part of the tradition. After the war (in Japan, any reference to "the war" means World War II), department stores brought the concept of Christmas to Japan as a way to boost sales, and it took hold. Families with small children are likely to have presents under a small tree and even give or attend Christmas parties.

I polled my students as to which holiday they liked better, *Oshogatsu* or Christmas. It was a dead heat. Students preferring Christmas had two main reasons. First, presents. Second, they have a good feeling on that day, as if everyone is nicer to everyone else for just a little while. The students who preferred *Oshogatsu* also had two main reasons. First, money. Children receive an envelope with the equivalent of $100 or more in it from their parents. Second, the whole family is together. They play with their cousins, and visit with grandparents, uncles and aunts.

I also conducted a poll in the various teachers' rooms. The older men prefer *Oshogatsu*, while the younger teachers and most of the older women tend to prefer Christmas. The younger teachers say they like the feelings of joy they remember from their youth (and no doubt the presents). The older women are expected to work like slaves for the whole family on *Oshogatsu,* so in comparison, Christmas looks better.

Yesterday I had about 15 people over for an impromptu Christmas party. After eating a pot-luck dinner we sang the usual Christmas carols: ALTs sang in English; the Japanese teachers sang in Japanese. During the party, Beethoven's Ode to Joy was played almost constantly. For some reason, that melody is a long-time end-of-the-year tradition in Japan.

When it came time to pass out the presents, I was elected Santa Claus, but no one would teach me how to say in Japanese: "The women have to sit on Santa's lap to receive a present." The Japanese, who are taught to be self-effacing, say *tsumaranai mono* (tsu ma rah na e mow no – it's nothing really) when handing someone a gift. Few Japanese will open a present in front of the person who gave it to them. To do that, their culture requires them to ask permission. Invariably, they are careful to not to rip the paper while unwrapping the gift.

While having nothing to do with the spirit of Christmas, during the evening I noticed how warm the house was. It was probably due to all the body heat. Maybe that is one of the reasons why in Japan the generations live together: body heat in winter.

It is Sunday night now and I am writing this while snuggled under the *kotatsu*. In about 20 minutes it will be time to watch the Sunday night movie. Aside from the national news which is translated on the subchannel, it is one of the few times during the week when there is a bilingual broadcast. (These are American movies or TV programs which were made in stereo. The right channel is the main channel – Japanese – and the left is the sub channel – English.) You would not believe how desperate you become to hear your native language. There have been times when I watched *Sesame Street* on Japanese educational TV just to be able to understand what was going on.

Unfortunately, the Japanese love American action movies and show more of them than any other film. Arnold Schwarzeneggar is a favorite. They call him Shua-*chan* (shoe ah chan). "Shua" is how the Japanese pronounce the "Schwa" part of Arnie's name. *Chan* is the diminutive of *san*, reserved for close friends or small children. If you know someone well, instead of saying *san*, which is more formal, you take either his last or first name, drop the last syllable or so and add *chan*. Tonight is one of shua-*chan*'s early efforts. I am not a big fan of action movies and do not think I ever saw a Schwarzeneggar movie before coming here. Because his movies are on TV often and he appears in commercials made for the Japanese market, I have seen a lot of him here. I am beginning to like his acting, and I am wondering whether he is good or if I am desperate for English.

Fortunately, the hands-down favorite American actress, among Japanese of all ages, is, for some reason, Audrey Hepburn, so I can look forward to many good movies with her in it. No doubt by the end of the year I will be well steeped in Audrey Hepburn movies.

I am not sure anymore which year that will be actually. The Japanese use the Western calendar, but the government officially uses a home-grown way of counting years as do the people for many everyday uses. The Japanese calendar is based on the emperor's reign. The emperor who led Japan to war in World War II, who we refer to by his first name (emperors do not have last names), Hirohito, is known to the Japanese not by his name but by the name for his reign, *Showa* (show wa – shining peace). The Japanese so rarely refer to the emperor by name that many have to think a bit to remember it, although *Showa* is an everyday word. Hirohito died in 1988, or *Showa* 63 (the 63rd year of his reign). His son, Emperor Akihito (again a first name), is the *Heisei* (hey – peace; say – becoming) emperor. Already people have difficultly recalling his name.

The year 1998 is *Heisei jyunen* (jew nen), or the 10th year of the reign of the *Heisei* emperor. Future dates are calculated in the emperors' reigns too. For example, the year 2000 will be the 12th year of the *Heisei* reign. If Akihito dies in 1999, it would start as the eleventh year of *Heisei* but would end as the first year of his son's reign. No one can say what happens if one emperor dies in February and his replacement dies in November. I wonder if the man (no women need apply) from February to November has a year named after his reign.

Ask a Japanese what year they were born in and they will say *Showa* (and youngsters *Heisei*) this or that, but ask them what year that is in the Western calendar and they must stop and use their left palm and right index finger to calculate. For example, being born in 1956 means you were born in *Showa* 31. Basing the calendar on the emperor's reign has one obvious drawback – emperors have a tendency to die. Perhaps in recognition of that, since Hirohito's death, most calendars are printed with Western dates. In spite of that, most Japanese just cannot seem to think in them.

Even today, the older people think in "*Showa*" time because they have done so for an entire lifetime. To them 1998 is *Showa* 73. For present and future dates, they convert from *Showa* into *Heisei*.

Well, I guess I am not sure when I am sending this letter, in 1997 or *Heisei* 9, but today for sure, whenever that is. As I sit here writing, I cannot stop humming "Silent Night." I just realized it is because at school on Friday, I could hear the music teacher who sits near me, but speaks no English, humming that song. Maybe there is something contagious about this Christmas spirit after all. I will try to stuff some of this carol in the envelope for you to hear when you open it.

Bye for now. Merry Christmas.

*D*ear Uncle Chet and Aunt Dottie,   January 4
I hope your holidays were happy. After the Block Conference, I started a two-week vacation that included touring several cities. Due to the way my vacation time worked, I had to return in time for work today, although there are no classes. So I am at the Board on the computer writing to you.

On Christmas Eve another ALT, Andy, and I drove to Fukuoka, where I had some business to attend to, on Christmas no less. In Japan, officially, December 25 was just Tuesday.

Andy is a bearded 26-year-old black belt from Atlanta with a computer degree. He claims to have been "exiled" to an island in the East China Sea called Goshonouura. It has 5,000 residents who are friendly but, he says, there are no females between the ages of 16 and 60. Not having women on the island is not really a problem for Andy. During college, when he realized his cute, fresh-out-of-college Japanese professor, Kodama Mie (Mie – me a [her first name]), was a year older than he, he decided to ask her for a date. At the end of the year, Mie returned to Japan. Andy signed up to be an ALT for the sole reason of convincing Mie she wants to marry him.

On Christmas evening, we went to see an American movie. Tickets were $15 a piece. The seats were narrower, with less knee room than an American theater. For many in the audience that did not matter because they had to stand. Land prices result in theaters packed to standing-room only.

As with most American movies, it was subtitled. Japanese would rather hear the English version than have the movie dubbed into Japanese. On the other hand, a common complaint is that when sitting in a theater they can often hear a Westerner laughing at some scene that is not funny in the Japanese translation. Many Japanese describe their goal in learning English as understanding the jokes in our movies.

I know the translations were not accurate, even with my limited Japanese. We use more swear words than they do. When someone is called a "fool" in a movie, it is translated as *baka* (ba ka – fool). When someone is called a "shithead," it is translated *baka*. When someone is called a "low-down, no-good, varmint-bait, belly-crawling snake," that too is translated *baka*. You get the idea.

The day after seeing the movie, we drove to Hiroshima. Between the cities are pretty valleys filled with small villages. About 70 percent of Japan is comprised of short, steep mountains. Instead of going around the mountains, the expressways go through them. Unfortunately, tunnel ventilation is poor. Newer tunnels have huge jetengine-like ceiling-hung fans. My guess is their purpose is to blow out vehicle exhaust fumes, but enough smoke stays in the tunnel to seep into the car. Rolling the windows up tight makes no difference. There is a visible pall of exhaust near the mouth's of longer tunnels. Upon exiting, we rolled down the windows to breathe fresh air. With many tunnels spaced only two or three hundred feet apart we had to roll the windows up quickly before entering the cloud of blue smoke drifting out of the next tunnel. I hate to think what would happen if the car stalled in the middle of a long tunnel.

We arrived in Hiroshima around suppertime. At our youth hostel, we met several ALTs who said that schools farther north have stoves in all the classrooms. Heat in the schools in winter: must be a wimpy school district. In keeping with the Japanese ideal of "We train 'em to be as tough as the Spartans," the ALTs confirmed that in their schools as soon as the room warms, the windows are opened.

The following day, the 27th, I explored Hiroshima. Parking in Japanese big cities is not cheap. A popular solution to the high cost of land is the enclosed tower parking structure, where 30 cars are parked in a space that otherwise could accommodate three or four. Think of a Ferris wheel that is not round but has the shape a rubber band would have if you put it around your thumb and forefinger and stretched it. Stand that image straight up and down, enclose it in aluminum, and make it grow several stories and you get the idea. To park at one of these towers, I pull onto the two tire racks and exit. The attendant presses a button and my car takes a ride up.

As customers back their cars out to leave, the attendant says, "Awrye, awrye, Okay, stowpu," which is from "Alright, alright, Okay stop." Attendants bow as customers drive away. The tower I parked at advertised that it is big enough to handle "Western cars," which means a Mercedes or the newer, large Japanese cars.

My most important Hiroshima visit was to the Atomic Bomb Museum. Hiroshima and its people were the first to suffer the ungodly fury atoms unleash when ripped apart. On August 6, 1945, at 8:15 A.M. the bomb called Little Boy was detonated at "Ground Zero" (600 yards above the ground in order to maximize the blast area). With the hope that the Japanese would not waste effort on them, only a couple planes flew the mission here and at Nagasaki. The spot directly under Ground Zero was the spot least affected by the blast. There on the banks of the river stands the remains of one of the few brick-and-steel buildings the city had. The brick walls still support the steel-frame dome top of the building. The dome's covering material was incinerated instantaneously.

The museum was constructed near Ground Zero in the small Peace Park adjacent to the river. The morning I visited was sterile: the sky gray, the ground white, the trees leafless. The day felt still. Preserving the building in its bombed-out condition was a wise choice. I cannot say exactly why, but for me, the building was an especially impressive reminder of what happens when the world throws sanity away.

The museum is a sombering experience. As many as 100,000 people died because of a single bomb – one that is a firecracker compared to today's bombs. Pictures of destruction and death were everywhere. There was a grizzly graphic movie from the 1970s in which doctors who were near Ground Zero were interviewed. They said in the first days after the bomb, there was no medicine for the thousands upon thousands who suffered from radiation, a disease the doctors had never heard of and did not know how to begin to treat. A couple of the doctors showed parts of their bodies that had been charred by the blast.

Surprisingly, the museum's exhibits, explained in both English and Japanese, are not strongly anti-American. One sign suggested that in the past the U.S. Army Air Corps had given advance notice of bombings, but not of this one. Another exhibit, however, contained leaflets that had been dropped warning the people to leave the city as it would soon be destroyed.

One survivor, an old woman, came closest to understanding the reason for all the suffering. She said if there had been no war, there would have been no bomb. I left with a better understanding of why the Japanese think of themselves as victims of World War II. Except for a brief comment about the Chinese and Korean slave laborers who were killed by the bomb, there was not even an oblique mention that anyone besides the Japanese had suffered one iota as a result of the war. If all you know about the war is what you hear from the Japanese government, you know that Japan was forced to attack Pearl Harbor because the U.S. cut off oil and scrap metal exports to Japan.

What the Japanese government does not teach its people worries me. It never teaches that the oil and scrap metal were being used to carry on a war of invasion against China. The government never teaches about the slaughters in China, such as the Rape of Nanking. In Nanking, the Japanese army went on a two-week rampage during which upward of 100,000 civilians were raped, mutilated and killed. An influential Japanese said the whole thing was made up by the Chinese to embarrass the Japanese. Apparently he believes that the testimony of the Chinese cannot be used to prove anything against the Japanese. The government never teaches that tens of thousands of mainly Korean women sought restitution for decades after being forced into prostitution as sex slaves to "comfort" Japanese soldiers. Japanese papers describe them as "comfort women." One Japanese war veteran was quoted as saying the women sought out the brothels because it was easier work than in the fields. Besides, as the ex-soldier said, Korean women all wanted to sleep with Japanese men. Hearing stuff like that makes it hard to decide what to do: laugh or cry.

While the government refuses to teach the children about the atrocities committed in the emperor's name and quietly pushs a that-never-happened message, Asian nations constantly demand apologies for what the Japanese did in World War II. It is confusing for Japanese youth. They hear demands for apologies on the news but are not taught the reason for the animosity. With the lingering resentment in Asia over the Japanese government's refusal to acknowledge any wrongdoing, there is much ambivalence toward Japan. Asia is angered by Japan's "War? What war?" attitude. At the same time, there is a mad scramble for the Japanese yen and Japanese manufacturing plants.

The Japanese know their neighbors distrust yet need them. The Japanese themselves do not trust their government. They are proud of their ethnicity, yet often they are ashamed of their government. They have mixed emotions about their national symbols, such as the national anthem, which they are embarrassed to sing. Their flag, with its red circle on a white field, is a source of ambivalence. Except for public buildings, it is rarely seen. When I pointed out the Japanese flag I saw on a house in Hondo, the Japanese person I was with looked at the house while making the Japanese gesture for "he's crazy" and said, "Right winger." The same thing happened when I pointed out the Japanese flag I saw on a house in Kumamoto. By contrast, the American flag can be seen everyday on a wide range of things: bags, T-shirts, notebooks, etc. I bet it is impossible to go to a Japanese school at any level and not find the American flag sported on something of some student's.

The government's it-did-not-happen approach is far different from the German government's. Three Germans in their mid-20s, staying at the youth hostel said German youth are tired of being made to feel guilty for what the Nazis did. I am sure the Japanese let's-just-forget-our-past-aggressions approach is better for the psyche of the individual Japanese, but the German approach leaves me less worried that future generations will repeat the same mistakes.

I have no doubt the average Japanese person genuinely believes in peaceful coexistence. Unfortunately, such beliefs make as much difference to Japanese power brokers as my opinion has on the ocean's tide. The reason for that is the Japanese are among the most politically passive people on the planet.

We had more of that same trait in our culture before our Vietnam experience. One result of that war is that Americans left behind the old America-right-or-wrong attitude and the feeling that what the government did was up to the government, not the people.

The Japanese suffered horribly for their emperor's willful decision to unleash World War II in Asia and the Pacific. Yet from the suffering they inflicted on others and endured themselves, they did not learn what we did in Vietnam. In fact, some too young to have experienced the war's horrors look back on it nostalgically, as a time when a tiny nation bravely fought numerically superior foes.

Until this decade the Japanese elected the same party into power since the war in spite of money and bribery scandals, which are about as common in Japan as drug-related killings are in the States. The Japanese do not control their government; it controls them. And it in turn is controlled by the monied interests, many of whom are the sons of Japan's World War II leaders. I left Hiroshima not very happy with the thought that Japan is a democracy not controlled by its own people.

The day after visiting the museum, I left for Kyoto. Andy headed for the Sea of Japan side of the country to visit Mie. The mountains between Hiroshima and Kyoto are plentiful, but not too steep. On the mountains sides, the trees are planted in uniform patterns. It looks like there is tree farming on most of the slopes. In every flat space between the mountains are houses and fields.

Kyoto was the second capital of Japan, from the 700s to 1868, when it was officially moved when the emperor moved to Tokyo. The area around Kyoto has its own dialect, which, because Kyoto was the center of learning and art for so long, the people here still consider to be the higher form of Japanese. Everybody else considers standard Japanese to have derived from a dialect of the Tokyo area. Kyoto is in an area called Kinki (kinky). There is a bank called, you guessed it, Kinki Bank. I am not sure I would want to bank there, but dating the tellers might be interesting. Not that they would be bimbos, at least not working for a bank. (In Japanese *bimbo* (been bow) means poor.)

I stayed at a Japanese family's house in Kyoto. I met the man of the house through the JET Program and he invited me to stay if I decided to visit that city. When he made the offer, he never mentioned that he has an attractive daughter. Meeting Reiko was a pleasant surprise. She volunteered to be my sightseeing tour guide.

Kyoto is the prettiest Japanese city I have seen, especially the eastern part. There are trees in various parts of the city, and a few parks with grass. The city, however, has a lot in common with the drab, gray poured-concrete buildings that are typically Japanese. I imagine that with the rapid growth after the war, beauty was not very high on the priority scale. The still out-numbered newer downtown buildings show the flair and artistry expected in a big modern city. For a reason that I cannot understand, Kyoto, like other Japanese cities, has a few rice fields left. Some next to factories.

Just off the main roads are the streets narrower than alleys that have businesses, apartments and homes mixed together. Cars and trucks come by, but mostly bicycles and foot traffic clog these tiny arteries. The roads are filled with sounds other than traffic. Merchants in small pickup trucks with steam whistles sell foods such as tofu and chestnuts (in the fall). The cry of the whistle is different for each product, such as "Toooofuuuu, Toooofuuuu." In Kyoto men push carts hawking sweet potato-like vegetables. Elderly women push carts or drive tiny pickup trucks selling vegetables.

From time to time Buddhist priests plaintively wail as they walked in a single file of four or five. The male priests wear full-length brown robes and straw hats reminiscent of Chinese coolie hats. The female priests wear brown robes, but no hats, perhaps to show off their bald heads. A male priest stiffly stands sentinel on the bridge over the Kamogawa River, which marks the western boundary of the ancient (as in before there was an America), bustling section of town called Gion. This priest has crisp, starched white linen wrapped around his neck and feet (which gives the impression of formality). He holds a big staff and stands in wooden slippers next to a donation plate.

I saw a bizillion temples on the tourist trail. Our first stop was at *Kinkakuji* (keen ka coo gee), which is multistory and extensively covered with gold (the "*kin*" in *Kinkakuji* means gold). We walked around the grounds but were not permitted inside. As I walked up to the temple, I saw its likeness reflecting off of the still pond in front of it. Behind it a stand of trees completes the beautiful picture. From there we went to a temple called *Ginkakuji* (*gin* rhymes with keen and means silver). Despite it name, this temple is a drab, wood one. Originally it was to have been covered in silver, but that never happened. I did not find the temple very interesting, probably because I saw it within ten minutes of seeing *Kinkakuji*, which was so impressive. One thing about *Ginkakuji* I will always remember is that nearby we found a *FREE* place to park. I could not believe it and asked Reiko if I read the sign correctly. I cannot tell you which was more surprising: finding something free in Japan, or accurately reading a sign in Japanese. For me, either is a major shock. We left the car and walked around from 9:30 to 4:30.

We strolled along a winding shop-lined road that had little traffic except pedestrians and followed the flow of people from one temple to the next. I especially liked the canal with trees on either side. It is called the "Path of the Philosophers," because 100 years ago a couple of philosophers would walk the path debating each other. Somewhere we saw a temple with a world-famous rock garden. I think I will never understand the charm of a rock garden.

Walking around the temples was a learning experience. First, it is costly. Each temple charges the equivalent of between $4 and $6 per person. After a full day of temple viewing, I was tapped out. Second, in December it is cold on the feet. You can walk inside some of the temples, but shoes are prohibited. Because the slippers are too small, I walked in my stocking feet. None of the temples have heat, and the wood floors were like walking on ice. After a few times, I passed on visiting the tranquility of the inner sanctuaries.

By the end of the day, it seemed like we visited all of Kyoto's reported 1,000 temples. They seem more to look at than to use. People milled about, but they only regarded the gardens and buildings. In the temple precincts, where admission was charged and souvenirs were hawked, I did not get any feeling that God was present.

The symbol reminiscent of Nazism did not help either. I took a double take the first time I saw it on the entrance to a temple. On inspection I realized that the symbol was what a swastika would look like in a mirror. Reiko said the symbol is an old Buddhist symbol that made its way to Japan from India a long time ago.

On New Year's Eve Reiko and I went to Nara. Although 35 miles from Kyoto, due to incredible traffic, the trip took one and a half hours. Nara has the biggest temple in Japan, called *Todaiji* (toe die gee – big eastern temple). Around the temple is a beautiful, spacious park with killer deer. They walk right up to you and pull on your coat sleeve to prompt food donations. Reiko and other women played tug-of-war for their purses with them.

Inside the temple, we were protected from evil spirits by the world's biggest cast-bronze statue of Buddha. Between 11 P.M. on New Year's eve and 1 A.M. the bell is rung 108 times, as are bells all over the country. Reiko says the Buddhists believe that there are 108 evil passions. Each gong of the bell cleanses the soul of one of them for the new year.

I doubt my soul was cleansed, but the trip cleaned out my wallet. When not staying with Reiko's family, I stayed at dirt cheap youth hostels. I started the trip with 100,000 yen (about $800). Four days into the trip I took another $800 out of the post office. I had to take out another $600 to finish the trip.

Reiko took the train home from Nara. Since I had known her for just a few days, I was surprised that on the train platform she cried when her train came into view. I have no idea what our relationship is at this point, I have not even kissed her except for a friendly one wrapped around a hug on the platform at the train station, but she invited me back for the holidays coming up in late April.

From Nara I drove 42 miles to Osaka, but due to Japan-style holiday traffic, the trip took two hours. I stayed in Osaka long enough to eat lunch, count my money and listen to my wallet scold me into going home. The trip to the ferry port was 24 miles, but took three hours. I decided to go home across the smallest of Japan's four main islands, Shikoku. At the ferry port I waited two hours even though ferries were arriving every 10 to 15 minutes.

On Shikoku, I traveled to the Pacific side, where I stayed at a temple located near the tip of a cape. As with many otherwise beautiful stretches of coastline, much of Shikoku's is concreted in. The road was usually two lanes wide, but sometimes it narrowed to one lane with pullouts. Along the coast for several miles, I saw several older men facing the sea and doing a form of slow-moving and light calisthenics, which I think was tai chi. I am not sure if they were part of a group because they were separated from each other by hundreds of yards.

My room was not quite the Ritz. It was six *tatami* and had a *kotatsu* with a frayed electrical cord. Other than the *kotatsu*, there was no heat. The futon was warm all night though and the room had all the privacy anyone could want, so long as all the privacy one would want can be protected by a rice-paper door with no lock.

The facilities were communal, right down to the rinse cup for brushing teeth. Dinner was Western style, the main dish being spaghetti eaten with *hashi*. It was tasty, but the Japanese made the usual sucking sounds while vacuuming the noodles into their mouths.

The cape itself was scenic, being embraced along its length by a beautiful beach. Although the next day's afternoon temperature was in the 50s and the gentle breeze was warm, I had the seashore to myself. After a certain date in the early fall, Japanese stop going to the beach until a certain date in the late spring, regardless of an unseasonably warm and beautiful winter day.

The next morning I drove to the Shikoku side of the Bungo Straights to catch a ferry to Kyushu. I had a hard time communicating with the man in the ticket booth. I asked for a ticket for one person and one car. In response he gave me a look which clearly said "What the heck you talkin' bout, boy?" After a few minutes of repeating the same thing over and over, he finally asked me to point out the car. He then asked me for about $90 for a 40-minute ride and gave me a ticket.

Later I realized the problem had been due to my pitiful use of Japanese counters. In Japanese almost any time you use a noun plus a number, you have to attach the right counter or it makes no sense. We have the same thing in English, but not nearly to the same extent. For example, we can say either six cows or six head of cattle. We can say six loaves of bread, but it is nonsense to say six breads. Six heads of lettuce makes sense, but six lettuces does not. The Japanese counter for houses is *ken* (the *kanji* is different from the *ken* meaning prefectural government); for cars, *dai* (die); for big animals, *tou* (toe); for small animals, *hiki* (he key); and so on. Later I thought about my conversation with the attendant and I realized I told him I wanted a ticket for one person and one house. *Dai*, *ken*, what's the difference?

On the ferry from Shikoku to Kyushu, men were smoking and children were playing. I sat next to a real lover of *Playboy*. He had two: one imported from the U.S. and one written in Japanese. Peeking over his shoulder, I saw the Japanese one had the pubic hair area electronically masked over and in the American one someone had physically scratched out the women's pubic hair. If the rationale for scratching that part out is because people's morals will be harmed, I wonder how long the guy who has to open every single *Playboy* coming into the country can be counted on as a rock-solid bastion of Japanese morals. Looking at *gaijin* pubic hair all day long to obliterate it will surely cause him to start foaming at the mouth, pull at the hair on his head and shout, "*Gaijin* pubic hair, *gaijin* pubic hair!!"

Taking a walk later, a Japanese man staggered up and grabbed my arm. "You American. Me Japanese. We friends. You drink with us." He had a powerful grip. When I told him I was not interested, he tried to drag me upstairs where his friends were. Finally I promised I would follow him in a minute. When he left, I went to another part of the boat and never saw him again. I still have no idea what would have happened, but no doubt I am better off not knowing.

Well, it is closing time now as the lights are going down. I put in a hard day at the office putting my notes together about the trip. What a job!

*D*ear Dad,   January 17
I have several free hours at Hondo-*chu* to write to you about my recent cancer scare. I did not tell you before because I did not want to worry you if it turned out to be nothing, which it did.

Before I left for Japan, I had a physical. My exam included what my doctor called a testicular cancer examination. I had never heard of it before, but she explained I should check my testicles for potential cancerous lumps just as women check their breasts. The next time I thought about that was at the Block Conference in December. I was astonished to find a lump. I made an appointment with a local doctor for the Friday before Christmas. The doctor did an ultrasound and said in Japanese, "Isn't that pretty." He said in English, "Merry Christmas. Benign."

Between making that appointment and going to it, I called Frank. Because he is a lawyer in the Mayo Clinic legal department, I asked him if there were any Mayo-trained doctors in Japan. I wanted a good doctor and one I could talk with in English.

The only Mayo-trained doctor in the specialty I needed is in Sapporo, a several-hour flight from Kumamoto city. He recommended a doctor in Fukuoka, Dr. Naito, who did postgraduate training at a university in Texas. My appointment with Dr. Naito was for Tuesday,

December 25.

I spent from 8:30 to 2:00 Christmas Day in the hospital being poked, prodded and in general having more people handle my testicles than if I were in a French bordello with an open line of credit. The gray-haired chief urologist at one point asked, "Does this hurt?" while putting pressure on my testicle. "No," I said. "Does this hurt?" while putting pressure to another area of my testicle. I responded with a whole string of blue words which conveyed the meaning "Yes, as a matter of fact it does." He smiled and said in a fatherly way, "That's good." At the time I did not think anything of it. Later I wondered if that was a valid test or a leftover score to settle from World War II.

Dr. Naito said the first ultrasound could not rule out cancer, but a blood test would help establish the answer. The results would take ten days due to the holidays. He recommended I go on my planned vacation without worrying. I thought the whole thing was pretty much over, and following his advice, I went on the trip.

Two days after I returned home, he called. My blood test was "a little abnormal." He guesstimated my chances at 50/50. He explained that if it were cancer, the only treatment was removal of the testicle. I would be in the hospital for ten days of follow-up therapy and extensive testing to make sure it had not spread.

I would have to be admitted to the hospital for a biopsy, which involved a two-hour operation. He had scheduled tests for Monday and the operation for Wednesday. I sat on the floor next to the phone stunned. Faced with such a serious problem, being thousands of miles from home did not help.

I left the house Sunday afternoon and stayed with Terri and Henry Rye, who live about 40 minutes from the hospital. They are an American couple I met on the program who brought their two carrot-top boys, Aaron, a fourth grader, and Thomas, a second grader, with them. The boys are nonstop talkers. I think they are training to be lawyers.

Dr. Naito wanted me to stay in the hospital from Monday through the following Monday – even if the tumor was benign. After we talked, he agreed that I did not have to spend Monday night in the hospital. I stayed with the Ryes again. The next day, Tuesday, I had many tests. Between them I had time with nothing to do and spent some of it walking around the hospital. The signs hanging from the ceiling in this hospital are low, which means that I whacked my forehead a couple of times when I was not paying attention.

The condition of the hospital did not help my sprits. The outside had not been painted in years. The inside was painted in a variety of dull colors that could have only been planned to take a depressed person and push him into an emotional tailspin. I decided to go back to my room. As I turned, a short, plump 50ish woman in a fluffy bright pink nightgown stopped to talk to me in the hallway. She pushed an IV pole with an IV stuck in her arm. She smiled so brightly and seemed so eager to please, she reminded me of a collie. She asked me the usual questions that I can handle in Japanese; "Where are you from?" "How do you like Japan?" She asked me why I was in the hospital. For a spilt second I considered trying to explain to her in my baby Japanese. Realizing I was not going to be able to communicate all that, I just pointed in the general direction of my groin. I had to restrain a guffaw when she answered, "Me too." I left her with a "Good luck" and a smile.

As I walked away from this plump, pink bundle of smiles, my outlook changed. I saw her as someone with an indefatigable will who was determined to continue making the best of things regardless of the unwanted and undeserved obstacles that were dropped in her path. I decided there was no alternative but to follow her example.

Later that day, Dr. Naito said he could leave a fake testicle in my scrotum if the real one had to be removed. If I wanted one, the surgery would have to be postponed because they did not have any "Western-size" falsies. All the ones on hand were made for Japanese men and therefore half the size I would need. I walked out of that meeting and saw one of my nurses walking toward me in the hallway. I had the urge to say "Uh huh, that's right, I'm twice as big."

Speaking of nurses, trade friction between Japan and the States could be defused by sending nurses instead of cars. These women were wonderful, sweet and understanding. This kind of treatment from nurses in Japan is standard and not *gaijin* treatment.

I had one Japanese/English and one English/Japanese dictionary, which were in full use while the nurses were in the room. Most of the time they stayed long after they had done their job because they wanted to learn English. I was happy for the attention to keep my mind off things, and they were eager to help me pick up Japanese vocabulary.

Picking up more Japanese was imperative to avoid incidents like what almost happened the first day at the hospital. My nurse gave me a thermometer and as it was heading for my mouth her eyes widened in shock. I suddenly thought: "Is this a rectal thermometer?" No. it was an armpit thermometer. Only young children have their temperatures taken orally.

Early in the morning on the day of the surgery, male attendants lifted me onto a gurney and wheeled me to the operating room. As I was going through the doors I wondered how much of me would be coming out. Once inside, I was relieved to see all the high-tech-looking gizmos. Dr. Naito complained that American medicine is still ahead of Japanese medicine. So I was not sure what to expect, especially since the rest of the hospital seems more of a MASH unit than a hospital. The next thing I remember is groggily waking up in the operating room looking at smiling faces all around. One of the smiling faces said "Benign."

The nurses wheeled me back to my room where three male attendants lifted me from the gurney and placed me on my bed about as gently as a teenager replaces his baseball glove in the closet after a loss. A few minutes later, with nurses coming in to say congratulations, my room looked like a family reunion.

By about 1 P.M. I was starving because I had not eaten since 7 P.M. the night before. The nurse said that I could not eat until 6 P.M. I asked to see Dr. Naito, who told me I could not eat because I had no *fulatcharence*. I looked at him and said a little unsurely, "Do you want me to fart?" He said, "Yes." I have no idea why that was important, but I could not do it. He listened to my stomach with his stethoscope and said I could eat.

The hospital's kitchen is not listed in the Michelin travel guides, and I think it is because they actually tasted the food, not through mere oversight. I told him the restaurant across the street served pizza and I would prefer that. He stared at the ceiling a while and finally said okay. One of my nurses picked up the pizza at the cost of a couple slices. She and I ate together in my room and we had a pleasant conversation.

After lunch I asked Dr. Naito if I could go home that night. He knew I was not serious because I am sure he knew the anesthesia could not have worn off to the point that I could totally feel my legs. He replied that maybe he could release me before Monday but "Not today." I asked him about the next day. He countered that he would like me in the hospital until at least Saturday. Since my Japanese insurance was paying for all but about $20 of the costs, price was not a consideration. I simply wanted out. The negotiations continued until the doctor agreed to let me leave on the second evening if I agreed to come back the following morning for a check.

Thursday evening I stayed with the Ryes again. Whenever I am with them, I have a good time. I went with the boys to rent a video. It was a night I will long remember. Being with friends in their home talking and watching a movie was so much better than spending another night in the hospital. There were a few times when I laughed so hard my stitches hurt. During the movie, I had occasion to sneeze. I never before realized how much the inguinal area is involved in the act of sneezing. Without any exaggeration, that sneeze caused me the most pain of the entire ordeal.

The next day the doctor checked me and said I could go home. Terri told me that I should apologize to Dr. Naito for refusing to eat hospital food and refusing to stay in the hospital until Monday. She said that Japanese patients always do what the doctor orders so my behavior was probably unnerving to the staff.

Dr. Naito said he and his staff were not put off by my behavior. When I came to the hospital he talked with his staff about how to "handle" an American. He confirmed that a Japanese patient does exactly what the doctor and nurses tell him to do, but he knows that Americans do not always behave that way. I go back to see Dr. Naito on the 26th for what I presume will be my final follow-up exam. I intend to bring chocolates for my nurses.

Bye for now.

*D*ear Barb,   January 24
As the new year begins, I feel like I am still on a ballistic learning curve, thoroughly enjoying soaking up as much of the Japanese language and culture as I can. I have recently learned that the Japanese believe that they are internally physically different from Westerners.

I noticed many children at school with red rough skin on their hands and ears, which I took for a mild form of frostbite. The teachers corrected me. It is not frostbite, it is chilblain. The dictionary defines chilblain as an inflammation of the hands and feet caused by exposure to the cold. The "reason" given for the prevalence of chilblain in their children is due to the "unique"Japanese circulatory system. Even those teachers whom I think are the most reasonable say that in the hands, feet and earslobes of a Japanese person, the blood vessels do not come as close to the surface as a Westerner's, thus making them more susceptible to "chilblain." They honestly do not make the connection between the kids freezing at home and at school and developing frostbite or chilblain.

On Monday in the seventh-grade room at Saiitsu-*chu*, one of the windows had a gaping hole; it had been broken over the weekend. Yet, except for the occasional breeze, it was no colder than any of the other classrooms, each of which was cold enough for me to see my breath. With conditions like this, many of the brighter kids (and the teachers too) wear winter jackets during class.

At all the schools, the seventh graders are sicker than kids in the other two grades. The teachers have no theories for this. Sometimes the sniffling is so noisy that I have to talk louder to make sure I am heard. Today the sneezing, coughing and hacking away was a dull roar as I walked into class. Two kids happened to blow their noses at the same time, resulting in the class sounding like a coughing, sputtering version of the *Queen Mary* blowing her foghorn.

Most of these kids should be home, but they probably would not be much warmer there. If they stayed home, they would miss out on an important lesson in what it means to be Japanese. They are to contribute to the group even when they should be home caring for themselves. So they alternatively sit and sometimes blow on their hands to stay warm.

The teachers are hit by all the bugs and germs that have taken control of the classrooms. But Japanese workers are expected to go to work if they are able to stand. It is not a union rule but a cultural mandate. They come to school with their contagious coughs and probably pass them on to the remaining kids who have not brought their own germs from home. Everybody, I guess, glories in the fact that they are all properly playing their cultural roles.

Many of those who have colds wear white surgical masks. This is a holdover from the 1918 flu epidemic in which worldwide about 20 million people died. Japan lost so many people that it is still considered good form to wear a mask in public when you have a cold. I have never seen so many people look like they were preparing to perform surgery.

The elementary schools are just as cold as the junior high schools, but the students do not dress as warmly. The boys wear white shirts, jackets, very short shorts and thin-soled sneakers that are used inside the school only. A few boys wear no shoes, running around on the cold floor wearing socks. The girls wear blouses and short skirts. Almost all of them wear their winter coats. Their attire is in marked contrast to that of the visiting *gaijin*. I wear two pairs of socks (one wool), a polypropylene T-shirt (which I use in the States only for camping in the mountains), a shirt and a wool sweater.

The classroom has windows on both sides and the hallway wall is made of windows. Assuming that windows are there to permit cool summer breezes is strictly non-Japanese thinking. The windows were open, letting in the occasional bone-chilling gust. Finally I told some students to close the windows. As they were doing that, I saw about 100 others on the playground doing calisthenics – wearing T-shirts and shorts. I thought, "What is wrong with this picture?" Maybe I am stuck in a solitary winter weather pattern and everyone else is experiencing some kind of spring weather. The Japanese constantly are talking about the importance of the need to *gaman suru* (ga maan sue roo – tough it out). I guess I am seeing the early stages of *gaman suru* training.

In class, the children wanted to play a game that is intended to improve their knowledge of *katakana*. On each one-foot by two-foot card is a *katakana* character. Under it is a picture of some animal or object that begins with the *katakana* letter on the face of the card with the complete word spelled out in *katakana*. Four children neatly placed the cards on the floor at the front of the class. When the teacher told the class to form a circle around the cards, students walked through the cards to the other side, tiptoing between the cards so as not to disturb them in any way. They quietly sat in a circle waiting for the game to start. When the teacher uttered a letter of the *katakana* alphabet, the children were to find and touch that card. The first student to touch the card was privileged to keep it. The holder of the most cards at the end of the game would be declared the winner.

The teacher said the first letter and the class reacted with a mad scramble; soldiers trapped in a foxhole by enemy fire searching to find a live grenade on the ground cannot move faster. Kids literally flew across the cards to grab the right one.

I knew I was way out of my league and my chances of beating these rocket-launched kids to the correct card were minimal. They wanted me to participate, however, and I wanted to make them feel that I was interested in their game. I had as much success with these kids as I would have had in a science quiz show stacked up against Nobel Prize winners. The class sensed that Ken-*sensei* was more than a bit dull and not willing to fling his body across the floor for the chance of winning a card.

Because most of the girls were not as hell-bent for leather as the boys, the teacher said that on the next turn only the girls and Ken-*sensei* could play. When that did not work, she asked when I was born. Only children born within three months of April were allowed to play. When that did not work, she resorted to giving me hints in English before she said the word in Japanese. By that time even the class hamster knew the teacher was all but handing me the card an instant before she spoke to the class. It did not matter. It was important to them that I participate and win a few of the cards. I ended up with a grand total of two. Both times the kids applauded, encouraging me to do even better.

In the next period, the same children had a math lesson. They recited 1 to 10 in English. The teacher asked me to quiz them using flash cards which had equations such as 7 x 6 = , 5 - 3 = , 8 + 9 =. I taught the students how we pronounce the "signs" ("x" and "=" and so on).

Japanese children are taught to pronounce English using *katakana* as a guide which results in a distinctive *katakana*-English pronunciation. In this system, English words are often pronounced much differently than we pronounce them. The difference can be humorous. In Fukuoka I saw a sign on a bank calling itself Fukuoka *Shiti* (City) Bank. Fukuoka and Bank were written in *kanji* but the word city was written in *katakana*. Of course they have a native word for city, but English is so cool that even dignified banks adopt names with words from English. The only problem for this bank is that in using *katakana* the word city comes out sounding more like shetee. So to my eyes the bank is boasting to the world that it is the Fukuoka Shitty Bank. There are also buses proudly proclaiming that they are Shitty Buses. I have been told there is a kind of hotel classification called, you guessed it, Shitty Hotels.

The *katakana* pronunciation of "equal" sounds like "ee coo ah roo." In Japanese, no word ends in "s." So when Japanese pronounce an English word that has an "s" at the end, they often drop the "s," ("equals" is often pronounced the same as "equal.") When the "s" is pronounced, "equals" is pronounced "ee coo ah roo zoo."

Kids forgot the English words I had taught them, so responses were mixed Japanese and English. The exchanges between myself and the students went something like this:

"How much is 4 x 3?"

"Four *kakeru* three *wa jyuni.*"

"How much is 10 divided by 2?"

"Ten *waru* two ee coo wa roo zoo five."

It was beautiful. Sixth graders not only trying to get the math right, but trying hard to do it in a foreign language too. I so admired their efforts that even the "zoo" sound for "s" was like music to my ears.

After each student recited I gave the student a cheer, a little applause, or a thumbs-up. They had no idea what the thumbs-up sign meant. I explained the Roman emperors used it to signal life for the fallen gladiators. A boy did a thumbs-down sign and asked if it meant anything. I grabbed my chest in mock pain and sagged at the knees as if dying. The boy quickly gave me a thumbs-up and was visibly relieved that I quickly recovered. Being an entertainer is a bigger part of being a teacher than I ever imagined. As I left school that afternoon, a few children shouted "Ken-*sensei*!!" from a school window. I looked up and they were flashing the thumbs-up sign.

As I pedaled home on my bike, I realized that my body heat from the exercise made me warmer than I was in the classrooms. Actually, the Japanese winter, except for the far north of the country, is not too cold. My Japanese hometown this year is milder than any winter I experienced as a kid growing up in Detroit. In fact, it snows in this town only about once a year. Without central heating at home or at school, though, it seems colder.

This past weekend I stayed at the house of another ALT, Kevin. He lives in a town located high on the slopes of an extinct volcano called Aso-*san* (*san* in this case comes from the pronunciation for "mount"), which is bone-chilling cold. He says the warmest place in his house at night, outside of his futon, is the inside of the refrigerator. He puts his contact lens solution in the refrigerator at night so it *will not freeze*! The other Aso-*san* ALT, Becky, has two kerosene heaters that she points at the spot where she sits under her *kotatsu*. Even wearing her winter jacket, she is barely warm at night.

Well, that about wraps up what is new here. Please write soon so I can read some English. If you do not have time to write, send the back of a milk bottle. Anything.

*D*ear Lynea,   February 14
Happy Valentine's Day!! It is Valentine's Day, even in Japan. The stores adopted it as they did Christmas to increase sales. It has a distinctly Japanese twist.

Only women give chocolate. I received chocolate from some of the students over the past several days and also from a few of the teachers. This is the concept of *giri choko* (ghee ree cho co). *Giri* means duty and *choko* is short for chocolate. Put the two together and you have a totally Japanese concept: the mandatory giving of a tiny gift of heartfelt appreciation. Women must give chocolate to their bosses and other men to whom they have become indebted over the course of the year. The day men give gifts of chocolate is White Day, a Japanese invention, which is March 14. The concept of *giri choco* does not seem to exist for the men so many women who give chocolate receive none in return.

On February 4 I was at Hondo-*chu*. It was the traditional first day of spring according to the Japanese calendar, but it was still freezing. The Japanese school year ends in March, which means the ninth graders will graduate soon. While I was in the teachers' room, two girls asked me to sign their personal yearbooks. Being a veteran of six months, I have a feel for the kids' English vocabulary. I wrote things that were both complimentary and understandable to them without a dictionary. They were so delighted they could understand what I had written that they literally jumped up and down holding each other's arms.

Watching two girls in navy-blue sailors' uniforms squealing and giggling points out to me how different these girls are from American teenagers. They are supposed to make our kids look sick in math and science, but individually, these kids act more, well, childish than American students of similar age. Girls walk down the hall holding hands; boys hold hands with other boys too and occasionally sit on another boy's lap between classes. I think the system somehow makes the students less mature but more responsible.

My students are more reliable than U.S. teenagers. They often ask me to bring my music so they can record it. Because I visit any given school only a few times a month, you would think trusting the children to return the tape or CD at my next visit would be a good way to deplete my music selection. Everything I have lent to the students at the various schools has been returned to me when promised and in the same condition as when I lent it.

Being in Japan is depleting my English. As I sat at my desk between classes, sipping *ocha*, Shiraiishi-*sensei*, a young, scholarly teacher, approached and announced we would teach his students how to use the adjectival form of the infinitive. He asked me how I use it and, not having a clue what he was talking about, I suppressed a smile because all I could think of was "By accident I'm sure." Instead I told him something like "Well there are many ways to use it. Could you give me an example of what you want to teach the children?" When he showed me his worksheet, I could rattle off examples (such as "We have four hours *to spend* on this project"). The good thing about rotating among several schools is that I knew I would see this lesson at the other schools. When the other teachers asked me the same question, I looked like I actually knew the answer.

As I was leaving school, I passed one of the rest rooms which are detached from the school. Several boys who were doing *soji* in and around it talked to me. One boy, eager to show off his English to his friends and embarrass a teacher at the same time, said "I like to masturbate."

Part of his plan worked. The other boys laughed. I decided that I would not give the boy the pleasure of shocking the teacher. I tried to put on a matter-of-fact expression on my face that would convey to the boys that I was seriously interested in learning what masturbation was and told him, "Show me." "Oh my God!" I turned to leave.

Within ten steps the boy said, "I have a big penis." I tried to put as much naive, surprised interest into my voice as I could when I said again, "Show me." He said no. I put my thumb and forefinger about an inch apart and asked with as much wide-eyed enthusiasm as I could fake, "Is it thiiiiis big?!?" The boy almost pulled a muscle stretching his arms as far as they would go. I could not repress a laugh.

Maybe the whole episode was not an English lesson that will be found or recommended in any book, but if the students can joke while using a foreign language, it may become more like a living language instead of dead words on a page they are doomed to mispronounce. After it was over, I thought it might have been the best class of the day.

At Kusuura-*chu* the kids were totally dead. During a time when they were supposed to be writing, most of the students had their eyes glued to their notebooks, so I did not try to suppress a yawn. One boy looked up and we both smiled. I felt bad about it. It had to leave the impression that I was bored, but hey, I was. It was my third class of the day, in a row, with dead kids. The phone commercial that shows a pin dropping makes a racket compared to the classes I had at Kusuura-*chu*.

The day was saved by the almost three-hour discussion I had in the teachers' room with an ever changing group of teachers. The school had no classes in the afternoon because a PTA meeting was scheduled. Many of the teachers found time to sit in on parts of the conversation taking place around the portable stove.

Our conversation was in a mixture of English, Japanese, sign language, gestures, and drawings. I am finding that when people want to communicate, the lack of a common language is no barrier. It was convenient, however, to have Kazama-*sensei*, the English teacher, at her desk in the teachers' room preparing for the PTA meeting so we could consult a living dictionary.

A couple of the teachers are very knowledgeable about the history not only of Japan but of the Japanese language. As you would expect, the Japanese-language teacher has a good knowledge of the history of the language. The history teacher, however, has almost no clue about Japanese history. He is an intelligent, dedicated teacher who studied and taught art until last year, when he was told that he had to teach history. Job switching without regard for training or preference is not unusual in Japan. The social studies teacher teaches English part-time. He is a pleasant, capable man, but his English speaking skill is genuinely not much above the students'. With this administrative, we-do-not-care-what-your-background-is attitude, I just wonder how anything gets done right. The science teacher, Funada-*sensei*, has had a lifelong interest in Japanese history. At this school, the science teacher knows so much more history than the history teacher that I wonder whether the kids could learn more history in their science class than they ever will in history class.

No one really knows where the Japanese people came from. They may be distantly related to Turks or maybe the Mongolians. Funada-*sensei* said that at one time Turkish people lived in the area of central Asia not too far from what is now Mongolia. He thinks the bulk of the Japanese stock came from the Mongols. He bases this on the fact that the babies of both Mongolians and Japanese have blue spots the size of softballs on their butts when they are born. No kidding. My impromptu poll revealed that all the teachers had blue spots on their bottoms when they were born. Within a year or two, babies of Mongolian heritage lose the blue spot. One way of calling someone wet behind the ears in Japanese is to call him a blue butt.

The conversation turned to the influence of foreign languages on Japanese. Before I came here, I thought English was the bastard of all languages, with influences from Greek, Latin, French, and so on. Borrowing from other languages, however, is a Japanese art form.

They developed a writing system relatively late. Well-developed writing systems and extensive literatures existed for at least 1,000 years in Western Europe, China and the Middle East before the Japanese felt a need for the written word. No one knows for sure, but somewhere between the fourth and sixth centuries A.D. the Japanese entered the world of the written word. When they began to write, they copied from China. In the average Japanese magazine today, for example, about 50 percent of the words are derived from Chinese.

Chinese is not the unified language I assumed it was. The differences in dialects are greater than the differences between American English and British English. A Chinese person from one part of China cannot understand the local dialect spoken by a Chinese from another part of the country. The *kanji* is fairly uniform, and the Chinese usually can read things written by people from other parts of China, but how they pronounce those *kanji* makes it mutually unintelligible.

The Japanese waded into this when they went to various parts of China centuries ago for many reasons: trade, study and religion, among others. Like tourists everywhere, they could not resist taking back souvenirs. Stuffed inside their suitcases were *kanji* by the thousands. They came back with vocabulary ranging across the whole spectrum. In this way sometimes the same *kanji* made its way into Japanese from two or three different places in China separated by a couple thousand miles, with of course pronunciation differences. Sometimes the same *kanji* made its way at different times from the same place but separated by a century or more, during which the Chinese pronunciation and perhaps the meaning, too, had altered slightly. One result was that Japanese sometimes incorporated both the old and new pronunciations and meanings.

Another was that the Japanese frequently ended up with one sound meaning several different things, but represented by different *kanji* such as the sound *tsuru* (tsu roo) meaning: (1) to wear; (2) to fish; (3) a cramp; (4) a bowstring; (5) a handle; (6) a vine; and (7) a crane (the bird). This is not a phenomenon limited to that sound. The sound *kaki* (ka key) is represented by different *kanji* and carries the burden of these words: (1) firearms; (2) as follows; (3) oyster; (4) persimmon; (5) a flowering plant; (6) the flowering season; (7) a fence; (8) a vase; and (9) summertime. Another example I like is *hashi*. The sentence: *Hashi no hashi de hashi de tabetta*; means: I ate by the side (*hashi*) of the bridge (*hashi*) with chopsticks (*hashi*).

All of this helps make the *kanji* so hard that it takes an above-average junior high school student to read the Japanese equivalent of *Time* magazine. I personally know well over seven *kanji* so it will not be long before I am reading like a native. As someone trying to cram the thousands of *kanji* into my head, I agree with the scholars who say that the written language is overcomplicated by *kanji*.

Of the thousands of *kanji*, most Japanese know only a fraction of them. After World War II, there were discussions about discarding *kanji* in favor of the homegrown alphabets derived from it. Instead it was decided to simplify the *kanji* by reducing the number of strokes needed to write the more complicated ones and reducing the number that would be taught at schools. The result is the Daily Use *Kanji,* the 2,000 *kanji* needed to graduate from high school. While large, it might seem that, with a committed effort of a month or two or three, that number could be memorized. The problem is that many *kanji* have up to 20 strokes and can be pronounced several different ways. The meaning can change with the pronunciation. So instead of 2,000 bits of information, you are dealing with many many times that number.

The idea behind *kanji* is that each one conveys a basic meaning. Two or more *kanji* are combined to form a compound and in the process a new word. These compounds can fit together well with the basic meaning of each *kanji* in the compound to make a new word which is logically related in meaning to the *kanji* from which it is made. The word "*kanji*" itself is a good example of a compound. The first character, *kan*, means Chinese, and the second, *ji*, means letter. The elements from which the word is made does not always tell the story of the word's meaning – just as our words "under" and "stand" when put together do not mean standing underneath something.

The Japanese call their country *Nihon* (knee hone – *ni* is "sun"; *hon* is "origin"), themselves *Nihonjin* (knee hone jean – jin means person), and their language *Nihongo* (knee hone go – go means talk). *Funada-sensei* thinks that "Japan" comes from the Italian pronunciation of a Chinese word for lacquer maker. Around 1200 A.D., at the time Marco Polo visited China, the Japanese were famous for making lacquered wooden trays. Marco Polo may have been told a word that meant in Chinese "those people make lacquer trays" and which sounded like jipanne. Run that word through Italian and you end up in English with Japan. *Funada-sensei* brought in a lacquered tray and a Japanese/English dictionary to prove it. He pointed to the tray and said "Japan" and then to the *kanji* entry in the dictionary that defined the *kanji* in English as lacquer or Japan.

There are two other traditional ways of writing Japanese: *hiragana* (he rah ghana) and *katakana*. By the ninth century *hiragana*, which has 55 characters, was developed, in part, to be an easier writing system for women. *Hiragana* characters are simplified renditions of some of the individual *kanji*. *Hiragana* represents all of the sounds in the Japanese language. Because it is a phonetic alphabet, Japanese words are easy to "spell." Any word that can be written in *kanji* can be written in *hiragana*. This is how children are first taught to write; foreigners too – including yours truly.

Katakana has the same number of characters as *hiragana* and is also a phonetic alphabet. It was developed before *hiragana* but was used by priests for writing poetry. Now *katakana* is used almost exclusively to write words borrowed from other languages.

Since the war, with English so popular, everyone also learns our alphabet, *romaji* (row ma gee – *Roma* is for Rome). *Romaji* is used to represent words in a form Westerners can more easily grasp. In some instance for Japanese too. Place names at train stations are written in *kanji* and *romaji* because without a phonetic clue, Japanese from other parts of the country could not pronounce the *kanji* for the names of the cities. *Romaji* is also how many Japanese companies write their names. There are *kanji* for Toyota, Nissan, Honda and the like, but even in the cars and advertising here, their names are written almost exclusively in *romaji.*

It takes so much effort to learn to write *kanji* that in subtle ways it is beginning to take a backseat to the other alphabets. In geography, except for Japan, China and Korea, almost all countries are now written in *katakana*, with the pronunciation more often than not the same as the English.

In typical Japanese writing there is a mixture of mostly *kanji*, a good deal of *hiragana*, a fair smattering of *katakana* and maybe some *romaji* thrown in for good measure. If that is not hard enough, Japanese can be written from right to left, or left to right or from the top to bottom, depending on whether the work is a book and whether it is fiction or nonfiction, etc. It is a wonder they can read at all. It all makes English seem easy and almost logical. I think you can begin to appreciate why writing Japanese is so hard.

After Chinese, English is the foreign language with the greatest impact on Japanese, although that is a relatively recent phenomenon. When Japan began its self-imposed exile from the rest of the world in the early 1600s, Portuguese and Dutch were the Western languages which influenced Japanese. During the 250 or so years of Japan's isolation, the Dutch were virtually the only Westerners permitted to visit specified ports. Consequently, many foreign words are from Dutch and to a lesser extent Portuguese (whose priests tried to convert the islands before the government kicked them out). When the Japanese reentered the rest of the world in the 1860s, German was the big influence for its medical and military terms.

Somewhere around the 1920s English started taking over. By World War II, there were aspects of Japanese life could not be expressed without using English. Baseball is an example. During the war umpires were jailed for accidentally using English in a game instead of the militarily approved Japanese substitutes. I watched a TV special called "No-English golf." The object of the game was for the players to describe in Japanese the round of golf they were playing without using a word derived from English. Players were penalized every time they slipped up. The players were literally falling down laughing at their ineptitude in describing a round of golf without using an English word.

With the influence from English come the words from foreign languages English has incorporated. For example, robot, from Czech; Aldebaran (a star) from Arabic; television, from Latin; beef, from French; and the list goes on. Japanese is an amazing, vibrant, bastard language. The languages that do the borrowing are the ones that become rich, and Japanese is becoming just that.

I hope to hear from you in time for White Day. Bye.

*D*ear Frank, February 27

I had another round of "Ken-*sensei* superstar" treatment. When I learned I was scheduled to teach on the 15th at Kita-*shogakko* (North Elementary School), I wondered whether anyone would believe me if I called in sick.

It was snowing outside. With no heat in the classroom, I feel bad about being so warmly dressed while the kids are horrendously under-dressed, but not enough to offer any of them my sweater. The kids "ahhed" when I told them that in America all the classrooms are heated.

After a question-and-answer period, they wanted to shake my hand. Next they sang "Old MacDonald" and "Frere Jacques," which reminded me of my own school days. I wonder how many adults across this planet can sing those songs. The thought made the world seem a little smaller.

In the next period I modeled so the children could draw pictures of me. While in the States my nose has not drawn much comment, many pictures depict my nose three times the size of my face. Toward the end of the exercise, the teacher told them to sign their works of art. They shouted, "Do we have to sign in English?!?" When she said yes, they pulled out their English notebooks, which have their names spelled in *romaji*.

As I walked to the class for lunch, a group of boys from another class pushed me into their classroom. Ultimately, the classes were combined and they all ate lunch with the *gaijin*. As in the junior high school, two students per class are responsible for handing food out to their classmates. The rest of the children to form a line and grab metal trays. Here too the captains lead the class in saying *itadakimasu*.

During the after-lunch play period, dozens of adoring eyes begged me to play *dojiboru* (doe gee bow roo – dodge ball). I wanted to refuse but somehow could not. At the gym, a boy from another class said, "I play judo." He grabbed my hand and tried to flip me. I grabbed him by the ankle and held him upside down. I think he realized that judo is all well and good, but after all, weighing three times as much as the other guy does not hurt either.

After the last class of the day, in the teachers' room, I was surrounded by giggling, bubbly children. Two girls with shopping bags approached me. The rest of the children swarmed around, pulling out their rolled-up, red-ribbon tied portrait of me. I accepted each with both hands, raised the scrolls slightly as a sign of respect and exchanged bows with the students. Leaving school, I waved to the bright-eyed children waving and shouting "*Sayonara*!!" All in a day in the life of Ken-*sensei* superstar.

On February 19 I was at Kamegawa-*chu,* where Ezaki-*sensei* teaches. I had a class was with Nomura-*sensei*, a dedicated, intelligent, young woman in her second year of teaching. As an English teacher, she is, through no fault of her own, a hopeless case. Her command of English is only marginally better than that of the students. She is another of the legion of teachers' teaching a subject for which she has no training. Although she is the school's Japanese teacher, this year she is being forced to pinch hit in English too. She is a dedicated teacher and works harder when she has a class scheduled with me.

The three of us have devised a way to overcome her lack of experience. Usually Nomura-*sensei* sits in on the first class Ezaki-*sensei* and I teach. Then during our classes together, she duplicates Ezaki-*sensei*'s role. On the 19th, she and I were together in the first class of the day. I was not sure we had communicated in our pre-class meeting. However, I had done this lesson with several experienced teachers' at other schools, so I felt confident that if we ran into trouble, we could muddle through.

The students were to write a letter complete with an envelope. It was a good learning tool as Japanese letters are structured somewhat differently (but not worth noting). The envelope is addressed entirely differently from ours, and that does bears mentioning.

Mentally lay an envelope ready to be addressed before you. Place the stamp on what we would call the bottom right. Now rotate the envelope so the stamp is on the top right. Below the stamp and to the left of it they write the address vertically from top to bottom from right to left. The address is written first with the addressee's name written last. It is one of those small things which points out the difference between our cultures. We address our letters with the name first, they do it last, which duplicates the individual's place in this society.

The model letter and envelope I wrote on the board were addressed to the emperor. The letter asked whether he could spare a heater from the Imperial Palace so the kids would not have to sit in class wearing their winter coats.

The children were to write letters in English to people of their choice. Most students addressed their letters to me or their friends and talked about sports or hobbies and the like. I called on several to read their letter aloud. One boy addressed his letter to "Rika" (Nomura-*sensei*'s first name). It was short but interesting: "Excuse me, but do you have a boyfriend? I don't like English." He said the word "don't" with emphasis and punctuated it with a definitive movement of his head. No doubt he has a crush on Nomura-*sensei*. It caused me to think back to my junior high school days and Mrs. Jordan, who I was sure was the perfect woman for me. Heck, maybe this boy thinks he really has a shot at "Rika."

Because there was a lot of writing during class, Nomura-*sensei* and I did not miscommunicate in front of the students. While the kids were working, in the music room the music teacher practiced the piano for an upcoming concert. The gentle tones of classical music drifted through the classroom in a very pleasing way. I admired the teacher's dedication to rehearsal. Without the body heat of 35 students, his room had to be colder than mine. Mine was cold enough for me to wander over to the windows where the sun was peeking in. I stood there for a few minutes to soak in the extra warmth.

On February 22 I was at Miyajidake. In the seventh-grade class I showed a homemade video of American mountains and beaches but the most interesting scenes to the students were the ones of Phoenix neighborhoods, my health club, a mall, and a big supermarket. The tape was broadcast over the school's video system in the classrooms and teachers' room. The female teachers' were especially impressed with the grocery store. It is about three times the size of one of their *supaamaaketo* (su pa ma ketto – supermarket). They laughed as they watched a woman thump a melon because they discovered women on the other side of the world do what they do. The prices were a shock to the teachers' too, usually half the Japanese price.

On the tape, I also have some shots of my niece, Nadya, who is three. When she talked the kids laughed, especially the seventh graders, who have been studying English since only last April. They finally found a native English speaker whose command of English is worse than theirs.

This was my last time to teach the ninth graders before they graduate, and at the end of class two students read short speeches. In one boy's three-sentence speech, neither Tahara-*sensei* nor I understood the second sentence. As do most Japanese, he pronounced the words with an "I" in them like "e." So the word "it" sounded like "eat." In the last sentence he thanked me for my efforts over the year in correcting his pronunciation, a word he stumbled on badly. Oh, well, I will have to work harder.

In the teachers' room after classes, Tahara-*sensei* took my picture with the teachers. It reminded me of the first time I was in this room. It was in August and only a few teachers were around. Two high school girls in blue jeans brought *mugicha* and snacks. When I came back to the school a week later for my first class, the two "high school girls" turned out to be the music teacher and the science teacher. In fact the music teacher is 25 and the science teacher is 27 and now several months' pregnant. I have become a better judge of the age of Japanese women, but they still seem to be younger to me than they really are. Women love to have *gaijin* guess their age, I think because they know the *gaijin* is going to miss by a couple of years on the low side.

After the picture-taking session, I spent some time in the tiny school library trying to read a newspaper article. Actually I do not read the paper so much as look for *kanji* I recognize to pick out enough in a sentence to guess the meaning. Soon, most of the ninth-grade class filtered in, as they were done for the day too. They all helped me with the *kanji* I did not understand, which turned out to be eight of every ten.

As I was leaving school the ninth graders were hanging out of the windows waving. Some were shouting "Bye bye," "Ciao!" or "See ya later, dude." I will miss them.

I visited Kusuura-*chu* on February 25. As I wrote this in my notebook I was in the *kocho-sensei*'s (co cho – principal's) room because there was a "secret" meeting in the teachers' room. I have no idea why I was excluded from it. Other ALTs complain they are excluded from teachers' meetings and are upset about it. One woman went home at Christmas vowing not to return. She cited the "unwelcome" feeling of being forced to sit outside the teachers' room during the daily 20-minute teachers' meetings. I was not happy about being excluded from this meeting but not because of any feeling of ostracism. I could see my breath and hoped for a short meeting so I could return to the heated teachers' room.

Now I am at home. When class started, I felt very cold. Probably because I did not have my daily blast of heat in the teachers' room. When the kids asked me how I was doing at the beginning of class, I told them that I was freezing because it was vvvvery cold. The kids enjoyed learning the new vocabulary word, "freezing." Practicing saying vvvvery was a good lesson to improve their pronunciation of the "v" sound.

Sitting in class wearing their winter jackets, the students could see their breath. When my nose felt like it was going to fall off, I snapped. I turned the lesson plan over and wrote in colored chalk "No stove, no school!" I chanted it and was followed by many of the students, all of whom were cold and most of whom had been bored up to that point. When I went to the teachers' room during the 10-minute break between classes, I taped the protest to the front of my desk.

Later, two students from that class entered the teachers' room and told another teacher, in English, "No stove, no school." During *soji* several kids from another class gathered around my desk to find out what the sign meant. Finally they translated it as "The school doesn't need a stove." Some protests are just doomed.

On February 26 I was at Saiitsu-*chu*, and the latest cold I was fighting was almost gone. I started driving to school this year. Boys in charge of the gravel driveway rake it making it look like a Zen rock garden. As I drove up the school's driveway, the boys doffed their caps to me as they would do to any of the teachers'. I bowed from the driver's seat. In my rearview mirror I saw them unable to hide the I-just-raked-that look on their faces.

The windows in the hallway were open, of course. Two birds flew in poking around the hallway looking for food. No one seemed to think much of it. It may seem quaint to have birds in the school, but I would much prefer the windows closed.

In the seventh-grade class we practiced saying "When is your birthday?" One girl said, "Today." The class sang "Happy Birthday" to her. I told the class of our custom of putting candles on birthday cakes and making a wish before blowing the candles out. Japanese use candles but do not make a wish. The girl said she would do it. I also warned her of the scientifically proven fact that if you tell someone your wish, it will not come true. She promised to be careful.

The class was interrupted by mother nature. It started to hail, slowly at first, then faster and with bigger balls. There was a mad scramble to close the windows. When the students settled down again, with each passing second they paid less and less attention to class and more and more to the hail. They were mesmerized by nature's display.

When the hailstones grew to roughly half the size of golf balls, the students' ability to concentrate plummeted. I told them they had 30 seconds to watch the hail. I held up my watch and became the official hail-break timer. Fortunately the hail let up when I announced time was up.

Time is almost up for the Japanese semester too. As I walked around the ninth-grade class for the last time yesterday, I reminisced about the past six months. When I arrived here I knew about Japan what the average American "knows" about Japan: big companies; people gladly working hard with little payback; nature lovers crammed in big cities; big savers for a rainy day; kids smarter, students better than their American peers.

I have learned a lot, about the country, about the people and about my students. Regarding the country and its people, I have learned that many of the "truths" we hold about Japan and its people are myths. About the students, I think that in a way I have done what Akane asked me to do back in August. I have become intimate with her students and with the students at the other six schools. They have found a spot for themselves in my heart. If you could be in class with them on a daily basis and see their bright smiles and the genuine interest they have in expanding themselves beyond the Japanese universe, you would be impressed too. And in the process, they are helping to broaden me. I do not know if teachers' usually learn as much from their students as I have, but if they do, it is just another reason why the profession is well stocked in spite of the low pay.

Take care. I hope to hear from you soon.

*D*ear Uncle Chet and Aunt Dottie,   March 13
You will be happy to know my complaining about the cold weather is over. It is warm enough to take my sweater off in the teachers' room. The downside is that I have to iron my shirts every day.

I want to tell you about some of the people I have met on the program. Though the majority of ALTs are stationed in cities, many are stuck away deep in *inaka* (e knocka – countryside). It makes for some lonely young people.

William, a bespectacled, bearded Canadian is in a village called Kawaura-*machi*, which would make Moose Jaw, Saskatchewan, seem like a metropolis. William said he, being the only *gaijin* most of the people in the village had met, is such a curiosity that if a letter were addressed to *Gaijin-san* (Mr. Foreigner), Kawaura-*machi*, it would be delivered to him. I did. It was.

Unfortunately, in the Japanese universe, that was not the end of it. Because my letter was job related, I used a Board envelope. The post office delivered the letter to the Kawaura Board of Education instead of William's house. William's Board then complained to my Board. They were civil and polite to me yet clearly irked when they asked me to refrain from doing that again.

In Japan everyone is connected with each other and everyone, at any given time, can be called on the carpet for something someone else in the group did. I will be more careful of my actions and how they reflect on others in my group. This Japanese personal responsibility to the group stuff can be tough.

Maybe not as tough as being the only *gaijin* in Kawaura-*machi*. William is becoming less lonely. He and Marion, from Scotland, are, according to the official ALT gossip hotline, definitely a "thing." Marion is friendly and has a wonderfully pleasing Scottish accent. William is trying to teach her how to speak without an "accent." Andy and I have told Marion it is impossible for a Canadian to teach anyone without leaving behind an accent, eh. They are not talking to us anymore.

Marion and William are trying to teach each other words of common objects and expressions in order to communicate. She says words like "bathers," "biro," "boot," "bum," "crisps," "dinner," "from the year dot," "lift," "loo," "lorry," "spot on" and "torch," which mean, respectively, swimsuit, ball-point pen, trunk (of a car), butt, potato chips, *LUNCH*, from way back, elevator, toilet, truck, exactly on point and flashlight.

The main problem Marion and William have, however, is not one of communication. Marion lives in a city called Yatsushiro. Their problem is the Japanese transportation system. Although their towns are not that far apart as the crow flies, as the Japanese transportation infrastructure works, it takes many hours by bus and ferry (and lots of yen) to get from Kawaura-*machi* to Yatsushiro. They can only see each other on weekends. As an alternative they are running up the bills on NTT (knee pone – *Nippon* [another way to say Japan] Telephone and Telegraph).

There is another *gaijin* in Yatsushiro, Phillip, from the East Coast. I spent a weekend at his place. I found him likable. Women apparently find him irresistible.

He gives private English lessons, which have amazing fringe benefits. One class is made up of five nurses. Another has seven young women: coeds and female professionals. He dates women from each class. Phillip's apartment is two doors down from a young professional woman who says she is his "pillow friend."

They are typical young Japanese women in that they refuse to introduce the *gaijin* to their parents. One ALT in his third year will not date Japanese women anymore because they refuse to take the relationship seriously. Part of the problem is that having a *gaijin* husband can mean the woman becomes sort of "foreign" herself, making it hard for them to feel as accepted into Japanese society after their marriages as they did before. Stepping outside the norm opens one up to the claim that you are somehow indefinably different from the Japanese "us." On TV I have seen programs where children who have spent chunks of their youth abroad are made fun of because they do not, according to their "pure" Japanese peers, know how to use *hashi* as well as a Japanese who has never been outside of Japan.

Despite this, *gaijin* are popular with Japanese women, because they believe Western men treat women better than Japanese men do. Japanese men have not lived through a women's liberation movement and still expect women to stand aside as they walk through a door and for the woman to jump when he orders another beer while watching TV. Besides, *gaijin* go home in a year or so, which means that no serious complications ought to arise. *Gaijin* men find the this-is-just-for-fun attitude too good to be true.

The Thursday night conversation class I go to is attended by two young women who are married to *sarariiman* and are almost by definition lonely business widows. Supposedly, some neglected Japanese wives gravitate toward affairs with *gaijin*. One often heard story is that middle-aged Japanese housewives walk up to *gaijin* men on subways or buses and say, "Sex with you." When it comes to me so far the lonely women of Japan have exhibited great self-restraint.

Since Phillip has been in Japan, he has not been to a grocery store nor has he paid for a meal in a restaurant. The only money he spends on "food" is on beer and chips at the 7-11 on the corner. He is taking advantage of the Japanese belief that single men do not have the vaguest clue how to cook. One question single ALT men are asked ad nauseam is "Who makes your suppers?" One ALT who has lived in the same small town for two and a half years is still asked that question. Women are shocked to learn that a man can actually cook food for himself.

Phillip's approach is that if the women insist he is incapable of cooking, he does not want to disappoint them. He accepts every invitation to dinner. He has zero interest in learning Japanese, so for the people who take him out to dinner, it is a cheap English lesson.

Four families have taken it upon themselves to feed him on a rotating basis on the nights he does not go out. By about four o'clock in the afternoon he receives a call inquiring about his dinner plans. If he is not going out, he either gets an invitation to come to the caller's house or they offer to bring food over for him. On Friday we were feted by some guy Phillip knows. Then on Saturday, when I suggested that we go to the store, Phillip told me we should wait till at least 5 P.M. before we do something rash like spend money on food. Sure enough, a woman called and said she was bringing food over. Phillip told her he had company, and the woman said she would bring more food.

My topic, however, is lonely ALTs, and that brings me to Andy, who claims to be lonelier than the Maytag repairman. He lives on an island he calls Devil's Island. He has had only one visitor so far: me. It was a dark, cold Friday evening by the time I arrived at the port of Kuratake, where I boarded a "taxi" ferry to the island. The passenger compartment was eleven feet by four feet with cushions thrown on the floor to sit on, so I had to take my shoes off before entering. It was heated by a portable kerosene heater, which I knew was operating because I could see the red-hot heating unit. My feet, however, which I let roam directly to the front of the stove, told me the stove being lit was a figment of my imagination.

I never told the boat's skipper where I was going. I assumed he would take me to the port. But he must have figured, correctly, "What would one *gaijin* be coming out here for if not to visit the other *gaijin*?" Instead of taking me to the port, he took me to the fish processing plant, which is about 200 yards from Andy's house. He turned his floodlight on to push back the dark. Gently nudging the bow of the boat up to the sea wall which is incorporated into the plant's concrete yard, he motioned for me to jump onto the sea wall. Then he pointed to an apartment building which I assumed was Andy's.

I wondered for a split second whether I was going to jump onto the sea wall only to be attacked by guard dogs. Or maybe that I would walk around to the front of the plant to find that to leave its property, I would have to scale a twenty-foot-high fence. Upon quick reflection, I decided that because the guy knows where Andy lives, he probably also knows that Andy works for the island government and hence is part of the ingroup. It follows that if I wound up in trouble because I did what the skipper told me to do, the repercussions would find their way right up his boat's wake. I therefore took it on faith that if I followed his advice, I would be alright. We waved to each other as he backed the boat away. Walking around to the front of the building, I found neither dogs nor a fence. There may be downsides to this wrap-around responsibility from and to the group, but it does permit a certain amount of trust in other people, if you read the relationships right.

I strolled over to Andy's in the pitch black, accompanied by the racket of the machinery keeping the day's catch frozen for shipment. Andy's Japanese was among the best of the ALTs when we arrived. In what he describes as a cultural anomaly, he has found perhaps the only group of Japanese who do not want to learn English. This gives him plenty of opportunities to practice his speaking.

There are two restaurants on the island. On Saturday night, we had dinner at the small one, which has three tables. We ducked to make it through the doorway, designed for the average Japanese height, and pushed aside the curtain that hangs down halfway to the floor. Then we stepped into the narrow hallway between the tables and the counter.

We sat next to the door because it was near the portable heater. Taking our shoes off, we stepped up a foot and a half onto the *tatami*. The tables stand about two feet high so of course there were no chairs, just cushions to sit on. The waitress immediately brought *ocha*. Many Westerners develop a taste for it, usually people who enjoy coffee. I do not like coffee either so I guess that may explain why I have not developed a liking for *ocha*. The waitress did not bring us a menu. As usual, Andy says, she brought out the food and at the end of the meal asked for 700 yen (about $6) each.

I reflected how far I have come since last July. There I was sitting on the floor, almost able to converse in Japanese, drinking *atsukan* (ah tsu khan – heated sake) (for which I have developed a real taste), downing my soup without a spoon, and eating raw fish. Who woulda thunk?

While we ate, the chef asked questions, which I fielded with my growing Japanese vocabulary and Andy's help. One odd thing about this traditional Japanese restaurant is the poster of the U.S.S. *Wisconsin*, a World War II era battleship. At the end of the war it bombarded Japan from Hakodate in the north to Okinawa in the south. The chef said he saw it in person somewhere as a child and thought it was the neatest thing since sliced bread.

After we talked, a group of five drunk vacationing *sarariiman* came in dressed in expensive-looking fishing clothes. They sat at the other two tables. We were disappointed to see them for a couple of reasons. First, if there are two Japanese men in the same room, one will smoke as if he is outside his boss's office, wondering whether his last screw-up is going to cost him his job. With five, there was a good chance the smoke would soon be hanging down from the ceiling like a thick blue fog. Second, because they were already tipsy, it would give them courage to take advantage of what would be a perfect opportunity to dredge up and butcher their rusty English on real-live *gaijin*.

Sure enough, the choking smell of burning tobacco filled the room like a sumo wrestler fills a doorway. With smoke coming out of their mouths and noses they asked the questions I hear from Japanese, complete with the identical grammatical and pronunciation errors. "Way ah do u who rum? (Where do you from?)"; "Whato izoo u a boo rah doe tie poo? (What is your blood type?)"; "How oldo ah u? (How old are you?)."

As we feared, the drunks invited us to join their party. If we did they would have paid for our food and drinks for the opportunity to speak English. They were content, however, with having their pictures taken with us. My face must be in 100 photo albums all over Japan. People all over want their picture taken with a *gaijin*. They think it gives their pictures, and hence their vacation, an international flair. My initiation into that aspect of Japanese culture came during the flight from Tokyo to Kumamoto. My seat was surrounded by several high schools girls who were on their way home from a class trip. After we landed, they insisted that I have my picture taken with them individually and in a group. As we posed, the person with the camera said the word the Japanese use to alert people to smile – cheese, or I should say, *chizu*. The mania even gets me in places. At an observatory near *gaijin*-scarce Hondo, I: (a) got in free, (b) had my picture taken with the entire staff, and (c) a young couple insisted I hold their baby for a picture with them.

Back at Andy's place, he said Mie still has not said yes. As do William and Marian, Andy and Mie have a distance problem. Andy lives on a minuscule island that is just past a tiny island, which is itself offshore of another small island. The small island is connected to another one by a bridge, which is in turn connected by bridge to a big island (Kyushu), which, hundreds of miles from Andy's house, is in turn connected by a bridge to the biggest Japanese island (called Honshu), on which Mie lives (several hours farther north and on the western side of the island) .

For all practical purposes, he is not much closer to her than he would be if he had stayed in Georgia. With all the ferries, buses, trains and what-not that he has to take, it would take only an hour or so longer from his house in Atlanta to Mie's house in Japan. Like that of William and Marion, Andy's long-distance phone bill is about $500 a month.

Mie and Andy have a problem that William and Marian do not have: a Japanese mother. (Mie's father is dead.) Mie has been reluctant to say yes to Andy in part because she is not ready to lose a mother to gain a husband. Many Japanese think a daughter marrying a *gaijin* is similar to being told you have cancer. Mie counts her mother in that group and has not mentioned a breath about Andy. Instead, at the insistence of her mother, she is going through the *omiai* process meeting fishermen with silver-rimmed teeth.

Andy will not take no for an answer. After coming all the way to Japan just to be nearer to Mie and enduring Devil's Island, I have no doubt that he is just the kind of persistent bugger who will only take yes for an answer.

For a while I wondered whether this my-mom-will-disown-me stuff was an excuse to keep him at bay while Mie finds someone in whom she is more interested. Akiko, however, a young woman in Hondo, introduced me to Robert, whom she met two years ago when he was an ALT. Robert told me that, without meeting Mie, he believes that her fear of being cut off from the family could very well be the main reason she will not marry Andy.

Akiko's father is the main stumbling block to Robert's marriage to Akiko. Robert has met many *kokusai copuru* (ko koo sigh ko poo roo – international couple) in the same boat. It took Akiko a year to gather the courage to tell her mom about Robert. The women agreed that it is still too soon to tell the old man that his daughter wants to marry a *gaijin*. When they will do that Robert does not know, but he wants to go home soon and would like to take Akiko with him as his bride. Another couple in Kyoto have been married two years and want to start a family. They were married in a civil ceremony and only the mother knows her daughter married a *gaijin*, a man about to obtain his doctorate in Japanese history. The couple want to start a family and they are considering how to tell her father of the marriage.

The reasons for this anti-*gaijin* phenomenon are not all based on bigotry. Old-fashioned financial self-interest plays its part. With housing costs outrageous all over Japan, the oldest son is still expected to live with and take care of the parents, in exchange for inheriting the house. A *gaijin* is not likely to do that. But bigotry is not a small part of the scenario either.

The Japanese consider themselves a racially pure stock. Where they came from is not clear, and their language is not closely related to any other. With their past shrouded in mist and their language unique, they believe that they are somehow not just unique but unique in a uniquely special bright and shiny kind of way. If you and I cannot understand it, well, it is because they are Japanese and we are not. I cannot tell you how many times I have been talking with someone when they say something that makes no sense at all. When I ask them to explain what they mean, they will just respond, "You are not Japanese, so you would not understand." It is aggravating to no end, and inexplicable in a people who are personally very self-effacing.

Take it easy, and I hope to hear from you soon.

*D*ear Dad,   March 20
        School is over for the semester with the new school
year starting the first week of April. On Saturday I went to
Miyajidake to take pictures of the school and the valley. The vice
principal let me in early so I could take my pictures before Saturday's
half day of classes started at 8:30. It was raining as I left the house at 7
A.M. Near Miyajidake high school students headed to Hondo squatted
under umbrellas at bus stops on the road's gravel shoulder. The rain
stopped as I arrived at school at 7:30 A.M. There were already a few kids
studying.

        I took a picture of a boy which makes me feel sorry for my
bright and eager students. It is of Tanaka-*san* whose desk is directly
beneath the class clock. It was not even 8 A.M. on a Saturday but the boy
was lost in study. Because the day was overcast, the little bit of sky in the
picture makes it look like 8 P.M. Which is just about right anyway. Many
of these kids will not get home until long after dark. To me, this
melancholy picture symbolizes all that I do not like about the Japanese
school system. It chews up their youth.

        Only the most dedicated workaholic can compete with these
kids. Seventh graders usually leave the house by 7:30 A.M. and return
about 6:30 P.M.; then they do homework for two hours. Eighth and ninth
graders are home earlier, about 5:30 P.M. but usually have between two
and five hours homework. Sundays are usually practice days for sports in
which many students participate.

        Whatever else can be said of the Japanese school system, it is
preparing students well for life in the Japanese universe. The struggle for
admission to the right high school is ferocious. On the national news this
week, students cried when they did not find their names on the list posted
outside their schools of those admitted to high schools. If they do not pass
the test, they cannot go to high school. To avoid that fate, about 30
percent of Hondo's students go to *juku* (jew coo – cram school) after
school to help them do well on their high school exams. In bigger cities,

attendance is much higher.

For a nation with a reputation for scholastic excellence, it is surprising that high school is not mandatory, and students must pass entrance exams to gain admittance. This test is the first major winnowing in the race up the ladder of Japanese society. Seniors in junior high are busy studying hours a day for the public school test. If they fail, they can retake it in a week, but if they fail that too, they must wait till next year. Public schools are more desirable because they are free and perceived to be of higher quality. Private high school entrance exams are somewhat easier. Private high school students also know they are already one step behind in the race for admission into the right college. High tuition is another disincentive to attending private schools.

Every year a small percentage of students from just about every junior high school fail to pass the entrance exams to either a public or private high school. For a substantial minority of those who fail, their education is over. Most study all year to retake the tests the following year. If they do not pass, they either go to a technical school or start work. The students groan with undisguised envy when I tell them that in America one's high school is usually decided based on proximity to one's home.

Public high schools are divided into three types: academic, trade and agricultural. Graduates from academic schools will likely go to some kind of college or advanced technical school. Graduates from the various trade high schools in large part will end up as mechanics for Toyota and the like. Other trade schools are devoted to the domestic arts of sewing, cooking and so on. The predominately female graduates of these schools become housewives or perhaps seamstresses, or some other trade that logically grows out of their studies. Agricultural high schools are the last type of trade school.

With farms being gobbled up by cities or golf courses, the dwindling gray-haired farming population is not being replaced. Graduates of agricultural schools consider farming a hick job and a back-breaking way to find a dead-end life. Most will not go to college (or they would have been able to pass the test for an academic school). They are likely to end up doing the "*San K*" jobs. Other agricultural school graduates end up filling their society's need for workers in low-paying menial jobs, such as the jobs with the green toilet trucks.

Admission to the "best" high school will later help with admission to the "best" college. The goal of the very best public high schools is simple: to help the student pass the college entrance exams. The struggle for admission to college is even more insane. High school seniors are now studying hours a day for college entrance exams.

Admission to the "best" college will later help them obtain a position with a socially prestigious company. A student's whole career is affected by what college he or she goes to. Since the last century, the majority of top leaders in government, business and academia have come from four or five schools. The best slots are actually reserved for Tokyo University graduates.

The Japanese system for college admission is, like so many things the Japanese have to go through, more difficult and expensive than can be explained rationally. The cost to apply is astronomical, about $1,000. Schools which have their own tests, give them on the same day as most other schools so even those students who have the financial resources to apply to 10 or 15 schools can probably only apply to two or maybe three schools. The tests are designed to weed out those students who have not given most of their waking hours for the last year to studying.

There are tests for jobs too. The teachers' admit that these tests which start in puberty and end in young adulthood, rarely test reasoning, ability. They are usually in yes/no or multiple-choice format. What they test is the students' ability to pack information into their heads and spew it out.

One young man I know is studying for the college exam. He is a studyaholic of epic proportions, but his dedication is not unusual. Last year he failed the college exam of a prestigious university, so he spent the past year attending *juku* during the day fulltime followed by studying at home until he passes out. If I pass his house on my way home on Friday night at 2 A.M., I see him in his living room studying. From the sheer amount of time he studies, I think the test must consist of memorizing the telephone books of Japan's nine largest cities.

To help kids face the pressure to study, there exists the concept of the *kyoiku mama* (kyo e coo – education; mama – mama). These women are so dedicated to their sons' educational needs that they can give themselves ulcers if their boy fails to get into the "right" preschool. The pressure never lets up. The *kyoiku mama* never asks that the precious boy take part in home rituals such as cooking, cleaning and the like, because she knows that the little one has a big chore ahead. To succeed in the fiercely competitive Japanese future, the boy must out study his peers or eat their dust. So his time is spent (in roughly descending order) attending school, studying, reading typical worthless comics and playing *famicon* (fa me – [fami]ly; con – [com]puter, which means video computer games).

Supposedly, as the young boys grow into puberty the *kyoiku mama* knows that their thoughts turn to the bodies of the girls in his life.

To keep the boys' noses in their books with a minimum of distraction, the truly dedicated *kyoiku mama* will sleep with her own son. Although undeniably a great rumor, I find it hard to believe more than a handful of truly strange women go so far.

Although Japanese women spread this rumor, they quickly disclaim any such behavior themselves. The prevalence of the rumor is explained, in part, as the Japanese reaction to the demands to which they must conform. This is how they voice their realization that the Japanese universe is set up with tests that are irrationally difficult, employers who are unyieldingly demanding of their time and a culture that brooks no slackers in its demands of conformity. While conforming as they must, they delight in telling of the person who conforms to an absurd degree. Having set up the straw man, they can believe that although they conform as they must, they have an understanding of what is reasonable. Therefore, they are "normal" in spite of the illogical demands placed upon them. Or maybe there really are *kyoiku mama* playing bedroom aerobics with their sons. Where the truth lies, I do not know. But the rumor being so juicy, I thought I would aid all the Japanese women who spread it to expand its reach beyond Japan's shores.

It is not surprising that there is a collective May letdown after all the March tests and new phases of life in April. The whole young population takes one gigantic collective sigh of relief called *gogatsubyo* (go gatsu be o – May sickness). Everyone is just emotionally exhausted and needs to regroup before getting back on the *gambaru* track (gam ba roo – *gambaru* can be translated several ways in English, but in this sense it is "hang in there") to endure the trials that await at the next level.

To help would-be slackers keep up with the day-to-day demands of the Japanese universe, everyday I hear three phrases that are a basic part of Japanese culture: *Gambatte* (gam baat tay – literally, try hard, but is also used to mean good luck), *gaman suru,* and *shikata ga nai* (she ka ta ga nah eh – there is nothing that can be done about it, as in "I do not want to be at school at 7:30 in the morning on a Saturday but *shikata ga nai*").

The Japanese are urged to *gambatte* because their duties are so *iya* (e ya – disagreeable) they have to *gaman suru*. Whether they want to do it or not, *shikata ga nai*. Expressions such as "I have rights" or "I'm not going to take it any more" do not exist or are such a minimal part of Japanese life that to my *gaijin* ears, they are drowned out by the cacophony of *gambatte, gaman suru* and *shikata ga nai*.

In all these ways school reinforces what it means to be Japanese: We are Japanese, the rest of humanity is not; you can think anything you want, but you do what you are told. Children are taught to work within the group. By definition there is the ingroup and the outgroups. The largest ingroup is the Japanese nation. The rest of us are in the largest of all outgroups, the *gaijin* group. Belonging to groups unfortunately breeds a feeling of solidarity with the group at the same time that it breeds a feeling of separateness from nongroup members. It is not the result of any deep dark conspiracy.

History's dead hand, a policy of the shogun period known as *sakoku* (sa co coo – closed country), still clutches to the heart of the Japanese culture. *Sakoku* refers to Japan's 200 years of self-imposed exile from the rest of humanity, which ended about 140 years ago. *Sakoku* intensified the notion of *shimaguni* (she ma goo knee – island nation), which refers not to a geographical fact but to a closed, insular mind-set. A mind-set that this is Japan and what is beyond our shores does not matter. The *shimaguni* mind-set combined with the power of the thoroughly indoctrinated *gambatte*, *gaman suru* and *shikata ga nai* results in teenagers whose outward-looking interest in things beyond the Japanese shores will, as part of the system's natural workings, be beaten down.

But somebody in Japan must think that that should change; after all, the program I am on exists. Kids in small villages like Miyajidake, who would never ever see a *gaijin*, let alone talk with one, have an opportunity to talk with Rosemary and me during and after class. What difference that will make, I do not know. But I am glad to be part of the process. I wish these kids had more of a life, and I hope that in some way I am helping to expand their horizons. I know they are expanding mine.

My students and I have talked about cultural differences between our schools. The kids groan when I tell them a typical American junior high schedule. Yes, they would like to go to school in America, especially because of the summer vacation. They cannot believe that summer vacation could stretch from June clear into September. When I tell them that I wore clothes of my own choosing and in high school drove my own car to school, I can see their eyes betraying their daydreams: girls wearing the "in" fashions to school and boys driving to high school in their own cars.

Even in tightly controlled Japan, however, kids cannot stay out of trouble. When you put together hundreds of teenagers whose bloodstreams are teeming with hormones, there are bound to be problems. This year a couple of pregnant girls were kicked out. Another was thrown out for being a weekend hooker in Kumamoto. Another was in a terrible car accident while drinking with other underage children. She was the only one to survive the crash.

Then there are the "Yankees" – immune-from-death teenagers

who ride motorscooters. In the ultimate of fashion statements, they buy helmets resembling batting helmets and wear them on the back of the head, with the bill of the cap pointing to the sky. It is kept on by a strap worn around the neck. A "Yankee" is never cold. Regardless of the weather, a "Yankee" is in short sleeves. A "Yankee" wears girl's socks with a picture of a lovable kitten sewn over the ankle and the English "Hello Kitty" over it. There is a whole line of Hello Kitty clothes, but the well dressed "Yankee" does not wear them or take Hello Kitty lunch boxes to school. If you see a "Yankee," do not giggle at his socks. They can be as bad as gang members anywhere. An American in Osaka was beaten by a group of "Yankees" when he tried to stop them from looking into his daypack.

Not long ago at Hondo-*chu*, there was a commotion in one of the side halls between morning classes. A crowd of boys and one of the male teachers' were watching two boys fight. A teacher who is six months' pregnant waded into the crowd. The fighting boys fell and the woman was thrown forward. Bent over, she held the nearest spectator for balance. I grabbed one of the boys by his belt and shirt collar. In a motion I perfected through countless hours of shoveling snow in Michigan, I deposited him on the floor on the other side of the hall. The other boy tried to get at him. I held him by the shirt but had to push him against the wall to keep them apart. When the windows rattled, I realized I had shoved too hard. With that I think everyone was a little worried the *gaijin* would kill them all. He meekly let the woman hustle him away. I knew all danger must have been over when the male teacher walked the other boy holding him by the ear.

At Kusuura-*chu*, between classes, three boys were wrestling on the floor in the hallway in an out-of-the-way part of the school. When they saw me they stopped, stood up and started to brush their uniforms off while staring at the floor. I looked at their expressions, which begged "We did not mean it and will never, ever do anything like that so long as we live." I motioned to the floor where they had been wrestling and said in Japanese "Go ahead." By the time I made it to the stairwell, I heard them at it again, which is probably exactly what would have happened if I had tried to chew them out instead.

Boys constantly sneak into *pachinko* parlors. Four boys at Hon machi-*chu* were caught last Wednesday night at one. Their punishment was to sit *seiza* for one hour outside the principal's office. This can be painful because the circulation to the feet is slowed. The punishment is less severe today than it would have been a couple of weeks ago. If they had been forced to sit *seiza* on the cold wood floor in the unheated hallway even three weeks ago, the punishment would have been entirely different. I walked over to the boys and asked them what they did. They said with angelic faces full of wonder at why they had been singled out, "We don't know." Some things are universal.

In a class last time at Kamegawa-*chu*, a boy played on his desk with two steel balls which his friends gleefully told me were *pachinko* balls. I confiscated them. The boy did not give them up without whimpering, which made me feel like an honest-to-goodness teacher. I gave the balls back to the boy at the end of class with a warning that I was going to tell his next period's teacher to take them away for good if he played with them again. Power! I love it.

When a child gets into trouble, more than the child suffers. For example, during February the whole school at Hon machi-*chu* stood at attention for one hour in the freezing gym because one boy stole money from a local merchant. And the students are not the only ones who suffer. Because two of his students dropped out of school, a teacher decided to take sensitivity training.

Before closing, I want to describe an incident that happened about five minutes ago. I crossed the hall from the teachers' room to the teachers' *tatami* mat room. Writing with the door open, I noticed one of the teachers enter the men's room a few doors down. Seconds later two girls stood outside the men's room door saying something to the teacher. He blasted out of the room as if it were on fire.

The girls could not control their giggles. I wondered what all the fuss was about when I saw out of the corner of my eye a green shape just outside the window. There was the toilet-cleaning green tanker truck. The girls were still in the hall so I left the *tatami* mat room as slowly as I could to maintain my dignity yet as quickly as I could to get away from what I knew was going to be an overpowering stink. I made it back into the teachers' room and sat down at my desk.

Unfortunately, the teachers' room was well within range of the smell. For five seconds the most disgusting stench enveloped the room. Just as at Miyajidake, no one reacted in the slightest. I wonder what the guys who work on those trucks must have been like as students to wind up with such a wonderful job.

Well, it is three o'clock and almost quitting time so I will wrap this one up.

*D*ear Barb,   March 29
          Last weekend I visited Nagasaki. It is a 20-minute drive to the Oniike ferry, followed by a 25-minute ferry ride to the port at Kuchiitsu on the Shimabara peninsula, followed by a 90-minute drive to Nagasaki.

I stayed, along with another ALT, at Sally's apartment. Sally is a 28-year-old East Coast Canadian. She moved out of the apartment her Board found for her because she wanted a more traditional one. Her apartment is a 1 LDK (a four-*tatami* bedroom, a four and one-half *tatami* living room, and a combined dining room and kitchen; 2 LDK, 3 LDK and even 4 LDK apartments exist).

Because she moved from the apartment provided, she has to pay her own rent. It is cheap by Japanese standards. She pays 30,000 yen a month, or about $240. She paid five months' "key money" (30,000 yen per month times 5 months = 150,000 yen or about $1,200), which landlords can demand because housing is in short supply. Usually half of the "key money" is not refundable, and in many cases less than that. In the biggest cities like Kyoto, landlords also command "gift money," which is not refundable. This can be a payment the equivalent of several more months' rent. At the end of the lease, sometimes a new payment of "gift money" is necessary to renew.

Her place is close to the Peace Park, the memorial to those killed by the atomic bomb. We met there because directions to her place were too complicated. The park's centerpiece is a huge statue that resembles a Buddha, except one arm is held straight out. Each part is supposed to be symbolic of something (the one closed eye, the way he is holding one hand, etc.), but Japanese pigeons are not impressed by the sanctity of the statue and make it their home, leaving ample "evidence" of their presence. Sally has never seen it without pigeons.

Her apartment is on the second floor. As I walked in I smelled an odor but could not place it. It was a musty smell but not very strong.

Although it was not pleasant, it was not strongly offensive either, and it did not travel as far as the living room. She explained that the rest room is so small that when I used it the door would bang against my knees when closed. The first time I walked into the rest room, I knew where the smell was from. It reeked. I lifted the seat and saw it is a drop toilet. I stuffed my shirt to my nose to fight the overpowering smell. No plumbing in the toilet for a 20-year-old apartment is not too unusual for Japan.

As I write this in my notebook, it is 11 A.M. on Sunday. I am twenty-five yards away from the black monolith erected under the epicenter of the atomic bomb blast in Nagasaki. The bomb was exploded several hundred feet overhead on August 9, 1945, at 11:02 A.M. It was overcast that day, and no doubt unbearably hot and muggy.

Today is a warm, blue-sky spring day. I look overhead where impending death silently screamed toward the ground so many years ago. Seeing a couple of crows circling, I recall that the crow is the symbol of death in some cultures. I just caught myself checking the sky above the birds to make sure there were no planes. No planes, but the roar of traffic from the road 100 yards away is in marked contrast to the secluded tranquility of the lush little park.

I just came from the building behind where I am sitting, the Atomic Bomb Museum. I was more emotionally moved by the one in Hiroshima, which is what I expected. Many Westerners and Japanese argue about which museum is better, and I have come to the conclusion that the most impressive is the first one you see.

The museum features an animated film reenacting the bombing. There are two scenes on the ground. In one the songs of birds are heard while a boy holds his hand out to his cat, which is stuck in a tree. In the other a woman is picking food in a field with her daughter nearby. A plane (at nearly six miles up resembling a silver needle) causes the air at ground level to reverberate slightly with the sound of its four far-away giant engines. Then a flash. The boy's clothes melt away at his death. The girl is trapped under a log. The mother, her hair burned away, lifts the log as skin falls from her shoulder to reveal bloody flesh. Later the mother dies in agony.

The theme of the museum is that innocent people suffered. The message, as far as it goes, is good. What is left unsaid makes me feel that ultimately the *truth* is the museum's victim. Nowhere is there evidence that territorial aggression is bad. Nowhere does the museum teach that it is not healthy to blindly follow military leaders who say they are ordered by an emperor who is a direct descendant of God.

I guess all this doom and gloom was brought on more than anything else by the eternal flame monument in the park next to the stairs on which I am now sitting. In 1983 Japanese officials went to Greece to bring to Japan flames kindled with the Olympic Flame. Greek tradition was that no war could be conducted during the Olympic Games. On the monument the inscription reads that as long as the flame burns, there will be no more Nagasakis. The flame is out today. I just looked at the crows again overhead and decided to move on.

On the way home I drove near an area called Unzen and stopped at an *onsen* (on sen – hot spring). *Onsen* abound throughout Japan. It is custom to skinny-dip at the *onsen,* and they are normally segregated by sex. Some of the more remote ones are coed. I admit I was hoping to find one. In a way I did. While I was bathing before entering the water, a man came in with his two children, one of whom was a girl of maybe eight. The worst part was the girl thought it was great to have a *gaijin* there. She stared at me the whole time. So I ended up wondering which parts I ought to wash and which parts I ought to skip.

The Unzen area is named after the nearby volcano, which, after two centuries of dormancy, recently began smoking again. The last time it exploded, part of the volcano slid into the Ariake Sea, causing a tidal wave. How high the wave was and how many people died varies with whom you talk to and how much he had to drink. Although the main wave traveled away from Hondo and it was not damaged too heavily, people are concerned.

I was at Kamegawa-*chu* on March 21 when Hondo had a midmorning earthquake. Most are tiny but this one knocked things off shelves. The teachers' room was suddenly alive with activity. People turned on the radio and TV. Someone called the Board. If the earthquake was caused by Unzen and had started the feared tidal wave, we had about 10 minutes before it would hit. After about 15 minutes of trying to decide whether to evacuate the students to higher ground, everyone just sort of gave up and went back to business as usual.

It was also graduation day. The afternoon ceremonies were held in the gym, which has a stage. It has red curtains on either side with writing in *kanji.* As I waited for the ceremonies to begin, I was pleased I could read most of it. At long last all the hours of study are beginning to pay off.

In school gyms, gym shoes (meaning worn only in the gym) or stocking feet are permitted. Slippers worn in other parts of the school are not considered clean enough. Most in attendance were in stocking feet. The sunny afternoon was no match for the cold wood floor, and the chill traveled up my legs.

The seniors spent a good amount of their time recently out of classes, practicing for this day. Everything went off like clockwork.

I was impressed how dressed up mothers were for the graduation. One wore a *kimono*, but the rest wore Western clothes. I was also impressed that of the big turnout of parents, there were only one or two dads. In Japan one does not even begin to think about taking time off work for such a frivolous reason as a big day in your child's life.

Behind the parents was the primarily female school band. Some things throughout the universe are constants. Junior high school bands come as close to playing beautiful music as politicians come to speaking the truth. I played the trumpet in my junior high school band next to a chubby girl who played the clarinet. She had an uncanny ability to make random squeaky noises. The vivid memories some of the clarinet sounds brought back made me wonder what the chances were that her daughters were in the band.

The ceremonies began at 2:33 P.M. by my watch. I moved my watch back three minutes. The teachers were introduced to the polite applause of parents and students. We stood as we were introduced, bowed to the audience and said "*Dozo yoroshiku, onegai shimasu* (doe zoe yo row she coo)." This is a stock phrase to be said whenever a Japanese person meets another with whom some sort of a relationship is to be established. It could be translated as begging for favorable treatment but is really considered nothing more than a polite thing to say under the circumstances.

When I was introduced, I stood, said "Hi," and waved. The parents quietly murmured at my break in decorum. Some of the kids giggled and several waved back saying, "Hi, Ken-*sensei*." The principal, whose stick-in-the-mud appearance belies a warm heart, looked out over the parents and flashed a smile that said "Hey, he's a *gaijin*, I can't be held responsible."

No ceremony in Japan is complete without endless speeches. Speeches were written on white folded paper, which was slowly, ever so formally, unfolded as each was read. The principal gave one, the head of the PTA gave one and the student representative of each grade gave one. I did not give one, nor did the woman sitting next to me, but I think everyone else did.

After the speech marathon, the principal opened up the first diploma, which unscrolled similar to the documents heralds read in the town square during the Middle Ages. An important part of the principal's job is to look good with gray hair. This principal has the classic stoic paternal look down pat. With the solemnity with which he read it, the diploma could have been a treaty between two countries sealing a lasting and heartfelt friendship. He read the entirety of only the first diploma and the last one. For the other students, he read only their names and to which homeroom they belonged.

The first student bowed to the principal who solemnly returned her bow. She claimed her diploma with both hands and raised it ever so slightly. Then she turned and waited on stage for the next student. They exchanged bows. The first student left and the second student bowed to the principal, and so on until the last student completed the ceremony. The scene I watched was the same scene repeated millions of times since prewar times. The just-graduated students marched out of the gym to the off-tune sounds of Sousa's "Washington Post." Most mothers beamed from ear to ear as their babies left the room. A few cried.

As I made my way to the teachers' room, several groups of students snagged me to pose in their photos. Being their teacher, I assume I was not asked to pose simply because *gaijin* are stylish in a photo album. I received a few small presents and an elaborate handmade card complete with the picture inside of the girl who made it. I also received several letters from girls addressed: "Love letter to Ken-*sensei*."

As I entered the teachers' room, a group of six or seven boys came in to ask if they could shake my hand and have their picture taken with me. One of the boys said, "You ah goo dough tee cha (you are good teacher)." Sure, his grammar was off, and my efforts had not improved his pronunciation one whit. But his sentiments made me feel pretty good anyway.

As the boys left, I saw Ezaki-*sensei* in a bowing marathon with one of the parents. I counted a total of 10 bows each, with the mother looking slightly sideways to make sure she was bowing lower than Ezaki-*sensei*. When the bowing stopped, the woman produced a picture of Ezaki-*sensei* taken with a group of students 30 years ago. She had taught the woman's husband and now her son.

I had known Ezaki-*sensei* as a *genki* gray-haired grandma who rides a bicycle to school and who bounces, not walks, to class. Looking at the picture, I saw an attractive woman wearing an optimistic smile with most of her life in front of her. She was ecstatic to hear that I thought she was attractive. We talked about the impact she has had on the lives of the thousands of her students until the reminiscing caused her eyes to moisten.

As my students leave behind one phase of their lives, so too my life as Ken-*sensei* only has a few more months to go. I wonder what impact I am having on the kids. I feel a part of an important process: the process of growing up. This time I am the one helping with the guiding. I feel in a way as if I have come full circle. It is a cycle that has existed for as long as there have been teachers and will continue as long as there are young people. As I take part in the process in a foreign country, I suspect that my teachers would like the idea of being rewarded for their hard work through my work helping children in another country understand our part of the world.

I may sound a bit like a broken record, but these kids have wormed their way into my heart. I did not expect it would happen and am a little surprised it did. It is one of those little things that creep up on you. Before you know it you are in the middle of something wonderful, but what that feeling is does not really bear description in words. When I leave Hondo and my days as Ken-*sensei*, I know these children will always be a warm memory in my heart.

I would go on reminiscing, but Tsuruta-*san* just leaned over and whispered, "U luke tie yard (you look tired)," my "shiftover" signal. I just have time to finish this, print it and hustle over to the main post office next door. What a tough job. Next week I will be in the office again so I'll write soon.

*D*ear Lynea,   April 7
Ever have the feeling everybody knows what is going on but you? Welcome to Japanese culture. As I walked to my desk on Monday morning, April Fool's day, there was a deathly silence. I asked Tsuruta-*san* what was going on. He explained that he, Tanaka-*san*, Funeshima-*san* (a middle-aged woman whom I have not yet written about but whom I have grown fond of) and two other people in the office, including my boss, Okabe-*kacho*, were being transferred the next day. They were to learn at 9 A.M. to what department within the city they were being moved.

I learned that government and big corporations shuffle office workers around every two to three years. The explanation is that with the social motivation for people to identify with the group, it is good to keep people moving around or the whole of Japan would ossify into little "cliques." Most of the Japanese I have asked do not really seem to know why they have such a strange system. They say, "That's just the way things are. I do not know the reason."

Being Japanese, when they are told to obey, they obey. They do not know why things are the way they are, they only know that they have to follow orders. Frankly, although for the most part the people I work with are fine people, their unquestioning devotion to following orders concerns me. They complain to their friends and moan and groan, but not to the higher-ups, and they end up doing what they are told anyway. A Japanese friend told me that Americans are taught about our "rights," Japanese are taught about their "responsibilities." Unquestioning obedience makes things efficient but efficiency can be a mixed blessing.

Before we found out where the people were going and who was going to replace them, one of the friendlier people in the office, Yokoyama-*san*, encouraged me to accept the changes because that is the Japanese way. Besides, he said, we would all quickly learn to like the new people. Later in the morning we found out Tsuruta-*san*'s friend, Nino-*san*, was taking his place. Tsuruta-*san* assured me that I would like Nino-*san*. I have sat next to him for most of a week now, and I think in time he will do a good job and we will get along fine. But I admit I am biased; I do not think I will grow to like him as much as Tsuruta-s*an*.

Because I have seen Tsuruta-*san* do his job many many times, I find myself in the odd position of helping Nino-*san* learn parts of his job. A woman visiting the office who owns a small business in Hondo sighed that the Japanese system makes it hard to conduct business with the city every April when so many people are learning new jobs. Apparently the Japanese expect the quality of service to go down just after April. As someone with rudimentary Japanese giving the new crew pointers, I can vouch for that.

Tsuruta-*san* was transferred to a department on another floor. It may be a more important position. All day Monday there was a trickle of gray-haired men going to the office of the superintendent (the only person at the Board with his own office). When they came out, the superintendent invariably walked over and introduced Tsuruta-*san*, who stood almost at attention and spoke in extra-polite language. He then bowed as formally as I have ever seen him do so. Instead of just having his hands casually at his side, his fingers lightly touched the side of his pants, he bent his neck more and he held the bows longer than normal.

Tanaka-*san*, who sat behind me, was transferred to a kindergarten. She was a teacher before and was ecstatic to be back in the classroom. Both she and Tsuruta-*san* had their desks cleared out by "closing time" Monday but stayed until Tuesday afternoon to teach their replacements the ropes.

All day Monday and most of Tuesday, people from all over City Hall and other city offices toured the building introducing themselves to people in the various departments. I was impressed with how formal everything was. A group of people would enter our office and we would stand. The new group was then introduced by their boss. Each person in the new group would introduce themselves and say, "*Dozo yoroshiku, onegai shimasu.*" Then the new group would bow to us and we to them.

This time of year is tough on the teachers too. They cannot teach for more than 15 years in the same district and no more than 7 years at the same school, with all transfers effective April 1. Because Kazama-*sensei* has been teaching in Hondo for 15 years and at Kusuura-*chu* for 7 years, she had to leave the district. She has to teach in another district for three years before she can return to a Hondo school. She was told on March 26 where to report on April 1. Short notice is par for the course in the Japanese scheme of things, but I think it is pretty shabby treatment of a woman who has worked so hard for so long. On top of that, her daily commute went from five minutes to almost one hour each way.

I am sad about Kazama-*sensei*'s transfer. She is a competent teacher and, like most of the people I work with, she is thoroughly dedicated to her students' best interests. I will miss working with her because in a world of cookie-cutter, mass-produced personalities, she is an individual. It is as if she is living her entire life five minutes late and hurrying not to fall any farther behind. Even more endearing, is that she can focus on one thing to the exclusion of all else.

Driving with her is always an adventure. While stopped at a light, she was so engrossed in answering my question, she forgot she was behind the wheel. I could not get a word in edgewise to tell her the light was green. Then a quite extraordinary thing happened in this rural Japanese town. Drivers behind us gently tooted their horns. She apologized profusely to them as if they could actually hear her.

People walking in the road seem to sense her presence and make room for her. Others get off their bicycles when they see her approaching. She shifts gears according to the when-I-feel-like-it school of thought, often shifting for no apparent reason. When she does put the car in gear, she is as likely to shift into the wrong gear as the right one: for example, she likes to start out in second gear.

Another time she was talking away and edged a little too close to the oncoming traffic. After she crossed the center line, the cars on the other side simply slid over as far toward the painted line on the edge of the shoulderless road as they could without falling into the rice paddy two feet below.

We only socialized one time, when she was doing translation duties at a drinking party. When a high Pooh-Bah stood at the end of the night, he swayed, grabbed the pole on the side of the booth and continued to hold the pole as he slid sideways to the floor. He finally let go, landing belly up. I could barely contain a guffaw when she quickly whispered informatively to me that the man was drunk.

Akane was transferred too, but not to Kumamoto, her annual aspiration. She will take Kazama-*sensei*'s place at Kusuura-*chu*, where I will still teach with her. On Tuesday Kusuura-*chu*'s principal introduced his new teachers, including Akane. She said she is happy with the move. At Kusuura-*chu* she will teach only her favorite subject, English, and not double as the girls' gym teacher as she did before. For her sake I hope her transfer to Kumamoto happens someday soon, but I am happy it did not this year because teaching with her is so much fun.

During the rounds of meeting new people, I met the new teachers at other schools. Hondo's second biggest junior high, Hondo *higashi-chu* (Hondo East) replaced both of last year's English teachers. The two new teachers are Mori-*sensei* and Sasami-*sensei*. Mori-*sensei* is a man about my age who speaks English as well as Akane and Tahara-*sensei*. Sasami-*sensei* is a 24-year-old man whose English amazes me. After graduating from college in Japan, he studied English at the University of Washington. His English is now the best of all the teachers in Hondo, including Akane. He and I talked for 15 minutes. In that short time, I realized that I could drop the communication strategies I use with most Japanese speakers of English, such as avoiding idiomatic expressions.

I am happy that both Mori-*sensei* and Sasami-*sensei* say they want to schedule four or five classes each visit. The old teachers avoided classes with me like I was a leper. In Japan, when you want to complain about somebody, it is considered bad form to talk to the person directly. You are supposed to go to a third person who acts as an intermediary. In January I spoke at length to the old teachers directly, and it did not go well. So I resorted to the Japanese way. I told Tsuruta-*san* and Yokoyama-*san* that the teachers were not scheduling enough classes for me. They promised they would look into it.

On my second visit in February the teachers still only scheduled one class. While still at the school, I called the Board, as I was instructed to do. That afternoon the principal talked with the teachers at their desks.

I could not hear a word, but by their hangdog looks I could tell they were being politely but firmly chewed out. I hated to get the teachers into trouble, because I realize that while this is a career detour for me, this is their lives. I said something only because I believe the main purpose of the program is to familiarize the kids with *gaijin*. After seeing that the average rural Japanese reacts to us as somehow otherworldly, I could not agree more that Japan's youth needs to see more *gaijin* up close and personal. I cannot take part in that educational process in the teachers' room.

There is a new teacher at Saiitsu-*chu*, with its Zen-like raked driveway. Last year's English teacher was temporary. She was made permanent but at an elementary school in another city where she will teach social studies. The new Saiitsu-*chu* English teacher is a fresh graduate. She seems nice, but with typical English skills, which means we will communicate with difficulty.

During the introductions, Hondo-*chu*'s Tsuruda-*sensei* was introduced as the school's new head English teacher. After we talked for a few moments, he told me he was getting a headache from speaking English, which he had avoided doing over the break. At least he is honest.

On Tuesday I called Tahara-*sensei*, asking her to act as an interpreter for a meeting Rosemary and I wanted with Tsuruta-*san*, Tanaka-*san* and Funeshima-*san*. We wanted to say good-bye to them properly. The meeting took place in the Board's small conference room. Funeshima-*san* started to cry at Rosemary's words, and seeing that sent a trickle down Rosemary's cheek too. I went out to get tissues for them and when I set the box on the table, it set them both off again which started Tanaka-*san* crying too.

As we returned to the Board's large office, a short woman, whose head did not come up to my chest and who looked old enough to be the widow of the last shogun, was hawking fruit from a big wicker basket nearly half her size. In it were native pearlike fruits called *nashi* (na she). She cut one up and gave a taste to everyone. I wanted to buy only one, but she would not hear of it. She sold them three for 1,000 yen (about $8), which was a deal considering the prices at the stores. I was hesitating when she smiled broadly. Not having any teeth, her tongue fell partway out of her mouth, à la Michael Jordan going in for a dunk. I chuckled to myself how a short, wrinkled, old-as-the-hills fruit peddler could remind me of a tall, youthful basketball player. I took the whole thing as a sign of some sort and bought the fruit.

Later that day, the office's electricity went out. A coworker using the computer lost everything he had been working on. He said in English, "Oh no!" I said, "No, not 'Oh no!' 'Oh shit!'" He plucked his dress shirt and said quizzically, "Oh *shatsu*?" *Wai shatsu* (why sha tsu – Y-shirt) is what they call a dress shirt because the collar and the tie form a "Y." I said "Oh shit" again, this time doing an aw-shucks and snapping my fingers. "Oh shit" caught on throughout the office, although they pronounced it more like "oh sheet." Even the prim and proper old *OL* hung up the phone, snapped her fingers and said, "Oh sheet." We all about died, but it wasn't until just before I went home that someone looked up what it meant in the dictionary. He told everybody else what they had been saying. Yokoyama-*san* stood over me and used our "Shame, shame" gesture, saying "Ken-*san* ee zoo baa dough boy. Berry baa dough boy."

As I left the office across the street in the curb lane, next to a loudspeaker van, was a political candidate with a microphone blaring out political slogans. He wore a green headband, white gloves and bowed to the drivers as cars passed. If a politician did the same thing in the States, *somebody* would swerve into him. In the paper recently there was a picture showing a politician in a *sento* washing the back of an elderly man, trying to soft soap his high-brow image. I guess stumping Japanese style can mean literally you wash my back and I will wash yours.

There was an *enkai* on Friday for the people who had been transferred. It was the first one I actually looked forward to attending. It was a formal affair at a hotel. Men wore suits and women wore fashionable dresses. Everyone sat on the floor. The women were in a super-domestic mode.

A new woman named Matsumoto-*san* piled food on my plate. The other new woman, Matsuoka-*san*, in the *seiza* sitting position, bowed with her head almost touching the floor before pouring the beer. In Japan, no one pours their own beer. You are supposed to keep your eye on the other's glass and pour the beer into their half-empty glass. Unless that person really protests, the glass is filled. The nondrunks usually never touch their glasses unless asked to do a toast, because they know that as soon as two drops spill out of their cup, three more will be poured in. I kept my glass full of orange drink.

I had a lesson with *hashi* during the meal, learning how to pry the raw lobster meat out of the shell with them. I am amazed at the stuff I eat now: sushi, sashimi, you name it. There are some things I refuse to eat, such as one of Hondo's specialities, *taco* (ta ko – octopus), which tastes like rubber with tentacles. Other foods I eat only on condition that no one will tell me what it is until after I am done. The Japanese eat things from the ocean probably not even ocean dwellers eat. If it is slimy or clinging to a rock at the bottom of the ocean so tightly it has to be scraped off, you can bet there are millions of Japanese who will call it food, eat it, roll their eyes and say *oishii*! (oh e she – it is delicious!).

As the beer flowed, the "conversation" began in earnest. A coworker had a little too much to drink when he stopped by my table to chat. I could not understand him so he started to pantomime. He ended up hopping like a frog. I still have no clue what he was trying to say because he quickly stopped trying to "communicate" when three people at the table nearly spit out their food while laughing at him.

Tsuruta-*san* said he will miss working with me and that I am his first American friend. I told him the high regard I have for him and was taken aback when he started crying. Neither of us is likely to forget that moment.

We ended up going to the *nijikai*, where I relaxed my orange-drink rule, probably too much. Spouses were invited, and Tsuruta-*san*'s wife and I did a karaoke duet. After the *sanjikai*, I decided to pass on the *yonjikai* (yawn gee ka e – fourth party) as it was going on two in the morning. I went home in a *takushi*. The driver showed me business cards of other *gaijin* he has taken in his cab. He asked me whether I had one and was disappointed that I had none. He pestered me about it, until I told him to be quiet as I was concentrating on not tossing my cookies in his cab.

Today I went with a few ALTs to Kumamoto for *hanami* (ha na – flower; me – see). *Hanami* means seeing cherry trees in bloom. The cherry tree has a special place in the hearts of Japanese with practically every man, woman and child participating. During *hanami* Japanese find a place packed with cherry trees in blossom and picnic beneath them. People take *hanami* seriously and so does the media. The *hanami* season starts in Okinawa and every night the TV news broadcasts a cherry-tree-in-bloom map of Japan. The line inches northward daily until it reaches Hokkaido, Japan's equivalent of Alaska.

During *hanami,* the Kumamoto castle grounds are packed with people who have in some cases waited since the night before to spread their blankets on the wide paths separating the grassy areas. The trees were at their peak. When the wind blew, the blossoms floated like fluffy snowflakes to the ground in numbers resembling a gentle snowfall. The delicately colored pink snowflakes landed in the long black hair of the Japanese women, making the scene seem tranquil.

When there is something interesting to do in Japan, the crowds come out in such numbers that even the Japanese question whether it is worth it. I hate crowds but this one added atmosphere to the day. We sat in an area clearly reserved for college students. Being *gaijin*, we knew that if we acted cute (used English), we would not be asked to leave. In fact, they asked us to share their *picunicu* (pea coo knee coo – picnic).

The students asked the ever-popular I-just-met-a-*gaijin* questions. During the interrogation, two groups of Japanese tried to join us as there was enough room to seat them comfortably. They were politely yet firmly turned away. As they left, the students called them *baka* in hushed tones. Being *gaijin*, we were "cool." Sometimes it pays to be a *gaijin*.

Probably most Japanese go to *hanami* to appreciate the beauty of the cherry blossoms, but many view it more as a socially acceptable way to get plastered. In fact, eating and boozing are almost as big a part of *hanami* as are the trees. After all, the people who go after dark must go for a reason other than the cherry blossoms.

Never let it be said that once a *sarariiman* starts drinking, he knows his limit. During a trip to the rest room, I missed some excitement. A man in the group next to us tossed his cookies. A man next to that group pawed a woman, starting a fight. The groper was arrested but not before the woman sported a black eye, the result of an inadvertent roundhouse from her would-be knight in shining armor.

I will close for now. Tomorrow begins not just another new week but a new semester too. I am interested to see if traditional patterns hold true. I am told the transformation is amazing. Last month's wild seventh graders supposedly will be the less *genki* more serious and quieter eighth graders. March's eighth graders now are supposed to be April's grimly serious ninth graders. Bye.

*D*ear Frank,   April 17
          On Saturday I started a four-day weekend. (We ALTs still do not know why we had Monday and Tuesday off.) I rode my mountain bike to Aso-*san*, a round trip of about 300 kilometers (180 miles). The weatherman predicted four days of beautiful weather, but I knew better. I think the real meaning of the word "Japan"

is "Country where it rains darn near every day." It was no surprise to me to read that Japan's average annual precipitation is ranked second in the world after the Philippines. Of the four supposedly beautiful days, it rained one day all day and for parts of two more, which is about right for this country.

I started the first day by taking a little-used narrow road through a lush valley. The old men and women who make up Japan's farming population were out in force that day. The fields were flooded and the men pushed hand-held tiller like rice planters full of rice seedlings. The women followed behind the men to fill in the places the machine missed. They wore the same kind of bonnets the old women on construction crews wear.

As I plodded past their fields, farmers stopped to watch me. Probably few people use this road unless they live here, so I suspect the *gaijin* was a brief dinnertime topic in homes along my route.

There is no road so lonely that it does not have a vending machine. I was so thirsty a few times, I had a sports drink called Pocari Sweat, which is put out by Coke, the market share king in Japan. The name is unappealing, but the drink is not bad. The cost of pop in a vending machine on this lonely stretch of road is the same price you find in stores in the city. Another example of "cooperative pricing" (what would be called monopolistic practices anywhere else) among Japan's big corporations.

As the little-traveled road climbed into the mountains, I rose above the farmed terraced hills we associate with Japan. The fields shimmered with endless rows of plastic in the shape of one-foot high Quonset huts. Inside the plastic was some kind of green plants, maybe lettuce. With whole fields covered in plastic, it is no wonder food is so expensive.

After crossing the last small mountain, I bicycled along the sea and encountered tiring headwinds so strong I had to pedal going downhill! Passing one river I noticed the wind pushed the waves *upstream*.

I spent the evening at the home of the Kellys (the Australian couple) in Kumamoto. American TV programs and movies are popular with Australians, which is not necessarily good. Their impression is that nowhere in America is safe and we have to be vigilant every moment. I have been telling Japanese since the day I arrived that no, I do not own a gun, and no, no one I know owns a gun. They assume that every single American owns one and carries it at all times. I cracked it up to the Japanese tendency to believe without questioning what they are told in the media. But Australians think the same thing.

I left as the morning rain stopped. The weather was great so I rode in my T-shirt, ending up with a sunburn. With no wind, going straight up most of the day was not too bad. The Japanese drivers, especially the truck drivers, really impressed me with their road etiquette. As I chugged up the hill on the shoulderless main road, drivers were often stuck behind me. They pulled up a discreet distance behind me until the oncoming lane of traffic was clear. Their attitude makes riding a breeze.

Along the way, I was in a small store and asked how much longer it would be to the Aso-*san*. The elderly storekeeper, seeing my bicycle, replied "Forty minutes." Only in Japan, where the bike is a daily means of transportation for housewives and businessmen, could I expect the average person to know that answer.

I spent the night at Becky's, who was vacationing in Kyoto and who left the key under the mat. If she were here, she would not have let me stay at her place. As part of the "ingroup" in our small towns, we ALTs sometimes experience members of the community meddling in our personal lives. I have not felt that in Hondo, but Becky feels like she is almost under surveillance. One summer Sunday evening, she went to the store and bought yogurt and chocolate. The next day the principal summoned her to his office to say he was concerned she was not eating right. When she asked what he meant, he told her that she needed to buy better foods than yogurt and chocolate. Japanese are accustomed to superiors taking such an unwanted interest in their personal lives.

In another way, Becky's experience has been different from mine. She teaches at an agricultural high school where the English teachers have no intention of speaking English, not even to say hello in the morning. From her first day in school, when she barely had enough Japanese skills for survival, she was tossed into the classroom alone. Becky, who taught in Chicago, said students there listen better than these students. She attributes the difference in part to the fact that she works in an agricultural high school. The kids know that they need a diploma to have any kind of chance in life but that a diploma from their school will count for little.

She has picked up enough Japanese to run the class, but the kids talk constantly and there have even been fights. They make her feel that they need English as much as they need Latin or Sanskrit. While struggling to maintain order, she stumbled upon an effective punishment. She tells the offending student to stand outside the classroom. Being separated from the group or the threat of it is something Japanese teenagers want to avoid.

Not wanting to eat alone, I went to a restaurant. Even in this small town, the infusion of American culture is strong. Disney posters hang on the walls, the chef/waiter wears a Snoopy apron, and the wall calendar sports a picture of the Grand Tetons. In other ways this town is hardcore Japan. Most of the stores are mom-and-pop ones with the owner's house in the back. Service is delayed while the owner slowly makes his or her way from the house to the store in response to my call.

I crawled under the *kotatsu* because the night on the mountain was cool. While sitting there, I was desperate for English so I popped Becky's Jane Fonda workout tape into the VCR. (I was not desperate enough to get out from under the *kotatsu* to do the workout.)

The next day I intended to bike to the volcano's rim, but my legs argued against it. They suggested I save the view of the rim of the volcano for a time when I had the car. The rain and fog convinced me to head back a day early. The fog limited visibility to 100 yards. I was even more impressed with the Japanese drivers, especially the truck drivers on the narrow, busy, steep, downhill road. I felt almost no anxiety about being on the road with them. I again spent the night at the Kellys'.

The last day of the trip started at McDonald's for breakfast. It is a hard meal to eat out in Japan. Many Japanese still have the traditional breakfast of rice, soup and fish. Many others eat a light breakfast of white-bread toast and coffee or *ocha*. A growing minority are tending toward a Western-style breakfast, but nonfast-food restaurants seem to think breakfast ought to consist of a thick slice of white bread, a little bit of salad and an egg (which costs about $4).

I ordered hotcakes. The young lady behind the counter was obviously nervous being in the presence of a flesh-and-blood *gaijin*. She used her high school English to smooth the transaction, politely asking "What's wrong with you?" I took that to mean "Hi, welcome to McDonald's. May I take your order?" She said she would bring the hotcakes to my table when they were ready. At the table, she bowed and apologized for taking so long. Wait for *that* to happen at your neighborhood McDonald's! Two college women struck up a conversation with me. Believe it or not, they asked me if we have McDonald's in America. When I told them that it started in California, they could not believe it.

The next day I attended a meeting of the principals. During the speech given by the supervisor of the Board, I wondered how many would be put to sleep by his monotonous droning. He is pushing 75 and was, I understand, dragged out of retirement early last year to fill the position that had been mysteriously left open. (No one admits to any knowledge of why the last man left suddenly.) If the supervisor were to wear a beanie, a robe and I could teach him to say "Nomini Patris," I think he could do a passable imitation of the pope. Whenever I see him he smiles and, walking a little bent over, does that little up-and-down gesture with his hand in front of his chest as if he is blessing someone.

I wish he had blessed us with a short speech. Standing in the back with the rest of the peons I was bored stiff. I was fiddling with the coins in my pocket when one fell out. Only the truly bored in the back of the room (my coworkers) heard it drop. Watching the eyes of ten people following the coin's progress till it bumped into a shoe and seesawed to rest, I realized knowing Japanese made the man's speech no more interesting. We all smiled but the speech droned on so I continued to fight to keep my brain from crawling out of my ear to travel someplace more interesting.

My first day of classes was at Miyajidake-*chu*, which had an opening ceremony. Miyajidake-*chu* now has a grand total of 29 students. Nine seventh graders, nine eighth graders, and eleven ninth graders. Actually, the first day of classes was only sort of the first day of classes. The eighth and ninth graders underwent a battery of physical exams, such as eye exams. I only had one class with seventh graders.

It was their first ever English class. They already know 1,000 to 2,000 English words but just do not know that they know them. The class worked out well. Like teenagers everywhere, Japanese kids hate to be singled out in class. I knew their anxiety levels would be high when they were told that on the first day of class, without having cracked open the book, they were supposed to give Japanese equivalents for English words they had never heard before. It is exactly what I wanted. I intended them to think on the way home, "You know, I shouldn't have been nervous, I understood all of those words. Maybe English ain't so hard."

I must be on my way to being a real teacher because I see how easy it is to spot the bright, adventurous kids who have an almost visible sparkle in their eyes. I called on those students first. I began with words that are pronounced so much alike in both languages there is little room for confusion; for example, piano, guitar and kiss. Once they had the idea, I slipped in words that have slightly different pronunciations but are still really close – words such as sports car, ice cream and beer. The class turned out to be a piece of cake. I mean *keki* (kay key – cake); maybe *chizukeki* (chee zoo kay key – cheese cake); maybe *sutoroberi chizukeki*; or maybe *buruberi* (boo roo bay ree – blueberry) *chizukeki*.

On the third day of classes I was at Akane's new school. Class with her was, as always, more fun than work. Our first class was with the newly promoted eighth graders. I told the students, who know me better than they know Akane, that she is a mean teacher and would throw a chair at them if they did not behave. At Akane's old school her eighth-grade class had a couple of boys who were a little on the trouble-maker side of life. When I entered the class for the first time in September, the students stood and said hello to me. Then they said hello to Akane. I told the class, through Akane, that since this is English class, we should follow the American custom and should say hello to Akane first because she is a lady.

When Akane translated that, one of the boys said something that sent giggles through the class. I asked Akane to explain but she would not tell me. When I insisted, she told me the boy said that she was no lady. I pointed at the boy and ordered him to report to my desk in the teachers' room immediately after class. Akane told me about the boy before he showed up. His father had deserted the family long ago and although the boy is bright, he has bad study habits, a poor attitude and is the classroom leader of a small group of mischievous boys. Talking to him at my desk, he put on the hangdog look students here assume when on the spot. I tried to impress upon him that although his comment had been wrong and that he needs to keep such comments to himself, I know he is intelligent and I was looking forward to teaching him throughout the year.

My relationship with his group has never been good. They are all bright kids but unruly enough to be a distraction to the class. In fairness to them, keeping a tight rein on her class does not seem to be in Akane's nature. She is reluctant to use a teacher's inherent authority to which the kids are willing to respond. She thinks she is a rotten teacher and "The children know it." She had trouble at Hon machi-*chu* only with that one class. I told her that she is one Hondo's best teachers.

In the end, I decided to stay out of disciplining kids because of an impromptu round-table discussion with other ALTs. The consensus was that as only an occasional visitor to the class, it is not for me to discipline students. My best intentions lasted until January, when the boys were in rare form. I asked them several times to be quiet but they continued to make teaching and learning difficult. Finally I could take no more. I looked at the group and said in English that if any one of the boys said one more word I was going to drag him out past the playground to the steep embankment of the creek, toss him in and drag him back to his seat, where I would knock their heads together if they even breathed too loudly.

Akane did not translate. The boys sat a little straighter in their seats and looked for all the world like they realized their death sentence would be overturned only if they did not allow one more peep to pass their lips. Since that day, the boys were well behaved in classes with me. The next time Rosemary was at the school, the boys asked her how to say various versions of "I like Ken-*sensei* but Ken-*sensei* does not like me." Several days later, when neither Rosemary nor I were at school, the boys returned to their usual behavior. They paid no attention to Akane and disrupted the other students. Out of frustration, Akane picked up a chair and threw it in their direction. Later she felt terrible about it. I ribbed her saying that by demanding more discipline I meant she should use stern words, not toss chairs. Akane translated my warning to her new students about flying objects by telling them that I think they have a pretty teacher. I raised my eyebrow.

We started the planned lesson teaching "this is my. . ." sentence structure. I looked quizzically at the textbook Akane was holding. I said, "This is my book," snatching the book from Akane's hand. She took it back, saying "No, this is my book." I said I was sorry, scanned the class, and with a look as if I had spotted something, walked over to a student who looked as if she could stand being put on the spot, grabbed her book and said, "This is my book." She took the book in both hands and said the magic words while trying to tug it out of my hands. I gave her the book and led the class in applause. By this time, the whisper grapevine was explaining the point of the lesson to those students who did not understand yet. As Akane wrote the sentence structure on the board, I was happy with how we had conveyed a concept to the kids just by using English and playacting.

After that class I had a free period, and while I was walking down the hall on my way to the rest room, I passed the classroom of the new seventh graders. The whole class stopped to stare at me. As the lesson had come to a total standstill, I introduced myself. (Only sliding windows, which were open, separate the classroom from the hallway.) After I had continued on, I heard a couple *sugoi* (sue goee). *Sugoi* means awful, but in this context, it means more like "Wow, it's not every day you meet a *gaijin* in the flesh." (*Sugoi* is used much like we use the word awful: "This steak is awfully good.")

I decided to have lunch in the classroom with those kids, as I was not going to have a class with them that day, and I figured the sooner they lost that Japanese awe of the *gaijin* the better. During lunch, they asked so many questions about me and America I barely had time to eat.

They also asked me to sing a song. I chose "O' Canada," which I had learned growing up in Detroit watching Hockey Night in Canada. I told them they had to sing the "O' Canada" parts and I sang the rest.

After lunch I went to the gym to shoot some hoops. Eight girls followed me while peppering me with questions in Japanese (to which I responded in English). As a group they deciphered my answers and in that way had an extra, real-life, English lesson. In the gym the school's newest students studied my shooting style and did their best to emulate me. I figure I set back the Japanese Olympic efforts in basketball at least a couple of decades.

So far, the new semester has been much more fun than the last. I am really beginning to regret I have so few months left as Ken-*sensei*. Write soon.

*D*ear Uncle Chet and Aunt Dottie,   May 9

Gorudan uiku (go roo dan – golden; ooh e coo – week) is a two-week period at the end of April and beginning of May when there are four closely spaced holidays. There is a Japanese name, but most refer to it by the English term, as if even the concept of relaxing and taking it easy is foreign enough that foreign words are needed to express the idea. Although *sarariiman* accrue vacation time as we do, most companies do not let them take it when it suits them, but when it suits the company. *Gorudan uiku* is one of the few times during the year *sarariiman* can use vacation time. As did many others, I strung together days off to end up with nearly a two-week vacation.

The first of the holidays falls on my birthday, April 29. It originally was a national holiday because it was Emperor Hirohito's birthday. (The current emperor's December birthday is a holiday.) Since Hirohito died, rather than give up a day off, they celebrate it as Greenery Day, because Hirohito was supposedly such a lover of nature. Another of the holidays is Constitution Day, commemorating the adoption of the constitution. I have no idea what the last two holidays are and have no inclination to ask anybody – what's life without a little mystery?

I traveled with Andy to visit Mie in her hometown, Izumo,

which is along the Sea of Japan, then went to Kyoto. I picked up Andy at the port at Kuratake. I made it there at 6 P.M. on a Friday, about the time elementary and junior high school kids are coming home. Near the port children walked toward me on the narrow road. With oncoming traffic, I stopped to let the other driver and the kids figure out what they were going to do. The other driver kept coming. On my right there must have been two or three inches clearance between the cars. On my left the kids scrunched up between my car and the wall and kept moving, with their chests scraping the wall and their butts polishing my car.

The next stop after picking Andy up was the house of Steve Armstrong, a Canadian ALT, to pick up a new batch of videotapes. Steve has the redeeming quality of liking *Star Trek*. He has the further redeeming quality of having parents who send him periodic care packages of *Star Trek* tapes. Andy and I spent the first night with the Ryes. Whenever I visit there I can count on getting to bed no earlier than 1 A.M. and that night was no exception.

The next morning we left for Izumo, where we stayed with Cynthia, an ALT from Texas. Andy was still officially *persona nonexisto* as far as Mie's mom was concerned. As soon as we arrived in Izumo, Andy disappeared with Mie. During the day I did some sightseeing and in the evening watched the first *Star Trek* tape, all six hours, with Cynthia. It was great to watch them with a fellow *esu efu* (a sue a foo – S.F., or science fiction) junkie. The next day followed the same pattern.

The third day Mie finally said "Yes!" and brought the *gaijin* home. Her mom asked Andy, born and raised in Georgia, "If there is another war between Japan and America, which side would you be on?" His answer? "The South!" They were thrown out of the house. Mie thinks her mother eventually will come around. The sad part is that the question was not a surprise to Andy. It shows how insular the Japanese are, reflecting the Japanese feeling that Japan is home and the rest of the world is a big scary unknown.

Andy and Mie celebrated their engagement that evening. Cynthia and I joined the festivities along with Mie's friends. At 2 A.M. I was at the counter asking the bartender to change the music when I felt warm breath on my neck and something on my left shoulder.

I looked around and two inches away were two big brown eyes and a pair of red lips surrounded by flowing black hair. I had been briefed by the experienced bar-hopping ALT males to speak English upon meeting a woman in a bar. I said, "Hi." She said, "Ha row." "I am Ken. What is your name?" "My name is Ai," which means "love." I took a good look at "Ai." She is undeniably cute. She is also undeniably a teenager.

I went to Ai's table, where two of her classmates were swaying in their seats. I called Cynthia over; she recognized Ai as one of her high school students. Her name really is Ai. We put the kids in the cab and told the driver to take them home.

Although the legal drinking age is 20, high school girls love to go to bars, and they are served alcohol because their IDs are not checked. Japanese men enjoy their company and pay for drinks. It is an open "secret" that bar owners look the other way. Why the police do so, I have no idea.

A day later I left on my solo trip to Kyoto. Arriving in the evening, I went to Reiko's house, where I stayed. I had heard that the average Japanese does not invite anyone but family and close friends to the house because space is so tight. My treatment by this family goes against those "myths."

Her mother introduced me to the grandparents, who now live there too. Shortly after I arrived, Reiko's mom joined the apron-clad neighborhood women picking out vegetables at the tiny vegetable store one block away and the grandparents went for a predinner walk. Two nicely dressed salesmen stepped into the *genkan* and announced themselves by saying "*sumimasen.*" A *gaijin* answering the door should have rattled their sales pitch. I "pretended" not to be able to speak Japanese (which does not take too much effort). I understood enough, however, to know they were actually Jehovah's Witnesses. They gave up with hardly a struggle in face of the *gaijin*, who was not ever going to understand their point.

During my several-day stay, I was never sure when the grandparents would catch me with my pants down. I was in the rest room when the hard-of-hearing grandpa asked if Kosuke (the oldest boy) was there. Unfortunately, the light switch is on the outside of the rest room. Not hearing my shouts, he turned the light off.

A day later I was taking a shower in the bathroom, which is in a separate room from the toilet. The bathroom consists of two rooms. The one just off the hall has the sink and washing machine and the one next to that is where the bath is. There is no lock on the sliding door that separates the sink/laundry room from the hall or the sink/laundry room from the bathing area. (In fact, the only room in the house with a lock, as with my house in Hondo, is the toilet.)

After bathing one dries off and dresses in the sink/laundry room. I dropped my towel to dress when Grandma asked if anyone was in the room as she opened the door. Grandma's hearing is worse than

Grandpa's, so my verbal response was mainly for my benefit. I just managed to position a fig leaf as she looked into the room.

In spite of these things I like the grandparents and they tolerated my presence. Grandma often talked to me and to my response she would reply "*Wakarimasen.*" Then she would ask me something else and I would answer. She would say again "*Wakarimasen*" and that usually ended the conversation. This noncommunication would not have been so bad, but, with her bad hearing and my bad Japanese, I ended up shouting incomprehensible Japanese for the neighbors to hear.

I never had a clue about the grandfather's Japanese. He mumbles rapid-fire old Japanese words and jabbered away as if I understood. He understood my Japanese if I spoke slowly and loudly. My last day, he tried using English. I gave up my seat for Grandma and Grandpa said, "I love you." Everyone stared at him and he said, "Doesn't that mean thank you?"

Grandpa adds humor to the house in other ways. One evening the youngest son was listening to some Bob Dylan tapes and I "played" the air guitar. They had never heard of it. It took awhile to explain in Japanese. Finally Grandpa understood and played the air violin, asking "Am I any good?"

At the dinner table, he continually puts the wrong sauces on the wrong foods and when someone tries to stop him he insists on doing just what he wants. Even Grandma laughs at him. I do not know what he is doing wrong as the sauces baffle me too. I assume he does the equivalent of putting ketchup in his coffee, because he leaves everyone in stitches.

We had fish (complete with the head and tail) almost every dinner. Watching Grandpa, I was reminded of a cat in a cartoon picking up a fish, sticking it in its mouth and daintily pulling out the complete skeleton. Grandpa picks up the whole fish with his *hashi*. After the first bite, the head is gone. With the last bite, the tail disappears forever. He eats the bones and all, although once he left a picked-clean spine. Following the others' lead, I used *hashi* to separate the meat from the bones.

He finishes the meal with a greenish-brown local delicacy consisting of superthin seaweed strips mixed with raw egg and soy sauce. He picks up the seaweed with *hashi* and, with the bowl almost to his lips, sucks the oozy gunk. He offered this to me, but I think I will never be quite that hungry.

The rest of the family finishes their meal with a dish called *ochazuke* (o cha zoo kay). It is a small bowl of rice that is mixed with *ocha*. You eat (drink?) it by bringing the bowl to your mouth and suck it in while shoveling with the *hashi*.

Many Japanese dishes are served in a big bowl in the middle of the table. Everyone uses their *hashi* to retrieve the food. In restaurants, one is to use the blunt end to put into the communal bowl. At home, the narrow "eating end" can be put in the bowl, maybe another reason guests are rare. In eating from communal bowls, Reiko's family is typical.

The two boys used their *hashi* to feed Chibi (chee be), the family dog, who sits on their laps. I kept track of who fed Chibi and what dishes they stuck their *hashi* into so I could avoid those bowls.

I had heard that the Japanese do not have pets because space is limited. Pets abound! There are zillions of cats (many without tails – the cropped-tail look is definitely in) and dogs (they all seem to be under 20 pounds). If you walk in the morning or evening practically anywhere in Japan, you will see someone walking his dog, ready to scoop up any present it tries to leave behind.

I had heard that pets were treated much worse than in the States, but Chibi is pampered. In some respects, she receives treatment I have never seen in the States. Before entering the house from the postage-stamp-size "garden," she gets her feet washed.

I am jealous of Chibi. When Reiko's mom shouted out, "*Gohan desu yo* (go han dess yo)," I wondered what that meant as it literally translates into: "It's rice!" Chibi, however, would blast off toward the table to take up a begging position. Now I know it is the Japanese version of "Supper's ready!" or "Come and get it!" Kosuke hollered while looking out the window. Everybody, including Chibi, looked. I, however, was searching in my dictionary for the meaning of "*Hora mite!*" (hoe rah me tay – hey, look!).

A Far Side cartoon had a dog and a person in it. The caption said something like, "WHAT WE SAY: Fifi, you are a bad dog. I have told you before Fifi not to do that Fifi and you still do it Fifi. Fifi is a bad dog." "WHAT THEY HEAR: *Fifi* kjd lkfji *Fifi* knfo itj *Fifi* kldf ioawk *Fifi* lkdjj iojjk." I know what Fifi feels like. In my conversations in Japanese, I hear "*Ken-san* kjkl oiu asd knsdu n;akdfjpu kljopdiu eat; *Ken-san* lkdfoipn hamburger?" To which I say yes and hope for the best. When I look at Chibi, I do so with envy because I have to admit she knows more Japanese than me.

Leaving Chibi at home, Reiko, her mom and I went to a "country western" bar, which is a *raibu hausu* (lie boo how sue – live house where live music is performed). After the first set, band members sat at our table. When the band went up for the second set, the band leader asked me to sing my request: the "Tennessee Waltz." I was not about to go up.

The drummer slapped his drumsticks together and soon half the audience picked up his "Mr. Ken" chant. The Japanese have the habit of using "Mr." or "Miss" in the same way as their word "*San.*" So when they speak English they say Mr. Ken or Ken Teacher.

Reiko's mom encouraged me and volunteered to sing with me. I gave in. She did a fine job as that song is one of her favorites. I stumbled over the words and floated from verse to verse realizing the music often left before I got to the words. I also added versatility to the song by changing the keys at times. As painful as the experience had to be for the audience, it was worse for me. I was ready to quit but they asked me to do a solo on the next song, "Jambalaya." I then had an interview with the band leader in Japanese, which resulted in yet another way to publicly humiliate myself.

The audience's capacity for truly god-awful singing was not satiated because later they asked me to sing again. I refused and again the audience chanted. I sang "I Can't Help Falling in Love." You know you are not musically gifted when the woman you are with grabs her stomach and doubles over with laughter while you are in the middle of what is supposed to be a tender love song.

Most of the band's songs were in what passes for English here. It is possible to listen to a song by a native English speaker and not understand all the words. For years I thought the Beatles sang "Lucy in disguise with diamonds." Even considering the muffled and slurred lyrics of some songs, this band's English pronunciations cannot be favorable compared with my skill as a singer. Reiko's mother asked me the name of a song, and it was then I realized the song was in English. For example, the band leader said they were going to play a couple "Bruce" songs, what you and I would call the blues. In spite of all that, listening to them was fun. I admired their effort to sing with emotion in a language so different from their own.

The next day Reiko and I went to a Tigers' baseball game. Baseball may be America's pastime, but it is Japan's passion. Even the national high school baseball championship tournament is televised. Homes and offices all over Japan are tuned into the spectacle for the several days it takes to decide the champion.

Reiko's team is the Hanshin Tigers, which is owned by the Hanshin Corporation. It also owns a department store chain and a railway and probably other stuff that they have not told me about yet.

It was a holiday so we reached the ballpark at eleven for a six o'clock game. We bought lunch and sat down in the box office line that already stretched 100 yards. I brought my Japanese books to study, and Reiko brought a book. An hour later a false rumor that the ticket window had opened caused a stampede reminiscent of a Godzilla movie.

The result was that the neat orderly line was now a crowd of people bunched up near and milling around the ticket window. I had never seen the Japanese exhibit such herd behavior before. I had assumed that everything would be conducted in a polite way. I walked to a point in the new "line" where I figured I would have been if there had been no stampede and stepped in line. My new neighbors were not thrilled, but in true Japanese fashion, they said nothing. When the ticket window opened, there was another stampede, resulting in the line being compacted to sardine proportions. I tried backing out of the line but that was harder than making it to the ticket window.

After I bought the tickets we made our way to the nearest entrance, which Reiko explained was the wrong one. Unwilling to fight the crowd to get to the right one, I employed a *gaijin* tactic. Reiko stayed back as I went to the entrance and handed the man my ticket. He said in Japanese that I was at the wrong gate. I told him in English that I would not go through the crowd. He repeatedly explained in Japanese that I was at the wrong entrance and I kept telling him in English that this was the entrance I was going through. Finally he waved me in. Reiko ran up and as he tried to stop her, I said in English that it was okay because she was with me. I grabbed her and pulled her with me. He gave up. *Gaijin* sometimes can get away with that sort of thing here, and I am not above employing such tactics.

The game would not start for several hours, but it was a nice day and the afternoon passed quickly with a mixture of conversation and studying. The game was interesting, with the overall experience nothing like watching a *dai ligu gemu* (die ree goo gay moo – literally, a big-league game), which is what they call our major leagues.

We sat in a section filled with fans of the opposing team, the Tokyo Giants. Each team has fan clubs whose members come to the game with trumpets and drums. They noisily lead cheers while their team is batting. I had the pleasure of sitting next to the two fans who had the trumpets – oh joy! The fans yelled the whole game. A large sign prohibited the "wave." Reiko did not know why. I tried to start a wave but she refused because the sign prohibited it. I did a wave by myself a couple of times but with 55,000 people not joining in, it is just not the same.

The team has two *gaijin*, the most that is permitted on the field at any one time for one team. The rule is based on a world outlook similar to one America is rejecting: We do not want the best, we want the best of "our kind."

One of the *gaijin* on the team can hit the ball a ton. Whenever he was at bat, someone a couple sections over waved a giant American flag. Flag waving is a big deal at Japanese baseball games. Diehard fans waved flags of both teams.

In the first inning, the Giants' pitcher was charged with a *wairudo piichi* (wa e roo dough pee chee – wild pitch), and later in the inning someone hit a *homu ranu* (hoe mu rah new – home run). Another player hit a *suree besu hito* (sueree baysue he toe – three base hit, or triple). The game ended with one out in the bottom of the ninth when the Tigers' starting pitcher hit a *sayonara homu ranu*.

The difference I lamented the most about the ballgame experience was no hot dogs! Who ever heard of such a thing? I could buy all the grilled octopus on a stick I wanted, and there was no shortage of fried buckwheat noodles sauteed in soy sauce, but a simple baseball prerequisite like a hot dog was not to be found. Boy, is this a foreign country or what?

Leaving Kyoto, I traveled through Shikoku, the smallest of Japan's four main islands. I had to wait five hours for the 20-minute ferry ride. Why these people do not clamor for better roads and an occasional bridge is beyond me. To drive from one end of Shikoku to the other, a distance of less than 200 miles, took me about one hour longer than it took me to fly from L.A. to Tokyo. I would turn my car off, write in my journal, start the car, move 25 to 30 feet, turn the car off, write . . .

At one point, I left my car in the middle of the road, walked to the gas station at the corner, used the rest room, then went to the convenience store, bought a pop and returned to my car. It was fortunate I returned when I did because within five minutes I had to move another couple hundred feet. Vendors came by selling noodles and other Japanese delicacies. This continued for two hours. The traffic finally started to move along at 20 kph, or about 12 mph.

On the trip's last night, I stayed at Kevin's place near Aso-*san*. This is his third year so he is quite settled into the lifestyle. His dog, whom he brought from the States, has a name that neither he nor the dog is likely to forget; "Come boy."

His house was packed with ALTs traveling home. There were two English women, Debbie and Fran. Brent and Trevor, like me, unexpectedly showed up asking for lodgings. By choice, Kevin lives in a "traditional" Japanese house. "Traditional" means one without a flush toilet, just an eight-inch by two-foot hole in the floor, which, when not in use, is covered with a piece of plastic. There is no hot water in the house so we would have had to boil water for six baths. We decided to go to an *onsen*.

Fran did not want to go to the coed *onsen*, which is the best one in the area, so we agreed to find a suitable one. While I was soaking in the *onsen*, Japanese females aged from 5 to 90 came into the men's section, looked around and then left. The Japanese men did not seem to think it was anything unusual. Back at the house, we talked until 1:30 A.M. Fran then went into the next room, stood just inside the doorway without closing the door, and with her her back to us, stripped and put her PJs on. It is times like that which make me certain of one thing: I will never understand women.

When I returned home the next day, Father Carroll, the local priest, called and we met for dinner. Arriving in 1962, the padre is part of the living history of Japan. After dinner we retired to the rectory, where he served homemade brandy.

He lived in Tokyo his first two years. Before Tokyo's '64 Olympics the subways were not air-conditioned. To cool off in the stifling summer heat the *sarariiman* would take off their pants on the subway after work. Men in shirt and tie stood in car after car stripped to their shorts, with their pants neatly folded on the overhead racks. For the '64 Olympics, with the first influx of *gaijin* expected in over 300 years (MacArthur's army of occupation excepted), signs were put up in the subways politely suggesting that men should not take their pants off!!

The sad part of the padre's story was that of the 150,000 people who live on the islands in this area, his congregation has 90 people on the books. Thirty show up regularly, 30 infrequently, and 30 hardly ever. He has gone back to the States only periodically and knows few people there now. When he retires he is not sure that he will go back to the States, although, in true Japanese spirit, he still feels like an outsider here. Loving God does not mean your life will not be lonely.

But having a family is no greater guarantee. As I write this, it is almost two weeks since Andy and Mie told her mom about their engagement, and Mie's mom still is not speaking to her. Bye for now.

*D*ear Dad, May 20

This weekend I went to the hometown of one of the teachers. It is in Kitakyushu, a large city on the northwest side of Kyushu. I left the day before he could so we met in the city. On Thursday night I drove to Kumamoto to catch the train on Friday because it does not come as far as Hondo. On Friday I threw my backpack on and walked to the trolley line that took me to Kumamoto *eki* (a key – station).

Japan has trains of all sorts and descriptions, but the features they all have in common are: They are electric, clean, and on time (to the point where I think the train companies hire only obsessively anal retentive employees). The most well-known train is the *shinkansen* (sheen khan sen), which our press calls the Bullet Train. There are a few Japanese words that *gaijin* (including those who have no interest in learning Japanese) incorporate into their vocabulary even when speaking English with another native English speaker. *Genki* is probably the most widely used, but *shinkansen* is always used too; no one ever refers to the "Bullet Train." I do not know why. I do know, however, that the train itself is fast, dependable and runs more often than bus lines in the States. It costs considerably more than the regular trains, but *gaijin* who are just visiting here can buy a two-week pass that is a great deal if you are going to do a lot of traveling. It is certainly one of the great trains of the world. If you want to get from door to door in entirely different parts of the country, it is almost as fast as air travel, and almost as expensive.

The trains below the *shinkansen* are the *tokkyu* (toe cue – limited express because it has limited stops); the *kyuko* (cue ko – express, which has more stops); and the *futsu densha* (foo tsu den sha – regular train), the "milk run," which stops at every station. Whenever a train comes the other way on a one-track section, the *futsu densha* is shunted off to the side until the faster train passes. You can travel cross country on the *futsu densha*, but only if you have a whole lot more time than money. They have a ticket called the *jyuhachi kippu* (jew ha chee key poo) that allows you to use the *futsu densha* all day long for about $20.

Taking the *futsu densha* on long trips is ordinarily not for *gaijin* because we are not well versed in Japanese train schedules. I took one with the teacher's help. He assembled the train schedules for all of the trains I would be needing and spent time at work poring over the schedules to come up with the most efficient route and schedule for me to take.

When I arrived at Kumamoto *eki*, the train was waiting but was already so crowded I could not find a seat. Part of the problem was the train strike for the area surrounding Kumamoto. Strikes are a little different from ours. When the union cannot come to an agreement with the company, the two sides negotiate to decide when a strike would be most convenient for both sides. Strikes take the form of well-publicized half-day or one-day work slowdowns, not stoppages. This seems totally screwy until you know one more fact. The president of the railway union (like the president of the auto union, like the president of the construction union) is always taken from company management and usually goes back to the company in a few years to assume a high position in it. So management is negotiating for the workers with the management. This is a totally Japanese concept: The guys at the top are supposed to be looking out for everyone's best interest. The theory is that they can be trusted to do their job fairly, even though the man negotiating for the workers someday wants to be the company chairman. It does not take a genius to realize that he is not only willing to cave in, he probably suggests ways to do it. No wonder workers here always get the short end. They are told their system is a better one than ours but why they believe it, I cannot understand.

This brings me to a subject that causes me to temporarily shunt my main story to the side track for a minute. They are told the company treats workers like "family." It sounds great, but the workers are the children in this family, with practically the same rights a child has in any family: The parents hold the purse strings with veto power over everything.

Many new workers must live in company dorms. Women with college degrees are often just *OL*. The women who make it to management have to quit by their late 20s to do the proper thing of raising a family, only to come back on a part-time basis in their late 30s as *OL*. The demands of this society do not stop with the women. If a *sarariiman* is not married by his early 30s, he feels the pressure from the higher-ups to follow the "Japanese way" of finding a wife and raising a family. An unmarried man in his mid-30s will find promotions harder to come by than a married peer.

Even their vaunted "lifetime" security is a double-edged sword.

They can see its lethal point, but they cannot feel the blade in their flesh. *Sarariiman* are pressured to succeed or be trampled by others in the company in the race to the top. If a Japanese man hates his job, he has a lifetime to hate it. Big Japanese companies usually do not hire laterally; they start workers right out of college or not at all. If the boss makes totally unreasonable demands, a *sarariiman* cannot say "Take this job and shove it." The *sarariiman* know it would be hard to find a job with another company in a society where you are expected to stay until you retire. They must do what they are told when they are told and do it with a smile. If not, they will experience the saying here: The nail that sticks up gets hammered down.

Culturally they are conditioned to prefer staying with the same company. Because of the importance of group affiliation, a *sarariiman*'s feeling of self-worth is bound up in the prestige of his company's name to a much greater extent than the company we work for gives us a feeling of self-importance. Even if a *sarariiman* could get a better-paying job with a tiny company, most would not leave the security and social status of the big one. It is that important to them.

I bring all this up to explain an incident I saw as I stood on the train with my fellow passengers who were packed in with me wall to wall. I felt sorry for the guys in suits around me. To them the strike is just another cost of being Japanese. Its biggest "impact" on me of the strike was actually on the several people around me who I wiped out with my backpack whenever I moved.

My train was bad, but another train pulling out of the station was worse. As its doors closed, a young *sarariiman* jumped onto the train. He could not quite get his whole body inside the doors and they would not shut. The man in charge of the *homu* (hoe moo – derived from "platform") motioned for the *sarariiman* to get off, but he refused. Perhaps he took the unusual posture of defying the authority figure because he was more terrified of not getting to were he was going on time.

The train worker pushed the young man farther into the train, wearing white gloves expressly for this purpose. It looked like the effort worked because the doors closed but the young man panicked. He was visibly agitated while pointing at the *homu*. Somehow his wallet had fallen out of his suitcoat. By this time the engineer was leaning out of the window, upset that he was being put behind schedule (and perhaps wondering whether he could explain the delay to his superiors). In what was a humanitarian act not appreciated by the casual tourist, he opened the doors again. The train worker who pushed the *sarariiman* in handed him the wallet, pushed him again and the doors closed.

The train started immediately. There were giggles from my train. The *sarariiman* was on the train, complete with his wallet, but somehow his tie ended up sticking outside, waving like a flag. To add insult to injury, the man's cheek was squished up again the window. It made me realize that while I am enjoying my time here, I am happy I am just a visitor.

I left Kumamoto at 8:03 A.M. on the *futsu densha* and was scheduled to arrive at 4:30 P.M. For the first two stops, a young woman's rear end was schmouched into my thigh by the crush of the crowd. She apologized profusely. I would have moved, but I could not. Just a little bit of dehumanization an *OL* must endure on her way to work.

Later in the trip I found a seat and then created a little excitement for myself. I know the train makes only quick stops at each station, but I was hungry and wanted to buy a candy bar at the *baiten* (buy ten – sales stand) on the *homu*. The station was in a big city where I thought the train would stop for at least five minutes. The woman next to me agreed to save my seat. (There is no reserved seating.) She looked confused, but I get that a lot when I speak Japanese so I paid no attention to it.

As I was deciding whether to buy another candy bar I heard the signal that the train was leaving. I grabbed my change in time to see the doors closing. As the train slowly pulled out, the conductor stuck his head out of the last compartment of the train. Slowing shaking his head, a how-stupid-can-you-be smile crossed his face as I told him I had luggage on board.

The platform attendant came over and, for a Japanese talking to a *gaijin*, he gave me an uncharacteristically strict lecture about jumping off a train on a two-minute stop to buy a candy bar. As I thought "Who do you think you are talking to?" it occurred to me that who he was talking to was a grown man holding a candy bar trying to explain that his backpack, including his laptop computer, was on a trip without him. Upon reflection, I humbly let him chew me out. After all, if he wants to take on the task of making me less stupid, good luck.

When his finger stopped wagging, it dialed the number to the next station. There I was reunited with my intact backpack. I was never too worried about it disappearing. Umbrellas are gone the second you turn around, bicycles ride away if left unlocked, but let a Japanese find a wallet with $1,000 and your name in it and you stand a good chance of seeing it again. When they get to be company presidents or politicians, they are probably less trusty than an Arizona governor, but at the personal level, where my backpack was concerned, they are very honest. My trip went well after I was reunited with my bags.

The teacher's dad has been a chemical engineer with the same company since 1969. He was transferred two years ago to another prefecture three hours away by car. It is part of the price one sometimes pays as a *sarariiman*. He lives in a company dorm Monday through Friday. Every Friday night he arrives home at about 9 P.M.; every Monday morning he leaves by 5 A.M. There is no end in sight to the forced separation.

The family cannot move to his new assignment for two reasons. The first is the emphasis Japanese families place on education. The youngest boy is in a good high school, which, as you know, gives him a decent shot at a good college, which gives him a shot as a *sarariiman* with a prestigious company.

The second reason is the cost of housing. Selling their house would be hard and buying just as difficult. They say the total value of all the real property in Japan is four times the total of the real property in the States (which is 25 times bigger than Japan). The people in the office took delight in telling me that land in Tokyo on a street called the Ginza is so expensive, if you stack thirteen 10,000 yen notes (roughly equal in size and value to a $100 bill) on it, you have enough money to buy the land under the bills. Land is so expensive the Imperial Palace is said to be equal in value to all of Canada. I wonder if a Japanese had enough money to buy either, which he would buy.

My house was one month old when I moved in. Compared to similar houses in bigger cities, it is inexpensive, $54,000. In a practice not unusual, the land is owned by someone other than the homeowner. The land is a separate transaction, usually a long-term lease. To buy the land would add another $70,000 to the price.

When talking about land values, the gasps started as they turned my 1,800-square-foot Arizona house into *tsubo*. When I told them I sold it with its three bedrooms and pool for $130,000, one woman grabbed my arm and said, "Are you sure the price of your house included the land?" When I told her about the two fireplaces, she clasped her hands to her chest and sighed to the ceiling. For the rest of the afternoon, she blushed when people mimicked her gesture and sigh. My coworkers calculated that the house would cost $250,000 in Hondo, without the pool (which no one has here) and without the land. They estimate the house alone would cost $750,000 in Kumamoto and even more in Fukuoka. I have no idea how they value their houses if the price is not based on what a ready, willing and able buyer would pay for it. There are plenty of ready and willing buyers, but able?

The teacher's family home, which they acquired the way many do, from the parents, is that of a well-to-do family. It has five bedrooms (two of which are about the size of walk-in closets) with a toilet upstairs and downstairs. The house is 1,600 square feet, which would make it as big to a Japanese as a 3,000 square foot house is to us.

With houses valued so high and salaries comparable to what ours are in the States, it is hard for young couples to buy *mai homu* (ma e hoe moo – my home). The concept of people buying their own homes while they are young enough to enjoy them is perceived as a personal freedom because it frees them from living with the extended family. The average person finds it a *chyarenji* (cha ren gee – challenge) to afford a home.

Modest-looking houses in Japan can be worth several million dollars. The teacher's family house fits that category. It has no insulation and is heated, as is mine, primarily by *toyu stobu*. It has wall-mounted air-conditioning in the bedrooms and living rooms. I mean no disrespect to this fine family, but I wonder if the U.S. government would be sued if it provided welfare mothers with houses in northern climates without central heating or insulation.

Bye for now; write soon.

*D*ear Barb,   May 30

Since the 19th, when forecasters called for fair weather for one week, I have seen the sun twice. Sometimes it rains nonstop for days, sometimes it rains before I leave for work, sometimes it rains at night, but a day without rain in Japan is like not being in Japan. I learned that Japan has a "Rainy Season," which is supposed to start very soon. I called for reservations on the Ark.

I was at the Thursday-night conversation class tonight. Helping people who are motivated to learn is not the only reason I attend. Equally important is the fascinating and wide-ranging topics that are discussed.

Over the course of the year I have kept a journal of our topics. We have talked about the watershed event in Japanese history that occurred at about the same time as our Civil War. The period from the early 1600s to 1867 is known as the *Edo Jidai* (a dough – edo; gee die – period, after the shogun's city, Edo). During the *Edo Jidai* the shogun was a hereditary privilege of the Tokugawa family, whose members ruled Japan by giving orders to the emperor in Kyoto. The shogun was, in theory, nothing more than the emperor's highest-ranking general, but it was well understood the emperor reigned but did not rule. Toward the end of the *Edo Jidai*, the shogun was too weak to impose his will on the country and powerful families pulled his strings.

Behind-the-scenes string-pulling has a long history in Japan. Centuries ago, when the real power in government rested with the emperor, at times an emperor would "retire" so his successor could ascend to the throne and the "retired" emperor would rule more effectively freed from the daily pomp-and-circumstance rituals of office. Sometimes the emperor who ascended the throne after the previous emperor's "retirement" also "retired," so there were two "retired" emperors and one "ruling" emperor all jockeying for power. For much of Japan's history the apparent authority figure usually has not been the person in power.

According to the history books, in 1868 the emperor was "restored" to power. Although called the "Restoration," in fact, the clan leaders of the various families who brought down the shogun ruled the emperor from behind the scenes. The emperor moved from Kyoto to Edo, which was renamed Tokyo. His reign was named *Meiji* (may gee – bright government). The *Meiji* emperor reigned for so long (until 1912) and Japan underwent so many changes in his time, the whole period is known as the *Meiji Jidai*. The *Meiji* emperor is as famous to the Japanese as George Washington is to us, but the tradition of referring to the emperor only by the name of his reign is so strong, few Japanese can remember his name.

Japan's distant past still pervades its culture. The U.S. government decided against charging Hirohito as a war criminal because it could use him to ease the people's acceptance of the Occupation. MacArthur is sometimes called the best emperor Japan ever had. It is probably more accurate to call him Japan's only *gaijin* shogun.

The ideal is still to be the power behind the public authority figure, pulling the strings. People would rather be the man behind the scenes than the "front man," even if the "front man" is the prime minister. I wondered aloud who is running the country. After a short debate, most agreed that until his corruption scandal several years ago, it was a man called Kanemaru Shin, who was officially just another member of the legislature but unofficially the most powerful man in Japan. A few people thought that Mr. Kanemaru's strings had been pulled also, but by whom, no one could say.

The *Meiji Jidai* was a milestone for the Japanese people because they were freed from their feudal ties. For the first time the average Japanese was entitled to an elementary school education. No longer would education be the sole domain of the nobles, samurai and wealthy merchants. The first universities were formed at this time too.

It is also when the average Japanese were given last names. The *Meiji* government sent priests throughout the country handing out simple, descriptive names. Those living at the bottom of a mountain wound up with last names like Yamashita (*yama* – mountain; *shita* – bottom). Those living in a house surrounded by fields wound up with last names like Tanaka (*ta* – field; *naka* – middle).

Until that time, most people were not addressed with the honorific "*san*." Quite a difference from Japanese society today, which is much more formal than ours. Today people (oftentimes including intimate friends or spouses) are not addressed simply by their names, but with some sort of honorific. Most of the people in this group call me Ken-*sensei*. When I am outside the context of the schools I am called Ken-*san*.

More polite still is "Ken-*sama*," a more elevated form of "*san*"" Some of my female students call me Ken-*chan*. Because "*chan*" is reserved for close friends, it is totally inappropriate for my students to call me that. A couple of boys call me by the word reserved for young boys, "Ken-*kun* (coon)." I do not mind. The students are just being a little sassy by bending the rules, and I also think it means that I have reached them on a personal level. It is gratifying to walk up to school in the morning and leave in the afternoon with kids leaning out of the window shouting "hello" or "good-bye, Ken-*sensei*" or Ken-*kun* or Ken-*chan*.

One woman brought up her family's tragic history. In the 1930s the military government encouraged Japanese nationals to move to Manchuria on the Chinese mainland, which was controlled by the Japanese army. One woman in her 40s said that her father was stationed there. After the war he and several hundred thousand Japanese soldiers were captured by the Soviets and sent to Siberia for three years. Just after the war, her mother and older sister trudged through Manchuria for six months. She never met her older sister, because she died of malnutrition before her mother finished the trek to the port city. It was a terrifying time for Japanese civilians on mainland China; food was scarce and winter was coming on. The Chinese and Koreans hated the Japanese for the atrocities their armies had committed, and the fleeing Japanese civilians had to evade self-appointed justice seekers.

Tonight we talked about another country occupied by Japan: Taiwan. The Japanese believe the Taiwanese have less antagonism toward the Japanese than other Asian peoples. The Taiwanese were, according to the Japanese, more accepting of Japanese occupation and consequently were treated less harshly. Unlike the Koreans who lived through World War II and were forced to learn Japanese, the Taiwanese who lived through that period are willing to speak Japanese when a tourist asks them a question. One of the teachers visited Taiwan last December. She said Taiwanese people in their 60s still have a good command of spoken Japanese, but the young people cannot speak it. With them, she communicated in writing, as the *kanji* are close enough in both languages.

The Taiwanese were subjected to "corporal" language lessons. Wrong answers or ungrammatical Japanese were corrected by whacking the student on the wrist with a ruler. A teacher with whom I have language exchange classes quipped that he could not use that method because *his* arm would get too tired. So much for the myth that the Japanese do not understand sarcasm.

The teacher who vacationed in Taiwan also spent one year in the U.S. on a teachers' exchange program. She was surprised at the intensity of religious feeling in the States. Japan is considered a Buddhist country and everyone in the Thursday-night group considers themselves Buddhists. However, most Japanese have a poor understanding of the tenets of Buddhism beyond the concept of coming back as a bug if they are bad. Buddhism seems to be the religion they turn to for the forms of conduct in times of grief, such as death or sickness. The substance of Buddhism seems to have penetrated only lightly into the Japanese psyche.

Most people also say they adhere to *Shinto*. *Shinto* teaches the Japanese that they will all one day become minigods after they die. Most every Japanese home has a small *Shinto* shrine. When a family member dies, he has a place in the shrine through which he can be fed (the descendants set out his favorite food or drink) and communicated with (family members clap their hands together to wake up the spirit when standing before the shrine).

How people view this "communication" varies. Most seem to believe it is one-way, with the ancestor hearing about how the children or grandchildren are doing at school or how everyone is progressing at work. Others think a well-informed and well-tended ancestor can intercede in the lives of the living. One person said once he was crossing a street without noticing a car coming at him. His dead father's voice warned him of the approaching car and he scampered out of harm's way.

Shinto is the religion whose gods are called on to bless new tunnels, the sumo ring at the beginning of the national tournaments and even the pool at Saiitsu-*chu*. When the new semester began I was invited to join the principal, vice principal and head teacher at the pool. They carried sake and fish on trays. At each corner of the pool they placed a whole cooked fish (eyeballs included). They spilled some sake into the pool, closed their eyes and briefly held their hands in prayer. The principal then drank from the sake cup, passed it to the vice principal and so on down the ranks till it got to me. I declined.

I hate drinking from communal cups. I assume the reason for them is the symbolic coming together of the group, but I do not seek such spittle comradeship.

A seventh-grade class watching the ceremony from their classroom giggled at the *gaijin* when I refused the sake. I shrugged my shoulders. I would rather have the class giggle than be the last guy to drink from the cup. (No women were there; I wonder if the pool gods do not like them.) No one seemed to be sure of the ceremony's significance. One teacher suggested it warded off injury to the children. No one, however, knows why fish are placed at each corner of the pool, or why the sake is important. This I believe is typical of the Japanese religious experience. They know the forms of the ceremonies but not the reasons for them. The fact that people in a modern industrial society give offerings of food and drink to the gods that lurk about the edges of human society is as curious to me as it is a natural part of the fabric of society to them.

Another thing woven deeply into Japanese society is the concept that there is a place for all Japanese and each Japanese had better accept the place picked for him or her. We touched upon the place women have in this society. In many ways Japan seems to be about 30 years behind the U.S. Certainly its treatment of women is.

Under the constitution husband and wife have equal rights. Judges interpret the phrase "essential equality" to mean "almost" equal, but not quite. A couple tried to have a passport issued for their seven-year-old son. The passport was refused because the boy does not exist under Japanese law. He does not exist because he is not on the husband's family registry, a list in the prefectural office listing births. The boy is not on the registry because the woman gave birth to the boy within 300 days of her divorce from her previous husband. The woman had been estranged from her ex-husband long before the day her divorce became final. She was married to her current husband, the natural father, before the boy's birth. Under Japanese law a child born within 300 days of the woman's divorce is presumed to have been conceived during the prior marriage.

In another case, a couple is fighting a law that prohibits women from marrying for six months after the date of their divorce. Men can remarry without any waiting period. This couple was married the day after her divorce was final. The government officials refuse to accept the proof of the marriage for filing. The court upheld the waiting period law in spite of the antidiscrimination law, saying biological differences between men and women justified the law.

A Korean man married to a Japanese woman is suing to give his baby his last name. Japanese officials registered the baby with the wife's maiden name because Japanese citizens, which the baby is, may have only Japanese last names.

In the process of obtaining all the necessary documents from both the U.S. and Japanese governments, an American woman on the program discovered that non-Japanese women who marry Japanese men are prevented by law from officially assuming the family name of their Japanese husband. She was told she could only use her husband's name socially. As an alias!

Were she Japanese, the woman's name would appear on the family registry and something called a "residence certificate," which all Japanese have. Because she is not Japanese, it is against the law for her name to appear on either. She says the family registry accurately reflects that her husband is married, but the space for "wife" is blank. It appears the Japanese bureaucrats have found a way to make a wifeless husband.

A female police officer in Tokyo (one of Tokyo's 10,000 police officers) was on the force for ten years when she made the news for doing something which no other woman in Japanese history had done: drive the patrol car. Driving any kind of public vehicle in Japan is a man's job. I have seen only a few women taxi drivers and no female bus drivers. In the 1990s the government allowed the first small group of women into its military academy.

In sports, women are not permitted inside a sumo ring during open or closing ceremonies because the rings are "purified." A book on hiking in Japan advises that there are mountains from which women are banned. One religious sect strictly bans them from hiking to the summit of "their" mountain. Women who have taken the prohibition lightly have encountered the faithful's violent exception to women trying to hike to the top.

Their supposedly meritocratic college system helps to perpetuate inequality. Everyone agrees that on the typical four-year college campus, about 70 or 80 percent of the students are men. At the less prestigious two-year colleges, about 70 or 80 percent of the students are women. The specialty schools are similarly segregated by sex.

In typical Japanese double-think, they have a steadfast belief, based on what they are told, that admission to college is based solely on merit. At the same time, based on observation, they recognize that women stand a significantly smaller chance of acceptance to a four-year college. The ability of the Japanese to believe what is manifestly not true leaves me a little uneasy. I worry that through this ability they can be taught to believe anything that is manifestly not true.

With that our discussion class came to an end. The women grabbed the teacups and took them to the kitchen to wash while the men lit up cigarettes while waiting to close up the school.

Tomorrow evening I am going to Hong Kong. I received a call a few minutes ago from an ALT in Kumamoto who a had weekend trip there planned but came down with the flu and was desperate to dump his round-trip ticket. With that I will close this letter.

ear Lynea,   June 12
As you know, at the beginning of this month I went to Hong Kong. It was so hot and muggy – even the act of breathing was enough to cause a full brow of sweat.

I thought there would be a lot of English-speaking Chinese. Although that was the case 10 to 15 years ago, many people who could speak English left Hong Kong in advance of the Communists' arrival.

In the cab at the airport, I told the driver the name of my hotel. Unfortunately he knew as much English as I do astrophysics. After telling him several times where I wanted to go and after hearing in Chinese "I have no idea what you are talking about," I decided to get out. Sensing a warm body with money about to exit his taxi, he put it in gear and took off. Being a linguist is not high on the priority list for becoming a taxi driver in Hong Kong. I can testify, however, that it has a higher priority than driving skill.

I showed him the hotel's phone number. He said what could have meant "No thanks, I have a girl friend." I pointed to the two-way radio in the car and gestured my way through the scenario where he calls his base, they call the hotel, get directions, and call him back on the radio and I get out of the cab sometime before the meter shows an amount equal to our national debt to Japan. Fortunately I made it to the hotel while I still had enough money to pay for the fare.

The whole weekend I explored and shopped. While shopping I had little trouble communicating. English was the most helpful but sometimes I drew the *kanji* for the word I wanted to say. Once I talked with a store clerk in Japanese. Prices in Hong Kong are reasonable. I bought things that would cost twice as much in the States and several times as much in Japan. One of the things I bought was a Chinese visa for my trip home this August on the Trans-Siberian Railway (from Beijing to Moscow). I decided to take what money I have saved here and blow it on a once-in-a-lifetime trip across China, Mongolia and Russia.

Hong Kong is quite different from any city I have ever seen. It has given me a different perspective on Japan. The buildings downtown are beautiful and show the genius of world-class inspiration. They are vastly superior in appearance to all but a couple of buildings in Japan. The newer Japanese buildings that diverge from the poured-concrete style are usually square boxes covered by glass and some variation of stone.

Once I left Hong Kong's downtown area, however, the ugliness of the city smacked me in the face. There are often awful smells, probably from the garbage all over the streets. The buildings have every kind of mold and fungus happily propagating while clinging to the outside walls. That people have to live in them is an indictment of the government that rules the city, and the previous one too.

The people also seem desperately poor. Beggars are a frequent sight in shopping districts, and even hardworking people seem to make just enough to hang rags from their bodies. The oppressiveness of the poverty was moving. This is the city that is going to rebuild China?

I wonder whether the leaders of Japan looked at their Asian cousins long ago and decided that they were not interested in living under similar conditions. Perhaps that is why they created a nation that while lacking economically, governmentally and socially in many important aspects when viewed from a Western perspective is, when compared to other Asian countries, in virtually every way the Star of the Orient. I still think Japan's leaders are unfair to their people, but they give them back more than the people in Hong Kong receive.

Back in Japan this past Saturday, Andy and I went on a bike ride with no particular destination in mind. We took back roads until we started seeing signs for Miyajidake. Then we decided to stop by the school. As my life as Ken-*sensei* draws to a close, I find myself dragging out the days to soak up the last drops of enjoyment from my students. During the week, I stay at the schools until early evening talking with the students, studying or writing.

We rode alongside a small bustling river for quite a while as the road narrowed to about the size of a good bike path, but of course it was a road, with two-way traffic. Occasionally big trucks passed us. The woods closed in on the road as it became steep. It was very pretty. Once the trees opened and revealed a rice paddy on the side of the road down a steep embankment. With all the rain Japan gets, it is luxuriously green this time of year and the scene was not only beautiful, but, with all the bushes and flowers bursting out with the spring, aromatic. That is, until we stopped for directions. Not long after that rice paddy there was an intersection with no sign. We stopped to ask a farmer for directions who was leaning on his shovel in the bed of his small Japanese-style pickup (which are smaller than the Japanese pickups they sell in the States).

As I approached the smell told me he was ankle deep in cow manure. I can understand how things in life can turn out badly and that one might find oneself working ankle deep in cow manure. I think, however, that to light up a cigarette and casually stand in it during a break can only mean that all hope in life is gone.

We arrived at Miyajidake at 2 P.M. expecting to see some students and a few teachers. We saw the entire student body. The boys were in the gym playing volleyball against a team from Kawaura-*machi*. They warmly welcomed us and were especially impressed with Andy's beard.

I showed Andy around. Our first stop was the view from the homeroom of the ninth grade class. The principal stepped in. He recently returned from a three-week trip to America on an exchange program during which he visited schools in several states. Although he talked enthusiastically about the trip, for three weeks he ate only three things: eggs (for breakfast), and chicken or hamburgers (for lunch and dinner). I can empathize with a traveler who is stuck eating not what he wants from the menu but only what he can translate.

He told us the girls were playing volleyball at the elementary school up the block. We stopped by to watch. Because the school's student population is so tiny, I have come to know these students well and they are among my favorites. They were between games when we walked in and they mobbed us. Ah, if only they were at least ten years older!

During the games the girls showed their usually *genki*ness. They were diving for the ball and making good setups for spikes. The Japanese are very polite and there is no in-your-face talk in the gym. In fact, girls from Miyajidake were the linesmen and were scrupulously fair.

Because Andy's Japanese is advanced he talked with the girls for a while. The enthusiasm with which they responded made me question a decision I had made back in the fall. When I decided to learn Japanese, several ALTs said these kids will have very few opportunities to speak English with a native speaker and if I spoke to them in Japanese, that would take away that rare chance. So I always speak in English to the kids, and I encourage them to speak to me in English, although I do not insist on it. Andy's view has been different from the start. He said that in class he speaks only English but outside of the classroom he speaks in whichever language the students want. His view is that he can convey more information to them about America using Japanese because their English is extremely limited. For the kids who are eager to expand their horizons beyond Japan's shores, he thinks speaking in Japanese serves that higher purpose. From now on, I will adopt Andy's view.

Last Monday at Saiitsu-*chu* I was faced with what I was sure would be the worst day of my life as Ken-*sensei*. The English teacher came to school to explain that a relative died during the night. On Tuesday the school would have a temporary replacement, but for Monday I was all the school had to teach three classes and the English club after school. Tuesday the entire school was having an English test, and I would have to prepare the children for it.

Until then I usually had been in class with a Japanese teacher. My most common role was to read the lessons aloud and correct the students' pronunciation. Now I had to be a real teacher, and I had to do it on my own. The teacher explained to the three class captains that I would be in class alone. My heart sank when the girls simultaneously leapt into the air, clapped their hands together and shouted "*Yokatta*! (Yo ka ta – Great!)." I thought their reaction showed they knew they could use and abuse their very own *gaijin* teacher. Ken-*sensei*: the ultimate in substitute teachers.

When the chime sounded for the first class, I trudged out of the teachers' room with the lesson plan. Teachers said, "*Gambatte.*" I faced the prospect of teaching Japanese teenagers with the fear and trepidation condemned prisoners feel as they are led down the dark corridor toward "the chair." In my mind the rattle of ankle chains made the only sound in this tragic march. Deep in the prisoner's heart hope flickers that the phone on the wall will ring and freedom will once again be his. I look around: The English teacher is driving away.

As I walked past the eighth graders in their classroom they seemed agitated and said things to me to which I did not pay attention. When I saw the empty seventh-grade classroom next door, the eighth graders told me that the other class was in the gym. The eighth graders had their English textbooks out. What a start for the know-nothing substitute. I had taken the wrong lesson plan. I returned to the teachers' room for the right plan accompanied by the laughter of 30 teenagers. Fortunately this class is among the best behaved in the whole city. When I babbled instructions in English or Japanese, they held conferences around the room to decide what it was I wanted them to do. They were always right and did it gladly.

The next class was seventh graders. As I entered the kids jumped out of their seats to stand at attention next to their desks. Every time I gave them an instruction in Japanese, they applauded with beaming smiles and I heard a couple voices say "*Jozu!*" They were almost overhelpful. If I said "Write this down in your notebooks," they would ask me: "Do we have to write in capital letters or small letters?"; "Should we print or write connecting the letters?"; "Should we write on the same page we wrote on in yesterday's class or on a clean page?"; "Should we use pencils or pens?" After the zillionth question, I answered each with a phrase I taught them: "It does not matter to me."

One boy asked a question and, without really listening to it, I answered that way. As he was leaving class I wondered where I had given him permission to go. I considered stopping him to ask but I thought seventh graders, like the savage beast, might be able to sense fear and uncertainty. The children settled down to a dull roar and things went fine because they were charged up about have a *gaijin* all to themselves for 50 minutes. I walked out of the class thinking that with their cooperation, I had actually accomplished the goal of preparing them for the test.

Before lunch I had my third and last class of the day. I entered the classroom with the thought "Hey, I can do this." I cannot help thinking that if a Japanese teacher with English skills comparable to my Japanese-language skills had tried to substitute in an American school, the guy would have looked like chopped liver at the end of the day.

I ate lunch with the ninth graders but I daydreamed about the teachers' room air conditioner. After lunch I went to the gym to shoot hoops. Several girls from the ninth-grade class shot baskets with me.

Another girl came into the gym wearing my suit coat. I got it back after several girls and two boys tried it on. As I waited for my coat, a few girls stood next to me and compared the height of our hips. I thought things were getting just a little too sexually suggestive for me so I told them good-bye. Two of them protested by grabbing my arms and pulling me toward the mat while inviting me to practice sumo wrestling with them. Envisioning the inside of a Japanese prison, I made my excuses and beat it.

Later I conducted the meeting of the English club. Almost every student is in some club or other. I walked with a couple students to the principal's office, where the meeting was held. A girl walked in ahead of me, and there stood the principal with suit pants down around his ankles showing off a fine pair of boxer shorts and a pair of Betty Davis knees. He motioned toward me and mumbled something. I did not understand but, based on common human experience, assumed I comprehended. I grabbed the girl, turned her around and started to usher her out of the room. She flipped on the light switch, twisted out of my grasp and continued walking toward the table and chairs near the principal's desk. The other students streamed in behind her. I tried to get them to understand that I wanted them out of the room but at that moment the principal nonchalantly finished pulling up his sweatpants. He put on his baseball hat and walked out without saying a word. Japan school life! It is not predictable, but it sure is not boring.

Since Tuesday the classrooms have become hot again. The *tsuyu* (tsu you – rainy season) officially started. There was a distinct change in the weather, not so much in the amount of rain but in the way it comes down and in the rise in the temperature and humidity. It is now so hot and muggy in the classrooms that even when I loosen my tie, I continue to sweat. Last summer was stifling, but this seems worse if only because I know that following the rainy season, the stifling heat returns.

I was at Hondo-*chu* when the rainy season started its muggy torrents. The rain comes in torrents, stops, then comes in torrents again. The kids are self-appointed rain watchers. When the rain starts, there is about a ten-second lag before the downpour really hits. The children run to close the windows in the classroom and in the hallway. Within a few minutes, the heat and humidity rise, steaming up the inside of the windows. The classroom is like a natural sauna. The kids use their writing pads to fan themselves. Fortunately, the heavy spurts are as short as they are violent. Between downpours we have either a very fine drizzle or no rain at all, so the windows can be opened again to cool off the room until the next downpour.

air-conditioned teachers' room. Since the new school year began, I have been to this school three times and each time I have a full day of classes. I guess I asked for it. Even at that, this is the easiest job I will ever have. The new seventh-grade classes are great. All the girls are as cute as a button and precious. Some of the boys are so short, when they are at their desks it looks like they are sitting in a hole. All the students have bright cheery faces, eagerly awaiting to hear what this *gaijin* has to say.

During one of the classes today we taught the "This is my. . ." form again. One boy was not getting it so I walked to his desk and took his pencil case in my hand. I said, "This is my pencil case." No response. I put a 10,000 yen note on his desk (about $80). His friends all shouted for him to say "This is my *ichi man en* (e chee maan en – 10,000 yen note)." The boy was too shocked to do or say anything. I am not sure if he learned anything from that, but everyone around him sure knows that form now.

My last activity of the day was to take over the English club for Mori-*sensei*. He had to leave school early because he is still not finished with his home visits. Every new semester, the homeroom teachers are required to visit the parents of each of their students. Normally the teacher goes to the student's home. The teachers try to keep the visits to 30 minutes, but some take hours. For the first month of this semester, the schools were let out in the afternoon (classes were scaled back to 45 minutes) to give the teachers an opportunity to teach and meet the parents too. Mori-*sensei* is not finished yet because he is new to the area and must introduce himself to all the parents, let them get to know him and then talk about the students. He is about average in his commitment to his students, which means it is genuine. I think calling him "average" is a compliment to him and the rest of the teachers here. As a group they are dedicated to teaching, which results in Japan's well-educated population.

The English club consists of five girls. When I spoke to them, they conferred among themselves to decide what I had said and then confirmed by saying in Japanese what they concluded I had said in English. If it was wrong they went back into conference until they came up with another version. One of the girls said that her favorite movie star is James Dean. Older Japanese have all seen his movies, and he is still popular as a pin-up poster with young girls. I told the girls that James Dean liked boys. The group had a little difficulty believing it. Another girl asked with concern in Japanese, "Is Tom Cruise okay?" I said yes and they all said with relief, "Good!" Actually, I thought about telling them the truth, which is that I have no idea, but I figure everyone needs a little certainty in their lives.

And I know with certainty that the chimes just sounded and I have to end another grueling day at the office. Bye.

*D*ear Frank,   June 28
Two weekends ago a group of ALTs and dependents camped out in my house. We planned a Saturday picnic on the beach on the far side of the island in the village of Reihoku. Naturally it was beautiful Friday and Sunday, but after we unloaded the cars at the beach on Saturday it started raining in wind-driven buckets. If you are not prepared for rain in Japan, especially in the rainy season, you are not prepared for life here. We had a Plan B, which turned out to be fun.

The English teacher in Reihoku made arrangements for us to use the cooking classroom if we could not cook on the beach. After all the last-minute changes in plan, we finally made it to the school 3 P.M. There were about 50 kids preparing for Tuesday's island-wide sports day, which was held in Hondo. Ten boys helped us set up the grill outside under the school's overhanging canopy and tracked down the school's boom box.

We shared the food with them. American-style potato salad was a hit. Japanese potato salad is made from mashed potatoes and often has cucumbers in it as well as bits of fish. The hamburgers were a hit too. Foods we take for granted at home are rare here. You can buy hamburgers at restaurants, but they are not something made at home. Tracking hamburger buns down proved so difficult we had to special order them.

Among the ALTs who came were Terri and Henry Rye and their boys, Aaron and Thomas. The boys attend the local Japanese schools. It will set them back when they return to school in the States this fall, but the Ryes see the year as an incomparable experience for them. The boys say much of what goes on in class is over their heads but they are picking up Japanese from the children in their classes, with whom they play after school. There are two girls in class who like Aaron, and Thomas has his eye on an older woman, a fifth grader.

The boys are getting a real-life education in intercultural

relations. Four girls came by. Thomas looked like he was trying to avoid them and I asked him why. He said that within a few minutes they would call him cute and start hugging him. I have to admit, the boy called it. They all took turns hugging him and saying in Japanese and English that he was cute. He hopes he remains cute in their eyes until he comes back to Japan after college.

When it came time to divvy up the leftovers, a high school teacher asked if he could take the meat. He is in charge of the boys' high school dorm and the boys are always hungry. They live in the dorms because his school is considered the best in this whole area and consequently it attracts students from the outlying areas, including other islands. These kids can only go home by ferry on Saturday after class.

Most of us returned to my house. We ate Terri's homemade cheesecake and as usual talked until late in the evening. Some ALTs were surprised that they could speak to Aaron and Thomas as they would to adults, using slang and everything. Several spoke to the boys as they would a Japanese teacher, slowly and with no homey expressions or slang. It is amazing that we have been here less than a year and many of us are forgetting how to communicate with children from our own culture.

As I mentioned, Tuesday was an island-wide sports day in Hondo. Each of the schools hosted different events. I was at Hondo-*chu*, which hosted track and field and girls' volleyball. I watched the volleyball from the gym's balcony. (It was inside and hence in the shade.) The Miyajidake-*chu* girls' team was great. Every eighth- and ninth-grade girl at the school is on the team and they play like a machine. The seventh-grade girls (all four of them) are the *chiagaru* (chee a ga roo – cheer girl). Girls from Kusuura-*chu* begged me me to sing O'Canada. Because of the setting they said, "Small voice ok." It reminded me of an ex-ALT I met who said earlier this year he ran into students he had three years ago. They still remember the words to "The Flintstones."

Driving home, I turned left from the school driveway. A telephone pole stands in the street in front of the school's wall. A middle-aged man with his pants unzipped urinated against the pole. The children and adults who passed by took no notice of him. Although it is against the law here to urinate in public, older men have no compunction against it, even in the busiest of places. You see this once or twice a month. When I am driving from Hondo to Kumamoto, it seems like every other trip I will see a man standing next to his car. Not only do they not bother to walk over to a nearby bush, they do not even bother to position themselves so their car is between them and the view of passing motorists.

The fact that they have decided to answer nature's call in a business area seems to make little difference. Not long ago I was on Andy's island with a group of ALTs who had gone there to meet his visiting dad and brother. We were returning from the restaurant as we strolled past the main village's harbor. Ringing the harbor is a U-shaped row of shops. At 9 P.M. they were all closed but there were still a fair number of people walking around. Andy's brother poked Andy in the ribs and said, "Look at that!" "Look at what?" Andy asked. "That guy right there [about 30 feet ahead of us on the left] standing on the harbor wall under the street light pissing into the harbor!" Andy and I had the same reaction: "So what?"

I bicycled last weekend to Hitoyoshi, which is the Japanese hometown of a married Canadian couple, Olga and Lawrence, both ALTs. They are leaving after two years on the program, and I came to attend the party in honor of their departure and Olga's 27th birthday.

I started out in the early morning and headed to the far side of my island to take a ferry to the main island of Kyushu. On the way, as I was puffing up one of the steeper hills, a crew from the electric company passed me. They leaned out of the windows and shouted "*FAITO*" (fie toe – from "fight" meaning "go for it"). My first stop was the port city of Ushibuka, where I ate lunch although it was too early for it. I had heard of a place called Miki House (named in honor of Mickey Mouse) with honest-to-goodness hamburgers. They were as good as advertised. The woman pulled out an album of other ALTs who had eaten there. She is quite proud that her hamburgers are famous among the American ALTs and told me, "Americans know hamburgers."

The road from the port on Kyushu to the main road was a steady incline, which I trudged up. I took a break two hours after leaving the ferry at a store where, about 50 feet away, there was a bench under a tree. It was a sleepy kind of store, where the cobwebs are seldom disturbed by customers. I had to make it past the white Akita dog snoozing in front of the door. He was big, about 70 pounds, I estimate. As I opened the door, I pushed his body several inches but he did not so much as open an eyelid. After the door opened enough for me to squeeze in I stepped over him.

I stepped over the dog again on the way out with my drink and sat on the bench in the shade. The girl behind the counter came out and hit me with the standard, I-met-a-*gaijin* questions. She went back into the store, returned with a rock-and-roll magazine and we talked about music. I stayed longer than I intended because she was so much fun to talk with. We talked in a mixture of Japanese and English. After the sun worked its way to the bench, I decided to leave.

I asked her how far it was to Hitoyoshi. She asked the meter reader who had just driven up in his company pickup. He said, "A long time." He offered a ride, but I told him I wanted the exercise. As I passed the store I noticed the dog had moved one of his legs sometime during my conversation with the girl, so I took it as proof he was not dead.

I took an exhausting tiny farming road up into the mountains. Two hours later I saw the same man again at a traffic light in a city where I had to make the same turn he was making onto an even smaller, more remote, steeper mountain road. He asked again if I wanted a ride and when I declined, he said "*Faito!*"

Later, when the river on my map did not show up on the side of the road as expected, I saw a few houses up the road. Then ahead of me I saw a junior high school girl bicycling home from school. I decided to say hello to her while I was far enough behind so that she would not turn and find a *gaijin* right next to her. I was about 40 feet behind her when I said hello in the softest voice I could muster. She was obviously startled. She looked behind her, let out a scream as if she were looking at the Texas chain saw murderer and hopped off of her bike. She jumped off of it so cleanly that before crashing to the pavement it continued forward for several feet as if being ridden by the invisible man. As I plugged away uphill, I reached the point where she had jumped off. There she was, crouched behind a bush narrower than her body and concealing nothing above her shoulders. I waved to her and said good-bye. For the next couple of miles I wondered if a cop car would come up behind me to arrest me for something the girl made up to explain her scream to the neighbors. I have never before seen such a spontaneous, acute fit of xenophobia in Japan.

Later construction workers confirmed I was on the right road. I still have not figured out what happened to the river. After the construction site, the road, which had been a long steady incline all day, became steeper, complete with hairpin turns. These remote mountain roads in Japan are so narrow they give the feel of being made specifically as bike paths through the thick green forests. This was the most grueling part of a totally exhausting day. Long gone were the rice paddies, which have a beauty I have come to appreciate. They were replaced by neatly planted, lush forest on steep slopes. Throughout this country can be seen the hand of man. I think there is not a weed unaccounted for in the whole country. It is the result of a population half that of America's crammed into "livable space" the size, I understand, of Connecticut.

After what seemed like an eternity of pedaling straight up, I reached the top and for the next 30 minutes, all the way to town, it was clear sailing downhill. It was great to feel the wind rush past my ears and not expend one single solitary calorie's worth of effort for all the speed I gained and all the ground I was covering.

When I finally made it to the city limits of Hitoyoshi, I saw my old friend, the man who had twice offered me a ride. I recognized him even though he was in his own car this time. He smiled at me and we both waved as I waited at the light while he made a left turn. I am not sure what, but I feel like I shared something small yet special with him that day. For a reason I cannot really explain, what we shared gives me a good feeling.

At the party I talked with a *genki* Australian woman, Verona, who is an ex-ALT now teaching at a university. She had a wild outfit on, a cross between Annie Hall and the Hell's Angels, if you can picture that. The only thing her outfit did not clash with was her pink and purple hair. If her students do not get a feel for personal freedom from her, they never will. Olga said Verona's hair had calmed down since she had seen her last. It was not arranged in shooting spikes of hair-spray frozen clumps.

The next morning Lawrence decided to bicycle with me to the port city. He knows the beautiful back roads, complete with streams, old weatherbeaten farm buildings and a tiny waterfall. The ride, mostly downhill, took about two hours and was as beautiful as advertised. On the way we made a side trip to Lawrence's favorite *Shinto* shrine, which is dedicated to the penis. Wooden replicas are scattered all around. They are in various sizes with the biggest one standing outside the shrine and reaching into the sky a Titan-sized 30 feet. Japan, not exactly in the same century as the rest of us, but never boring.

At the port city, Olga and Verona met us and we ate lunch together. They all gave me a warm send-off as the ferry pulled out. Waving back, I thought about the kindness they had extended to me, and it made me sad to think what the odds are I will ever see any of them again.

Next week is the students' finals week. Because I would sit at the Board all week, I will use up the vacation time I have left. Tomorrow I go to Hokkaido, which is the northernmost main island of Japan. Although it has 25 percent of Japan's landmass, it has only a small percentage of its population. Japanese equate Hokkaido with wide open spaces. Their general image of Hokkaido is somewhat equivalent to the image we have of Alaska.

The last remnants of the original inhabitants of these islands are still found there. Japan was originally settled by the Ainu (eye knew) , a Caucasian people. Sometime later the ancestors of the Japanese, then called the Yamato, landed in Kyushu. As the Yamato slowly spread north, they pushed the Ainu farther into the undeveloped spaces. Although Honshu and Hokkaido are now connected by tunnel, only in the last century (during the *Meiji Jidai*) did the Japanese begin to push in earnest into Hokkaido. The government policy was to absorb the Ainu. Now they are almost gone as a distinct race and were long ago forced to take Japanese names and speak Japanese.

If there is a place in Japan other than Tokyo Disneyland all Japanese would like to visit it is Hokkaido, yet almost none of them I know have. No doubt because it is cheaper to go to Hawaii than Hokkaido. Even more than Hokkaido, most would prefer to go to a foreign country. The majority of overseas travelers have been to the States (Australia is second on the list of foreign countries to visit). Their favorite vacation spot in America is Hawaii. Because so many Japanese go there, they almost do not count it as being a trip to America. I know how they feel because as a kid in Detroit I did not count Canada as a foreign country.

People who cannot afford a trip to Hawaii visit Guam, which they regard as a sunny island tropical paradise. I have not had the heart to tell them that Americans, when we think of Guam at all, think that it is the island closest to the point in the ocean where you can sail off the edge of the earth.

Well, it is quitting time now so I am going to mail this tonight.

ear Mark,   July 9
I left for the airport at 7 A.M. Saturday morning. On the way I saw students silently trudging to school.

My first night in Hokkaido, I stayed in the apartment of a fellow *Tatami* Timeshare ALT, Kerri, who lives in Sapporo. My house is used on many weekends as a hotel by traveling ALTs, so I do not mind asking others for the privilege.

Kerri would not be home until 8 P.M. so she left the door key under the mat. It is nothing short of amazing how comfortable ALTs are with one another. I had never met Kerri. I simply talked with her over the phone after finding her name in the ALT *Tatami* Timeshare directory. In spite of never meeting her, there I was letting myself into her apartment while she was out. It really gives one the feel of being part of a large, trusting, extended family. The money I received from pawning her things is going to help stretch my vacation too.

During the day, I went to the train station and bought a *furichiketto* (foo ree che kay toe – free ticket). The name is deceptive; it is not free. It is a $200 two-week, unlimited-mileage rail pass good anywhere in Hokkaido.

Walking around Sapporo reminded me more of an American city than a Japanese one. The city's layout reflects that it was planned toward the end of the last century by an American. It has broad, straight streets, all of which are named. There also were sections that had underground utilities, instead of the constant overhead thicket of vinelike utility lines. The houses do not have typical Japanese tile roofs with gargoyles as rain spouts. Many have bright red or blue aluminum roofs to keep the weight of the roofs down, so that when snow falls (the city is famous for its winter ice festival), the roof does not crash through the ceiling.

People in Sapporo are quick to point out that although the city's winter is long, it is not too cold and it does not get the most snow in Japan. That honor is reserved for the mountainous region in northern Honshu. People there shovel snow from roofs. Some houses have a door on the second floor with no stairs. They are used when the snow piles deep enough. When the passes are so thick with snow that the roads look more like a path through a steep, narrow canyon, the roads are closed.

Whatever the winter weather, while I was in Hokkaido it was conducive to wandering around. For a month or more the sun has been an infrequent visitor in Hondo. Hokkaido skies are blue. The weather is neither hot nor muggy. Most days a cool breeze gently streamed across Hokkaido. To complete the un-Japanese feel, I was not rained on during my stay!! It was almost like being in another country. Sapporo has the vice all Japanese cities have, though. I think the Japanese concrete companies have a religious objection to rivers without concrete beds.

Upon returning to Kerri's, I watched the news. Her Board bought her a small satellite dish she uses to pick up the premium Japanese TV channels. These carry American programming, CNN, TV programs, movies and sports. A channel called Wow Wow carries the most American movies and is one the average Japanese wants but it is over $100 per month. Kerri's is free.

She is leaving after two years here to resume her teaching career in Halifax, Canada. Her experience has been a little different from mine. Two of her friends had their houses broken into and two other friends had been robbed at knifepoint! Quite a difference from the supersafe Japan we hear about in the States and which, frankly, I have experienced so far.

Her work, though, which she says she will miss, has been like mine. She rotates among nine schools, spending a week at a time at each one. The smallest has only 14 students, with only two eighth graders! She told me of another ALT who visits one school that has a full complement of teachers, but only two, count 'em two, students! Something that made me envious was that all of her schools have central heating. (The locals may say it is not cold here but Hokkaido is notorious for blasts of Siberian winds in the winter.) As at my schools, when the room warms up, the windows are opened.

The next morning I left by train to a town called Sounkyo, at the base of Kuro-*dake* (coo row dah kay – Black Peak). The scenery is different from the terraced rice fields of the rest of Japan; undulating plains, far-off horizons, brightly colored roofs of the farmhouses and silos next to the barns that remind me of scenery on the back roads in Michigan. Kerri said Hokkaido reminds her of home too. After speeding by several fields with gentle dips in them, it came to me what the biggest difference is between farming here and in the south of Japan. The fields in the other parts of Japan are flat, even if terraced. The land in the south needs to be exactly even for each rice plant to stand in just the right amount of water. Up here where they grow things besides rice, the land does not have to be leveled with laser accuracy. Then I saw something for the first time in Japan: a field of weeds.

Arriving in the early afternoon, I rented a bike to head up a box canyon to look at waterfalls. Following the highway I saw evenly spaced tall poles on both sides of the road. Arrows pointing down to the edge of the road were attached at the top. Contrary to what people in Sapporo said, the snow in this area piles deep enough to make the arrows useful in showing where the edge of the road is. Glad it's July! I was disappointed to learn as I rode up the canyon that even here at the base of a mountain, rivers cannot run free, but are picked up and laid back down in a bed of concrete.

The next day I hiked with a group at the youth hostel to the top of the peak. I found that I cannot hike up a steep rocky trail and speak Japanese at the same time. I have to concentrate so much on what I am saying that I slipped a couple times. At the top the others turned around, but I took the alpine trail over to Asahi-*dake* (ah sah he dah kay – Sunrise Peak), which turned out to be an all-day hike. It is the only place so far in Japan where I could get a 360-degree view as I can in Arizona.

At the town of Asahi, I took the train to the other side of Hokkaido to the small town of Shiri. At the train stop in Abashiri, several high school girls boarded. Two sat next to me and three sat across from me in the facing boothlike seats. They asked me all the I-just-met-a-*gaijin* questions then left two stops before mine.

As arranged, an ALT, Barbra (no, not Barbara), picked me up at the tiny train station. Barbra is a statuesque blond Canadian from Alberta who is also ending her two years here to return home. On the way to her apartment, she said the girls on the train called her to tell her I was coming. It is a small world when you are a *gaijin*. Because her schools are far flung and the bus service is sparse in these parts, her employer supplies her a car.

As part of my "rent" I gladly taught with her. Students in her schools have more personal freedom than my students. They wear watches and a couple girls wore earrings. In some ways the school is built differently too. The headroom in the doorways is sufficient so that I do not have to duck (maybe it is my imagination, but the boys seem taller and stouter than my students too), and there are ducts for that marvel of marvels, central heating in a public school!!

In the late afternoon I headed for the tip of a remote peninsula called Shiretoko. Barbra teaches at a school in a small town near the base of it and we made plans to team teach there after I hiked for a few days. I took a bus to the small town and started to walk along the dirt road for the last 12 miles to the youth hostel. As I walked I kept my thumb out for a ride. Japanese do not hitchhike. They know a fellow Japanese will not pick them up. They are happy, however, to pick up a *gaijin*.

Thirty minutes after I started, a small red car stopped next to me. The driver stammered slowly, just barely managing to say "You are going youse hoe stay roo (youth hostel)?" "Yes (he would not have understood 'yeah'). "I take you by this car?" In the car we had a choppy conversation in English. I asked him, "What is your job? (he would have not understood, "whacha do for a livin'?"). "Teecha (teacher)." "What kind of teacher?" "Ing ooh reesh teecha (English teacher)."

From the youth hostel, I hiked to an area called Five Lakes. Then I made my way down to the beach not too far from the hostel. As

I wrote down the day's events in my journal, I was sitting on the sandy beach on the shore of the Okhotsk Sea while the waves crashed with a roar and a force I could feel. As I finished writing, the sun was a big red ball slowly sinking into the ocean.

The next day I left most of my stuff at the hostel and hiked on the largely deserted dirt road several miles toward the trail head at the tip of the peninsula where there is a *rotemburo* (row tem burro – an outdoor, natural hot spring). From the trail head it is a 30-minute scramble up the middle of a fast stream which is crowded by thick undergrowth down to both banks. It flows from its source to the ocean as many Japanese streams do, in a short, steep course. This one has steep waterfall after steep waterfall, with the consequent slippery rocks for hand- or footholds. In short, it was death defying. The *rotemburo* is a four-foot deep by eight-foot across oval pool just off of the main channel. The water was nice and toasty.

I enjoyed the walk back along the road. I counted 14 foxes (including one mother standing on the side of the road with two pups nursing, until the family saw me, that is). A couple hours into the walk, two passing construction workers asked me if I wanted a ride. I accepted to get back to the beach in time for sundown again.

The next day I taught with Barbra again. This school rarely sees one *gaijin*, let alone two. As we walked through the school the children streamed out of the classrooms. The school has a room dedicated to Brazilians of Japanese ancestry as there is a sizable Japanese population in Brazil as a result of significant immigrations there before World War II. Now their grandchildren are coming back to take part in Japan's economic miracle sporting names such as Gomez Yamaguchi.

Barbra drove me to the train station. We drove by the harbor full of lumber ships unloading Siberian wood. In exchange, the Russians buy old Japanese cars, which she says sell well in the Russian Far East.

The day I returned to Hondo the rainy season ended. The next day the typhoon season started. On the plane I took the opportunity to start writing a good-bye speech. When I finish it the teachers have already agreed to translate it for me. I will give it at each school during my last visit. In less than ten days I will be leaving the best job I ever had. It is time to go but I want to capture these moments in a bottle and over the years take the bottle off the shelf to take a sip and let the memories flood back. I will always miss this place and these people.

*D*ear Uncle Chet and Aunt Dottie,   July 18

It's over. I left school for the last time 20 minutes ago. I am Ken-*sensei* no more. When I returned from my Hokkaido trip, I made the last round of visits to all of the schools. At each one I gave the speech I have printed at the end of this letter. Here are highlights of my last days at school.

July 10. Saiitsu-*chu*. A few girls made *origami* (or ree ga me – the art of folding paper into designs) *tsuru* (tsu roo – crane: the bird, not the construction tool). The crane is a symbol deeply imbedded in Japanese culture. Teenage girls seem to be the *origami* crane experts.

In an eighth-grade class we taught superlatives (good, better, best). It led me to an impromptu student poll about the hardest classes and most popular sports. Sixteen of 31 said English is the hardest subject; three said all are hard; the rest were evenly split between science and Japanese. Most agree baseball is the most popular sport, closely followed by soccer. One said sumo and one said *geto baru* (gay toe bow roo – gateball: croquetlike game played only by bent-over grammas and grandpas).

July 11. Miyajidake-*chu*. My last time here. This will no doubt be my saddest ending. I sound like a broken record, but I really like this school: the view, the students, the staff and above all Tahara-*sensei*.

After lunch the entire school gathered in the ninth-grade classroom to hear the principal and me give our speeches. On the board the students wrote a bright, multicolored message saying thank you for teaching us. After my speech, I told them I was happy that the ceremony was being held in that room, as it is my favorite view in Japan.

As I left school, the gardener (i.e., the principal) handed me flowers picked from the garden. Kids were hanging out of the windows shouting goodbye as I drove down the driveway.

July 12. Hon machi-*chu*. When I came here last fall, this was Akane's school, but in April a teacher took over that resulted in the school descending from the top of my list of most-liked schools to near the bottom of the barrel. The kids did not know it was my last day. As I left school, I walked from the teachers' room to the *genkan*. About 20 students said their good-byes.

July 15. Hondo higashi-*chu*. My last classes were with the two seventh-grades and as I walked in each class I received applause. (I thought about telling them that bowing and begging was enough.) At the end of each class, they wanted me to sign my name on books, notebooks, foreheads, you name it. I shuddered when they started to ask to shake my hand because I knew that someone would try to squeeze the blood out of it, but I went ahead anyway and it turned out their bone-crunching hand-squeezing days must be over.

July 16. Kamegawa-*chu*. I was here on July 13 (Saturday) to say good-bye to the seventh graders who as I write this are now on a school trip. Today was hot and sweaty but the entire school assembled in the gym to send me off and listen to my speech. Afterward, Ezaki-*sensei* brought out her camera. The students proved once again that in Japan it is a virtual impossibility to pull one out a camera in front of two or more people without one of them flashing the V sign. In my impromptu polls over the year, I have found that some do it to signify peace, some do it to signify victory, but by far most do it because everybody else does it.

July 17. Kusuura-*chu*. The new Akane-*chu*. I had five classes with Akane. In one class we were doing a story about the *Titanic*. One girl showed how easy it is to screw up in a different language. As she was reading from the text, she said that the *Titanic* was surrounded by iceburgers (hold the pickles?). At lunch the one seventh grade class that I did not have a class with asked if I would eat with them and sing "O' Canada."

I had my good-bye party on the 17th, the night before my last teaching day. It started at the *shimin senta* (she mean sane ta – Citizen's Center). The superintendent of the Board was there as were the Mayor and a couple other dignitaries. There was a big poster saying thanks and we will miss you. The spread was nice too.

The mayor led off the event by giving a short speech followed by a equally short speech by the city council representative. Finally the superintendent gave a speech that made me feel appreciated. He said that he saw one of my classes and he thought the students were in good hands. Later he told me that a copy of the speech I had prepared for the students had made its way to him, and he thanked me for my efforts on behalf of the kids. I told him that I did not think of them as Japanese students anymore. I think of them as *my* students.

The mayor led the group in saying *kampai*. His official duties done, he promptly disappeared. Everybody poured my beer, as is the

Japanese custom, and we were back to swapping glasses again. At the end everyone lined up and I went down the isle to their applause. In the hallway the principal of Miyajidake-*chu* hugged me.

From there about 20 of us went to a *bea gaden* on the top of a hotel. The evening was clear, with just a few rosy clouds colored by the setting sun. There was a quarter moon and Venus was up. I ordered a large glass of beer, which looked more like a pitcher than a glass. We reminisced over many beers.

July 18. Hondo-*chu*. My last day on the job and I have a heck of a *futsuka yoi* (whost ka yo e – hang over). As I was leaving school many kids lined up outside the teachers' room to shake my hand. When I walked down the path toward my car, children were leaning out of the windows on the upper floors and waving. Those who were leaving the gate as I drove past bowed to me or waved.

I went to the Board to pick up my salary for July. Just like that I was Ken-*sensei* no more.

Tomorrow morning (the 19th) no longer am I going to be a semicelebrity, just another *gaijin*. A very happy chapter in my life is over. I do not know what jobs I will have in the future, but I doubt I will ever enjoy one as much as I have enjoyed this one.

Next week I head to Kyoto, where I will stay for a few days before taking the train to Kobe, where I will board a ship for Shanghai. From there I will start my trip across China, Mongolia and Russia on my way home.

Well, that wraps up the report from this side of the world. I will write again when I am back in the States in late October. Bye for now.

P.S.

Good-bye Speech

It has been almost a year since I came to Japan. When I arrived here, like most Americans, I knew little about Japan. I came to experience and learn about your country. Since then I have visited each of the four main islands and many of your major cities. My knowledge of Japan is certainly much greater now.

As you know, I will not be a teacher in this school after today. I have never had a job that I liked so well. The reason is primarily because of you, the students.

Many times during class, you may have seen me write on my lesson plan. Usually I did that because I had heard one of you say something in Japanese that I had never heard before. After class, I would ask the English teacher about it, and in that way I learned from you. So many interesting and funny things have happened that I began writing a journal to remember them. Many times after class the English teacher and I talked about something funny that happened in class and we laughed about it again. Each of you has brought a little bit of sunshine into my life.

One thing I have learned is how similar you are to American students. You work hard because you want to do what you think is right and you want to make your family proud of you. And, like American students, you would much rather be outside playing or in the house watching TV, but you study because you know it is best for your future.

Many of you must be wondering about your future. I have a suggestion. I encourage you to learn a foreign language, whether it is English or another language. Learning another language helps you to question things you always took for granted. For example, I have had difficulty communicating with some other native English speakers I have met on the JET Program. Australians have expressions that are unfamiliar to me, as do New Zealanders. I had a hard time understanding a man from England because of his accent. It made me realize how fleeting language is. Those people and I speak the same language but we speak it differently enough to make communication choppy at times. As I thought about it, I remember words that were current when I was a boy that have fallen out of use. Language keeps changing over time and distance. Nothing stays the same forever.

Learning a language may start you to wondering what communication is. To communicate an idea to another person, you must use a predetermined system of sounds or symbols. This is called language. If you stop to think about it, you may realize that all languages, Japanese, English, all of them, are a collection of sounds that, over time, came to be arranged in standardized ways. There was no plan, it just happened.

Why learn English when you can already communicate in Japanese? Using Japanese you can communicate with people in this country, which is about the size of the state of California. California, however, is not the biggest state in the U.S., and there are 49 other states in which English is spoken. English is also spoken in huge countries such as Canada and Australia and smaller countries such as England (including Scotland, Wales, and Ireland) and New Zealand.

It is frequently used as a second language in India and the Philippines. When I visited northern European countries, such as Holland, Germany and Denmark, I discovered many people can speak English.

You may wonder if there is a concrete reason to learn a second language. There are several jobs in Japan that require knowledge of English. Your teacher has one. Some other professions are medicine, translator, airline pilot and workers in airport control towers. If you want to be doctor or scientist, without at least a reading command of English, you probably cannot graduate because some of the texts are in English only. English is the language most scientists communicate in when they have international conferences. It is used as a sort of international language. Not long ago I watched tennis from another country broadcast in Japan. After the match a Japanese reporter interviewed one of the players who is from Argentina. They communicated in English. So if you learn it you have more of an opportunity to speak to people of different cultures.

This leads me to my last point: TRAVEL. I know that in Japan the emphasis is on hard work and duty, but I think you should consider a lifestyle of your own choosing. When the man who works hard all his life to make money dies, he is just as dead as a poorer man who did the things that he wanted to do. Work is good for the soul and you should not shrink from it, but work alone does not enrich the soul enough. To do this, I think, you must experience different things. The best way to do that is to travel to see different cultures.

If you had two lives, one in which you are to always do the duty imposed on you and another one in which you could do all the things you dream about, then life would be easier. But we are all given just one life. Because we are not given a second chance to live, we must do our best in this life. If you never dream any dreams, if you never try to make at least some of your dreams come true, none of them will.

If you try, you can make some of your dreams come true. You can do it while still fulfilling your duty to yourself, your family, your society. In English we have a saying, "Where there's a will, there's a way." It means if you want something badly enough, you will think of a way to make it happen. So start thinking now. You are young, but not too young to think. Start making plans for your journey through life.

I am glad that my journey brought me here and that our paths crossed. I am richer for it and I thank you. Good-bye and good luck.

*D*ear Dad,   November 1
    When I stepped outside of the L.A. international
terminal on my way to the domestic terminal, a thin, withered
old man with long, silver, unkempt hair was sitting against one
of the concrete pillars. His skin hung from his arm so loosely the tattoo
on the side of his biceps was only an indecipherable collage of faded
colors. Screaming to no one in particular, with a heavy dose of
obscenities he conveyed his main message: "Keep away from me." Happy
to oblige him, I thought "I am home!"

I have been in Arizona two weeks now. I found an apartment,
put my truck back in running condition and loaded it up trip after trip
with all my things from storage. I found myself looking forward to
opening each box wondering what was hiding inside. The feeling
persisted in spite of the fact that in each box what I found was the same
old junk I threw in storage when I packed my bags and headed to Japan.

My first letter began with an allusion to the Wizard of Oz. Like
Dorothy, who told her family and friends what she learned from her
experiences, since I left Japan, I have sorted through what I learned.

The Japanese have a deep pride in their culture. They feel a
connection to their past stretching back 2,000 years of recorded history.
With that background, they view American culture as in its infancy. They
are reluctant to change and do not want to import American ideas on
masse. But paradoxes abound in Japan. The influx of American culture
is sometimes like a waterfall, sometimes like a glacier, but it is relentless.

I never had any idea the influence American culture has on the
Japanese. It is impossible for a Japanese to listen to the radio, watch TV
or read a newspaper or magazine without being exposed to English and
American cultural motifs. They have incorporated so much English into
Japanese that they are now creating their own "English" words such as
OL, BGM, Y-shatsu, CM, ensto and on and on.

They know who our popular singers are. American music of all
descriptions plays on the radio everyday, including the latest American
musical fads. The typical Japanese person of any age will name either an

American among his favorite singers or an American song among his favorites. During karaoke at least one Japanese in the group will sing a song in English. Go to any music store and you will find music from France, Germany, etc., in the "foreign" music section. American and Japanese music is commingled under the usual sections such as "Jazz," "Rock" and the like.

They know who our perennial favorite and current "hot" actors and actresses are. The women are as crazy about the latest heartthrob as American women are. The men debate which Hollywood actress is the world's most beautiful woman. The typical Japanese will list among his or her favorite actors or actresses a Hollywood star. It follows that American movies are the most popular. At video stores, American movies are not found in the foreign movie section or the majority of the titles would be there.

Although most of us cannot name a single Japanese sports star of any era, they know both our sports legends and currently-popular sports figures. Young men wearing jerseys bearing the numbers of their favorite American sports stars are as much a part of Japan's daily life as ours. Products hawked by American sports stars sell well too.

American players populate Japanese professional sports, especially baseball (to the per-team limit imposed by the Japanese league). Some of the best sumo wrestlers are from America.

Unfortunately, we are helping to downgrade the vaunted "Japanese" diet. Burgers, pizza and fried chicken (no Kentucky Fried Chicken store would be complete without a statue of Colonel Saunders outside), and Coca Cola are all a growing part of the contemporary diet.

They know who our political leaders are. They have an interest in our politics because what we do politically affects them in ways we do not even realize. When Bush pressured Japan to contribute to the cost of the Gulf War it caused a debate about Article 9, their constitution's "peace clause," which renounces war and the maintenance of armed forces (in the debate many believed helping to pay for war was no different from waging war). Few Americans ever heard about that debate. If we have a constitutional or other kind of national debate, it is reported in the Japanese media.

When Japan compares itself to another country, it is America to which it does the comparing. Yet they do not readily accept all things American. Many Japanese resent our government's *gaiatsu* (guy aht sue – outside pressure) to reduce trade barriers even though privately many admit it often produces laws more favorable to the average consumer than the Japanese people could force their government to enact. While resenting American pressure, they know the sad fact is that often the Japanese government has to be forced to do the right thing. *Mawari ga urusai* (ma wa ree ga ooh roo sigh) is the expression the Japanese use to describe their government's actions in international cooperation. Essentially the phrase means that the government will act for the common good when it is tired of hearing those around it complain of its inaction.

Individually, many look to America as "the way." They see our emphasis on personal choice and see little of it in their lives. They often are locked into their parents' home until their late 20s or early 30s by sky-high rents and an unforgiving-on-young-wallets cost of living. The Japanese admire the "American" personality, which they think of as the best features of the cowboy incarnate. Those anxious to make their own way in the world instead of leaning on mom and dad are *hanguri da* (hone ga ree – hungry, in the yearning sense; da – is). A person who will buck the system is said to have *gatsu* (ga tsu – guts).

Perhaps because they see their cultural traditions being replaced by ours they reflexively react with "*Yappari, Nihon no ho ga ii* (ya pa ree knee hone no hoe ga e – after all, Japan is better)." The notion of superiority conveyed with this phrase may be an understandable feeling of hurt pride in reaction to their knowledge that for all the impact our culture has on them, we do not feel the need to acquaint ourselves with theirs.

For all of their exposure to American culture they have in their store of "common wisdom" about the U.S. some wrong beliefs. Time and time again I was asked about the kind of gun I own. They were surprised when I told them that not only do I not own a gun but that I know no one who owns a gun. One widely shared belief is that our society is falling apart (of course they get this idea from our press – and every American who speaks on the subject).

Their main gap in knowledge about the U.S. ironically comes in the one area where Americans know something about Japan: Big companies. A few American companies are so ingrained in Japan some do not realize they originated in the States, such as McDonald's, Circle K and 7-11. A few other American companies most Japanese know are Ford, Chrysler, IBM, Kodak and Apple. The typical Japanese, however, has no clue what General Motors, General Electric, Whirlpool or Exxon are. Although I name but a few big American companies with which the average Japanese person is unfamiliar, in reality the shorter list is of the American companies that they do know.

One thing most Japanese are absolutely convinced of is that

products made in Japan are superior to those made in the States. A group of engineers at a Japanese company told me without a hint of bragging, rather in a "we are convinced of this deep down in our bones" matter-of-fact way that not only is every product their company makes superior to that of their American competitors, but that every Japanese product made is superior to its America-made counterpart.

Japan, however, is nothing if not full of contradictions. The so-called cultural gap that makes American products "unacceptable" to the Japanese has largely been closed – by the Japanese consumer. There is a limit to high prices that even they will pay. Buying the best product for the lowest price is important to them; buying "Japanese" is a secondary concern to consumers intent on stretching their pay. They are willing to buy "inferior" American products to save significant amounts of yen. In fact, like people anywhere, "foreign" can have an exotic ring to it.

Their willingness to buy American products may come as a surprise to those who know Japan mainly through the actions of its protectionist special interests and the *keiretsu* (kay ray tsu – conglomerates of monopolistic proportions and inclinations). For years people have scratched their heads and wondered what kind of people the Japanese are: notorious for being big benefactors of free trade but denying access to their own market. Any argument that the Japanese consumer will not buy foreign products confuses the Japanese consumer with various powerful special interests and the *keiretsu*.

As changing world conditions bring more of us to Japan, the rest of the world will discover what I did. Far from being a monolithic Japan Inc., poised to keep the *gaijin* at bay, there are people eager help make their own finances go farther buying, or selling, foreign products.

Whatever happens, trade friction between America and Japan is unlikely to go away, which says something good about both countries. It means that we both make lots of products, we both fight for the same markets and we are competitive with each other. With any luck, Japan and America will be trade rivals for as long as our two peoples exist.

For good and for bad the Japanese have had their international reputation made not by themselves, but by self-serving power brokers. Many in America believe that we are being taken advantage of by the Japanese because of the trade imbalance. I believe it is the Japanese themselves who pay a dearer price on a daily basis for the success of their big corporations.

The genesis of their current condition was World War II. Before the war they were controlled by the military. Immediately after the war Japan was desperately poor. The Japanese acknowledge that their economic miracle began when America decided to buy materials for the Korean War from the Japanese. From the 1950s to the early 1990s one political party ruled. All acknowledge it had more than its share of money scandals, but the Japanese were not willing to turn that party out, or to question its activities too closely because following its lead resulted in the highest standard-of-living in Asia. (Eighty-nine percent believe they are middle class. It is a middle-class lifestyle, however, to which most Americans would not want to adjust.) So, even though free to do so in theory since the end of World War II, the Japanese have not ever truly exercised their right to control their government.

Ask an American who rules America, and the answer may be something like: "the people," "the President," "the Congress," "the military-industrial complex," and the like. Ask a Japanese who rules Japan, and the answer often is "I do not know." They just do not know whose hands are on the political puppet strings. One thing they do know is that the Japanese people do not rule.

Money, as everywhere else, rules, but money rules more directly in Japan than in America. No Japanese suspects that their legislature is free to rule the country according to the constitution because they all seem to have an understanding that there are still two constitutions in Japan. The written one and the unwritten one, with the unwritten one, based on "how things have always been." When there is a serious conflict between them the latter prevails.

One instance revolves around Article 9. The Japanese people have a genuine anti-war feeling. In spite of Article 9, Japan has one of the largest armed forces on the planet, which the government calls the "Self Defense Force." The people's sincere belief in the goals of the constitution cannot stop the government from doing what it wants to do regardless of the people's wishes.

This is a closed society and the law reflects it. It is closed to outsiders in general, but "outsider" does not simply describe people such as myself. The government, it would seem, considers itself the biggest ingroup, and plaintiffs against it the most unworthy of outgroups.

The Japanese government has no equivalent to the Freedom of Information Act (FOIA). Several years ago an American-built jetliner owned by a Japanese company crashed near a major Japanese city. The Japanese plaintiffs unsuccessfully sought information about the crash from their government. The plaintiffs received the information from the U.S. Federal Aviation Administration because the American manufacturer was required to provide the FAA with everything it had concerning the crash.

Japanese pressing claims for faulty drugs made by a Japanese company obtained information about the drug through our FOIA, because the drug had been investigated here too. Information about a nuclear accident in Japan was obtained by citizens in the same way because the pump which allegedly failed was designed by an American firm.

Although fighting the government is never easy, the Japanese accept the notion that "We do not need lawyers. We prefer to settle things through compromise." The reality is they have no choice. With only 700 new lawyers admitted and 100 new judges appointed yearly in a country with a population approximately half of ours, the courts are the last place the average Japanese could expect to resort for a resolution of his legal problems.

Until as a people they successfully assert control over their government, I think Japan should be viewed through a jaundiced eye. They know the let's-just-accept-it attitude has to change before the government will be as responsive as they would like.

In the long run, the economic downturn of the 1990s may help the Japanese to force their government to become more responsive to them. They have the right to do it, and now that the system is failing them, they do not have the same incentive to look the other way when their rights are ignored or abused. I wish for them just enough economic discomfort to complete the break with their cultural tradition of quietly enduring.

Ultimately I have learned two things about Japan. The first thing is, I like the Japanese. The average Japanese is just the kind of neighbor or coworker most of us appreciate. The other thing is, I have never been through anything as hard as being Japanese. They have made their country great through hard work and self sacrifice with comparatively little pay back. They deserve more in return and I hope they demand it.

Well, that is all I have to say. Through my letters, I hope your understanding of Japan has moved past the beyond-sushi stage.

adaruto (a dah roo toe – adult)
Ainu (eye knew – Caucasian people who originally settled Japan)
apuru pai (ah poo roo – apple; pa e – pie)
asa shan (ah sah – morning; shan – shampoo)
Aso-*san* (*san* in this case comes from the pronunciation for "mount")
atsukan (ah tsu khan – heated sake)
baiten (buy ten – sales stand on a train platform)
baka (ba ka – fool)
ban (ban – bang)
banira (ba knee ra – vanilla)
basuketo boru (ba sue kay toe bow roo – basketball)
BGM (bee gee emu – background music)
biagaden (be ah ga den – from beer and garden)
bideo (be day oh – video)
bimbo (been bow – poor)
bon enkai (bone en ka e – forget the year party)
bonsai (bone sigh – small sculptured tree)
buruberi chizukeki (boo roo bay ree – blueberry; chee zoo kay key – cheese cake)
chan (chan – diminutive form of *san* reserved for close friends or small children)
chiagaru (chee a ga roo – cheer girl)
chika (chee ka – basement)
chizu (chee zoo – cheese)
chizukeki (chee zoo kay key – cheese cake)
chocoreto (cho co ray toe – chocolate)
chu gakko (chew – middle; ga ko – school; junior high school)
chyarenji (cha ren gee – challenge)
dai (die – counter for cars)
dake (dah kay – mountain peak)
damu (da moo – dam)
denki kapeto (dain key – electricity; ka pet toe – carpet)
dai ligu gemu (die ree goo gay moo – how they refer to American major league baseball)
dojiboru (doe gee bow roo – dodge ball)
doriburu (doe re boo roo – dribble)
dozo (dough zoe – please)
dunku shooto (daan coo – dunk; shoe toe – shoot)

eacon (eh ah cone – from *air con*ditioning)
Edo Jidai (a dough – edo; gee die – period)
eki (a key – train station)
enkai (en ka e – drinking party)
ensto (en stow – *engine sto*p meaning stall)
erebeta (eh lay bay ta – elevator)
esu efu (a sue a foo - S.F: science fiction)
esu, emu, and *eru* (eh sue, eh moo, eh roo – "s," "m," and "l," [*s*mall, *m*edium and *l*arge])
faito (fie toe – go for it)
furichiketto (foo ree che kay toe – free ticket: a rail pass)
futsu densha (foo tsu den sha – regular, and slowest of Japan's trains)
futsuka yoi (whost ka yo e – hang over)
gaiatsu (guy aht sue – outside pressure)
gaijin (guy jean – foreigner[s])
gaman suru (ga maan sue roo – tough it out)
gareji (ga ray gee – garage)
gatsu (ga tsu – guts)
genkan (gen khan – similar to vestibule or an entryway)
genki (gain key – a variety of meanings, but when describing a personality it means lively or energetic)
geto baru (gay toe bow roo – gateball: similar to croquet)
Ginkakuji (geen ka coo gee – a temple in Kyoto)
giri choco (ghee ree – duty; cho co – *choco*late)
gohan desu yo (go han dess yo – "It's rice," means dinner is ready)
Gorudan uiku (go roo dan – golden; ooh e coo – week: A two-week period at the end of April and beginning of May when there are four closely spaced holidays)
gu choki pa (goo cho key pa – said during *jyan ken pon*)
hai (hi – yes)
hambaga (hah moo ba ga – hamburger)
hanguri da (hone ga ree -hungry, in the yearning sense; da – is)
hanko (han co – personal seals used to "sign" contracts)
haro (ha row – Japanese children's pronunciation of hello)
hashi (hah she – chopsticks)
Heisei (hey – peace; say – becoming)
hiki (he key – counter for small animals)
hiragana (he rah ghana – phonetic alphabet used as supplement to and in conjunction with the *kanji*)
homu (hoe moo – train platform)
homu ranu (hoe mu rah new – home run)

hora mite (hoe rah me tay – hey, look)

ichi man en (e chee maan en – 10,000 yen note)

ichinensei (e chee nen say – seventh grader[s])

inaka (e knocka – countryside)

irrashaimase (e rah shy ma say – welcome)

Itadakimasu (e ta da key ma sue – I (or we) receive)

jozu (joe's ooh – skilled or good)

jozu desu ne (you are good aren't you)

jyan ken pon (john ken pone – paper, scissors, rock game)

jyuhachi kippu (jew ha chee key poo – all-day pass on the *futsu densha*)

jyunen (jew nen – tenth year)

kacho (ka cho – section chief)

kampai (kaam pie –- bottoms up)

kanji (khan gee – Chinese characters with which the Japanese write)

karu pisu (ca roo pee sue – sports drink)

kashu mashin (kashoe masheen – ATM)

kashu kado (kashoe ka dough – cash card)

kashu kona (kashew co nah – cash corner, where they put ATMs)

katakana (ka ta khana – phonetic alphabet used to represent words from foreign languages)

kechapu (kay cha poo – ketchup)

keiretsu (kay ray tsu – conglomerates of monopolistic proportions and inclinations)

keki (kay key – cake)

ken (cane – prefectural government, similar to our county government)

ken (cane – counter for houses)

kaki (ka key – persimmon)

Kinkakuji (keen ka coo gee – a multi-story, gold-covered Kyoto temple)

Kinki (kinky – a geographic area in Japan)

kiritsu (key reets – command for students)

kiro (key row – *kilo*meter)

kocho-sensei (co cho sen say – principal)

kotatsu (co tat tsu – knee-high coffee table combing the idea of a rug, a blanket, and an electric stove)

kun (coon – a familiar form of address usually used in reference to boys)

kyuko (cue ko – express train which has more stops than a *tokkyu*)

macudonarudo (ma coo dow new roo dough – McDonald's)

mai homu (ma e hoe moo – my home)

mai kaa (ma e ka – one way to say passenger car)

man tsu man defensu (mahn tsu mhan de feign sue – man-to-man defense) *mawari ga urusai* (ma wa ree ga ooh roo sigh – people around are complaining)

Meiji Jidai (may gee; gee die – the *Meiji* Period)

Meiji (may gee – bright government)

mikan (me khan – a tangerine)

minicompo (me knee come poe – minicomponent stereo, or boombox)

misoshiru (me so she roo – popular type of Japanese soup)

misu (me sue – miss)

mugicha (moo ghee cha – barley tea)

mushi atsui (moo she a tsu e – hot and muggy)

nakodo (na ko dough – person who arranges *omiai* meetings)

nambapureto (numba poo ray toe – number plate)

natto (not toe – food made of fermented soy bean)

nice shooto (nice; shoe toe)

Nihon (knee – sun; hone – origin: Japanese name for Japan)

Nihongo (knee hone go – Japanese name for their language)

Nihonjin (knee hone jean – Japanese name for themselves)

nijikai (knee gee ka e – second party)

ninensei (knee nen say – eighth grader[s])

NTT (knee pone – *Nippon* [another way to say Japan] Telephone and Telegraph)

obasan (oh ba san – older women)

Obon (o bone– a national holiday when spirits return to homes)

ocha (o cha – green tea)

ochazuke (o cha zoo kay – a small bowl of rice that is mixed with *ocha*)

ohayo gozaimasu (ohio go zai maas – good morning)

oiru cheinji (oh e roo change e – oil change)

okane (o ka nay – money)

OL (oh a roo – women office workers: *O*ffice *L*ady)

omiage (o me ah gay)

omiai (o me eye – Japanese form of matchmaking)

omonjyu (oh mohn jew)

onegai shimasu (oh nay guy she maas – dictionary defines as "I ask [beg, request of] you;" at beginning of class is means "Please.")

origami (or ree ga me – the art of folding paper into designs)

oshi (o she – regrettable)

Oshogatsu (oh show ga tsu – New Year's)

pachinko (pah cheen ko – a pinball-like machine and a game of chance)

pasonaru fauru (pa sone na roo fa ooh roo – personal foul)

pasu (pa sue – pass)

Pokari Sweat (po ca ree – sue way toe)

poteto furai (po tay toe – potato; foo ra e – fry: french fry)

potto (poe toe – a Thermos-like container)

PTA (pea tea a – PTA)

raibu hausu (lie boo how sue – live house where live music is performed)

raji (rah gee – large)

rashu awa (rah shoe ah wa – rush hour)

reboundo boru (ree bown dough bow roo – rebound)

rei (ray – command for students to bow)

romaji (row ma gee – name for our alphabet)

rotemburo (row tem burro – an outdoor, natural hot spring)

rukii (roo key – rookie)

ryokan (ree yo kahn – traditional Japanese hotel)

saido mira (sa e dough – side; me rah – mirror)

sain (sa een – sign)

saizu (sigh zoo – size)

sake (sah kay – rice wine)

saloon (sa roon – family sedan)

san K (Jobs considered hard *kitsui* [keyt sui], dirty *kitanai* [key ta nai] and backbreaking *kurushi* [koo roo she] and not wanted by today's youth)

san *ko* (*san* – three; *ko* – high or tall: high education, salary, and tall)

san (*san* – unisex equivalent of "Mr." "Mrs.," "Miss," or "Ms.")

sanjikai (san gee ka e – third party)

sannensei (san nen say – ninth grader[s])

sarariiman (sa ra ree man – white-collar worker)

sayonara homu ranu (sa yo na rah hoe mu rah new – game ending home run)

seiza (say za – sitting on the floor with legs, from the knee to foot, in contact with the floor in a martial-arts style)

sensei (sen say – teacher)

sento (sen toe – public baths)

shaken (sha ken – government enforced inspection of all used cars)

sheku (shay coo – shake)

shiemu (she emmu – TV or radio commercial abbreviated to *CM*)

shimin senta (she mean sane ta – Citizen's Center)

shinkansen (sheen khan sen – the Bullet Train)

Shinto (sheen toe – religion native to Japan)

shirimasen (she ree ma sen – I do not know)

shirubia (she'll be a – Silvia)

sho gakko (show – elementary; gakko – school)

shodo (show dough – calligraphy)

shoji (show gee – wood and paper sliding doors)

Showa (show wa – shining peace)
shoyu (show you – soy sauce)
soba (sow ba – buckwheat noodles)
soji (so gee – cleaning done by the students every day at school)
sonkeigo (saun kay go – respectful language)
sugoi (sue goee – great)
suihanki (sue e han key – an automatic rice cooker)
sumimasen, wakarimasen (sue me ma sen, wa ka ree ma sen – I'm sorry, I don't understand)
sumimasen (sue me ma sen – excuse me)
supaamaaketo (su pa ma ketto – supermarket)
suree pointa (sue ree po een ta – three pointer)
suree pointo rain (sue ree po een toe rah en – three point line)
suree besu hito (sueree baysue he toe – three base hit, or triple)
sutoroberi chizukeki (sto raw bay ree – strawberry; chee zoo kay key – cheese cake)
sutoroberi (sto raw bay ree – strawberry)
taiya (tie ya – tire)
takushi (ta coo she – taxi)
taoru (ta o roo – from towel)
tatami (ta ta me – tightly woven straw mats 6 feet long and 3 feet wide)
tekunikaru fauru (tay ku knee ka roo – technical foul)
Tenno Heika (ten no hey ka – Imperial Majesty)
Todaiji (toe die gee – large temple in Nara)
toire (toe e ray – toilet)
tokkyu (toe cue – limited express train with limited stops)
toneru (toe nay roo – tunnel)
tou (toe – counter for big animals)
toyu stobu (toe you – stow boo: portable kerosene heater)
tsu pointa (tsu po een ta – two pointer)
tsubo (tsu bow – unit of measurement equal to two *tatami* mats)
tsumaranai mono (tsu ma rah na e mow no – it's nothing really)
tsuru (tsu roo – crane: the bird not the construction tool)
tsuyu (tsu you – rainy season)
umai (ooh ma e – skilled or good)
waipa (why pa – wiper)
wairudo piichi (wa e roo dough pee chee – wild pitch)
wakarimashita (wa ka ree ma she ta – I understand)
yakuza (yah coo za – the Japanese equivalent of the Mafia)
yappari, Nihon no ho ga ii (ya pa ree knee hone no hoe ga e – after all, Japan is better)

yokatta (yo ka ta – great)
yukata (you ka ta – a thin cotton house coat)
zon (zoe – zone)

ORDER FORM

 On-line orders: www.beyondsushi.com

 e-mail orders: colken@beyondsushi.com

 Postal orders: **Colken Publishers**
207 West Clarendon
Suite 20C
Phoenix, Arizona 85013
PLEASE INCLUDE COMPLETE RETURN ADDRESS

Please send the following books:
I understand that I may return any books for a full refund–for
any reason–no questions asked.

_____

_____

_____

Sales Tax:
Please add 6.8%

Shipping:
Book Rate: $2.00 for the first book and 75 cents for each
additional book.
(Surface shipping may take three weeks.)
Air Mail: $3.75 per book

Payment:
Check